# *The* CANADIAN GARDENER'S GUIDE TO FOLIAGE & GARDEN DESIGN

# The
# CANADIAN GARDENER'S
# GUIDE TO
# FOLIAGE &
# GARDEN DESIGN

*by Marjorie Harris*
*Photography by Tim Saunders*

RANDOM HOUSE
*TORONTO*

To Jack, for the passion and the patience. And to Susan, Stuart,
Kathy, Sheila and Sally who guided us so well.
*Marjorie Harris*

❧

To Adele, for her help and her love.
*Tim Saunders*

❧

In memoriam Murray Haigh

Text copyright © 1993 by Marjorie Harris
Photographs copyright © 1993 by Tim Saunders

All rights reserved under International and Pan-American
Copyright Conventions.

Published in Canada in 1993 by Random House of Canada
Limited, Toronto.

**Canadian Cataloguing in Publication Data**

Harris, Marjorie
    The Canadian gardener's guide to foliage and garden
design

ISBN 0-394-22231-8

1. Foliage plants.   2. Landscape gardening.   3. Gardening –
Canada.   I. Saunders, Tim.   II. Title.

SB431.H37 1993    635-9'75    C93-094045-8

The author has tried to be as accurate as possible with
information supplied by gardeners and acknowledged
authorities. We regret any errors or omissions.


*Design and art direction:* Andrew Smith
*Editorial:* Lorraine Johnson, Barbara Schon
*Production co-ordination:* Alan Terakawa
*Page layout and composition:* Andrew Smith Graphics, Inc.
*Line illustrations:* David Chapman
*Color separation:* Bradbury Tamblyn & Boorne Ltd.
*Printing and binding:* SFERA

Printed and bound in Italy

10 9 8 7 6 5 4 3 2 1

COVER: *Neil Turnbull designed Dr. Glenn Renecker's exquisite midtown garden. Hedging is* BUXUS SEMPERVIRENS *'Green Velvet'; the large evergreen is* PICEA GLAUCA, *white spruce; at the base is a mixture of rhododendrons and azaleas. Against the trellis arch:* ROSA *'New Dawn' with* HYDRANGEA PETIOLARIS; VIBURNUM CARLCEPHALUM; RODGERSIA PODOPHYLLA; POLYGONUM MULTIFORUM; ASTILBE. *Ontario Z6.*

PREVIOUS PAGE: *Sally Bryant has a fantasy gazebo decorated with paintings of her pets by Lyndon Andrews. Around the gazebo: Bourbon rose 'Kathleen Harrop' and* HUMULUS LUPULUS, *hops;* CLADRASTIS LUTEA *and Bourbon rose 'Mme Pierre Oger'. Left:* MISCANTHUS SINENSIS *'Zebrinus';* CORYLUS, *hazelnut. Right-hand bed from left:* ERICA; CALLUNA; HELLEBORUS; PRIMULA *in front of* CORNUS KOUSA, *Japanese dogwood;* CERCIS CANADENSIS, *redbud. To the right:* RHODODENDRON *'Roseum Elegans' and* AZALEA *'Silvery Pink'. Ontario Z6B.*

FOREWORD, PAGE 7: *Mrs. Peter Laing's garden has wonderful old stone benches and a table that belonged to her parents. In the background:* KOLKWITZIA, *beautybush, and late-flowering Persian lilacs; the ground cover is* VINCA MINOR. *Quebec Z4.*

# CONTENTS

# ACKNOWLEDGMENTS

Murray Haigh, one of Canada's finest landscape designers, died during the making of this book. He was a good friend and a hortguru of the first order. His wise and gentle counsel was one I always sought. Canadian gardening will be much diminished by his absence, but his beautiful gardens will live on and evolve. There will be a permanent record, we hope, of a small part of his enormous talent in the pages of this book.

Thanks to the wonderful people who gave us such good guidance: Stuart Robertson, Susan Ryley, Kathy Leishman, Sheila Paulson and Sally Bryant.

Thanks to all the kind people who let us stay in their homes: Helene and Jack Major; Pam and Roy Dalglish; Susan Ryley; Garry Clarke and Julie Cruickshank; Ted Phillips and Ken Woodman. They were gracious hosts who put up with late arrivals and 4:30 a.m. departures. To Liz Primeau and Bayla Gross who were so generous with their contacts. The landscape architects and designers who were so generous with their time: Janet Rosenberg, Murray Haigh, Ruth Dynbort, Ron Rule, James Floyd, Michael Dampf, Dennis Winters, Dorothea Lovat Dickson, John Thompson, Wendy Bond, Jon David Schulery and Neil Turnbull.

To David Tarrant and Gerald Straley of the UBC Botanical Garden; and Allen Paterson and Ann Milosoroff of the Royal Botanical Gardens in Hamilton. Dugald Cameron of Garden Import.

To Barbara Stevenson and Pamela MacKenzie at the Civic Garden Centre in Toronto, who always made themselves available to help.

And of course to all the wonderful gardeners who let us come into their most private sanctuaries:

Don Armstrong, Janet and Trevor Ashbee, Bella Balaz, Ned Baldwin and Marilyn Field-Marsham, Margaret and David Barham, Cecily and Norman Bell, Caesar Blake, Richard Birkett, Maureen and Brian Bixley, Peter and Jose Braun, Joy Brigham, Joan and Joel Brink, Mary Anne Brinkman, Beverley Burge, Audrey and John Burrows, Sally Bryant, Francis Cabot, Eloise Carmichael, Adrienne Clarkson and John Ralston Saul, Donald Combe, Wendy Cook, Elaine Corbet, Al Cummings, Pam and Roy Dalglish, Francisca Darts, Jackie Dean, Louis de Niverville and Tom Miller, Mr. and Mrs. Robert DeLuce, Linda Dowling of Happy Valley Herb Farm, Dr. and Mrs. A. Earp, David and Ronny Fingold, Mr. and Mrs. John P. Fisher, Pamela Frost, the late Barbara Frum and Murray Frum, Columba Fuller, Dr. R. L. Goossens, the late Murray Haigh, Paul Hamer, Linda and Peter Hamilton, Ralph and Carol Hansen, Thomas Hobbs, Humber Nurseries, William J. Hurren, Marion and Alex Jarvie, Popsie Johnston, Louise Kappus, Claire and the late Peter Kerrigan, Mrs. Peter Laing, Anna Leggatt, Kathy Leishman, the late Dr. Henry Landis, Marilyn Lightstone and Moses Znaimer, Juliana Lynch-Staunton, Sue Macaulay, Marion Macdonell, Philip and Katherine MacKenzie, Gina Mallet, Mary and Burt Manion, Rick and Gail Marshall, Renate and Herb Mayr, Annette McCoubrey, Wendy and Gordon McLean, Audrey Meiklejohn, Audrey Mellish, Lynne Milgram and David Kaye, Bill and Betty Miller, Mary and Terry Mills, John B. Mitchell, Heather Morgan, Leslie and Allen Morgan, Heather and Richard Mossakowski, Rex Murfitt, Arthur Oslach, Glen Patterson, Rosemary Pauer, Sheila Paulson, Dr. and Mrs. R. M. Peet, Laura Rapp, Dr. Glenn Renecker, Dorothy Richardson and Jacques Daoust, Dr. Joseph Ronsley, Janet Rosenberg, Susan Ryley, Marilyn and Charles Sale, Richard and Sandra Shannon, Richard Silver, Sheila Simmons, Mr. and Mrs. Michael Simpkins, Amy Stewart, David and Gillian Stewart, Gerald Straley, Tim Tanz, David Tarrant, Rosemary and Bill Terry, Francine and Peter Trent, Louise Weekes, Gary White and John Veillette, Elaine and David Whitehead, Vivienne and Michael Wiggan, Barbara Wilkins, Aileen Wolff, Carol Woodward, Carmen Varcoe and Ed Kowalyk, Andrew Yeoman, Robin Wilson, Al Zinn.

Special thanks go to Ted Johnston, who worked on the listings; to Jacqueline Rogers for her help in research; and to Marion Jarvie, who identified plants when no one else knew what they were and was the outside reader for the listings. Her suggestions were invaluable. The book was copy edited by Shaun Oakey. Lorraine Johnson, who edited the main text, and Barbara Schon, who did all the botanical editing, deserve medals. Andrew Smith, who is the best in the business, designed this book as he has done all the others—with grace and style.

All 120 film used in this book was processed by Steichenlab Limited, 500 Richmond Street East, Toronto, Ontario.

Marjorie Harris

# FOREWORD

*After The Canadian Gardener* was first published in 1990, my style of gardening changed rapidly. From a profound devotion to the evanescent pleasure of blossoms I found myself being more drawn to foliage plants—trees, shrubs, vines and ground covers or any plant that depends for its beauty on its leaves, texture and architecture rather than on its flowers. Putting these plants together, moving them into new designs, became increasingly important in my garden. It struck me then, and even more so now, that the skillful use of foliage plants is especially important for anyone gardening in the north.

Foliage plants, for instance, have a much longer season than perennials. And it's this kind of longevity that helps gardeners facing the extremes of climate that we do here in the northern part of North America. Foliage plants are, as well, the basic tools for the structure of all garden design. It's difficult to get fascinated by one without the other.

Since *The Canadian Gardener* was published, I've seen hundreds more gardens. If I found unhappy gardeners, they all shared one thing—besides the usual divine dissatisfaction of all gardeners—something missing from the garden. The missing link was usually a plan. Not something rigid but the element that adds soul to a garden: a sense of cohesion that gives subtle and profound meaning to the garden as a whole.

This, then, is what this book is addressing. The design of the garden per se and the successful use of foliage plants to accomplish that design vision. To further that end we have photographs of some of the most beautiful gardens in the country. We hope they'll inspire you to try out new design ideas and ways of putting plants together for a four-season garden.

Maintenance information for many plants can be found in my book *The Canadian Gardener*, which covered the essentials of gardening, especially with perennials. There is extensive information about xeriscaping, mulching, soil, fertilizing and pest management in my book *Ecological Gardening: Your Path to a Healthy Garden.* There is an essay at the end of this book with more thoughts on ecological and xeriscape garden design.

Once again Tim Saunders and I were treated incredibly well by the gardeners we met. And once again the team that was gathered for the first book has worked on this one.

Marjorie Harris

# CHAPTER ONE

# THE PRINCIPLES OF DESIGN

*"You cannot step into the same river twice."*
HERACLITUS

*T*he garden has much to teach us about nature and about the nature of this planet and the universe we live in. We have only to observe its wonders in microcosm to be impressed with the macrocosm. Whenever we touch nature we change it irrevocably; therefore, this touch must be done gently, with sensitivity and respect.

It is both the curse and the beauty of gardening that it never remains constant. No year, nor day, nor hour can render it exactly as before. This fact turns gardeners into poets, philosophers and sometimes tedious bores when they go on about it.

Gardening is, like all the performing arts, changeable, not only with each performer but with each performance. Even though we work with similar materials—plants, soil, water and sun—none of us ever gets precisely the same results as anyone else.

Garden design is the art of illusion: to make small spaces appear larger; and to make large spaces feel comfortable and enclosed—humane, because we wish to bring all things to our own level.

Gardening is also the art of allusion. Each object in a garden has a history behind it and a reference to some symbology or myth. Garden furnishings connect us with history. Personal totems make a garden an even more abundant and fertile place.

The garden is a source of solace when we need it, a place to alleviate gloom and misery. It is the refuge from the city. It is the taming, if you will, of the untamed wilderness.

The garden is the place of my only real contact with nature; it is part of my creativity. I depend on it to get through tough times. I want it to reflect the best part of me as well. It is the poetry in my life.

For many of us, the garden is a place for the retrieval of memories: in the scent of a plant, the shape of a border, the curve of a path toward some secret place. We are drawn back again and again.

If all that puts a lot of baggage into the activity of gardening, it also adds a great deal of pleasure. I find it incredibly boring when people come into my garden and say, "Oh, but it must take so much work. How many hours a day do you spend here?" To me this is not work, this is fun. Any work is irrelevant to the amount of joy I get back from the garden itself.

Gardening has taught me that if you love doing something you will probably do it well. The garden compels us to make it, and thus ourselves, better and better.

## CREATIVE GARDENING: TAKING STOCK

Gardening is a very curious activity. You can get pretty good results without knowing much about what you are doing. Yet the more you learn, the more you are destined to be gloomy about what you've accomplished. Eventually you'll become very discontented and want to change things.

The minute this primal urge takes over, you've got a problem on your hands. You can move things

---

RIGHT: *In Susan Ryley's garden a rose arch welcomes the viewer to mixed perennial borders divided into garden rooms. Left:* COTINUS COGGYGRIA *'Royal Purple'. Over the arch:* SOLANUM JASMINOIDES *'Album', the annual potato vine, runs rampant along with* CLEMATIS LARGESII. *To the right: leathery stems of* STIPA GIGANTEA *lean out over* ANTHEMIS CUPANIANA *and* VIOLA CORNUTA *'Alba'.* HYDRANGEA PETIOLARIS *clambers over the potting shed. British Columbia Z8.*

around quite happily and even end up with an attractive garden. But putting plants about in a helter-skelter manner will usually not make a great garden. Pretty perhaps, but not magnificent. And what are we gardeners if not optimists, always reaching beyond our own grasp.

Though a truly magnificent garden requires basic planning, the results will far outweigh whatever time it takes. Winter was given to us as a gift of time—for planning. This is when you can see the garden in its essence, stripped to the bare bones.

Having said that, however, the overdesigned garden is just as unsatisfying as the underdesigned garden. A garden with a bridge, a gazebo, a pergola, a folly, a pond and a terrace all shoved into a small urban space will be nothing but hilarious. Somewhere in between too much and too little design is the ideal garden.

Moving from purely instinctive gardening to creative gardening, using basic design principles but allowing for spontaneity, is the great leap most of us crave. Although this requires more thought, reading, research and planning—no way around it, more work—it's a lot more exciting as well. The results are like the gardens in this book—inspirational.

The first discipline of creative gardening—gardening by design *and* spontaneity—is an exercise in reality. Exactly what kind of a site do you have and what do you really want it to do for you? What does the site inform you about its light and soil? What's possible and what's not? A brilliant design filled with sun-loving plants won't work in a shady site; and a ravine lot might not be the best place to put a pond but it might be great for a waterfall.

What kind of feeling do you get from the land you live on? How will you marry the new design to the architecture of your house? If you are going to go beyond simple borders filled with a combination of annuals and perennials, then you have to put in time doing what I call Creative Staring.

This involves memorizing almost every square inch of your space. Once its spirit has entered your imagination, you can project ideas onto it the way a painter projects images onto a canvas.

There is one rule about gardening that is carved in stone. The minute you turn your back on the place, it gets larger. You will dream of having everything—all the things I've mentioned plus a rose arbor, pond or stream (maybe both), a small greenhouse, patio, deck, stone walls, a rock garden. Such fantasies will streak through your imagination. Everything is possible. Or so it seems. But what you are probably dealing with is space that is something less than majestic, unable to accommodate even a quarter of those *objets*.

The only surefire way to get started on a new garden design is to get out pen and notebook and make lists. First of all look around at the interior of your house. It will give you lots of information: what colors you like; whether you prefer things simple or complicated, romantic or classic in form, fussy or tailored.

Making the garden relate to the house is one of the cardinal rules of garden design. It seems obvious, but too often we turn our backs on the house and see only the land around it. The garden should be an extension of your house. Having a cluttered landscape around a formal house doesn't work, just as having a Japanese garden next to a Victorian cottage looks absurd.

## STYLE

Style is an ineffable thing. If you feel you're still searching for an appropriate style, do not feel alone. So are the rest of us. There are, however, a few ideas that might help in the quest. We have a vague idea of what romantic and classic styles look like. But when you break down either style into how it applies to the garden, you can get some very specific information.

The simplest way to find a suitable style is to take stock of what you already have. You can't borrow style from somewhere else. Or parachute it into

**LEFT:** *This skillfully designed compact garden by Bill and Rosemary Terry emphasizes evening fragrance, and the small pond creates a serene mood. Nicotiana, hybrid lilies, stocks,* MATTHIOLA BICORNIS *and* MIRABILIS JALAPA *provide scent. On the fence to the right:* WISTERIA SINENSISIO; *Bartlett pear and climbing roses are espaliered along the fence. Near the pool:* LAVANDULA ANGUSTIFOLIA *'Munstead'; pelargoniums and portulaca fill the pots. Ontario Z6.*

**BELOW:** *Marilyn Sale's garden was divided in two by designer Elisabeth Tschopp. Various clematis cover the pergola. Pink-flowering lilac 'Katherine Havemeyer'; white-flowering* EXOCHORDA X MACRANTHA *'The Bride'. The gray arching shrub is* COTONEASTER DIELSIANUS *var.* MAJOR; *coming forward: yellow flowers are* AURINIA SAXATILIS *'Citrina'; white flower of* IBERIS SEMPERVIRENS; COTONEASTER HORIZONTALIS; *pink- flowering low shrubs are* DAPHNE CNEORUM. *The . conifer is* MICROBIOTA DECUSSATA; *backed by* STEPHANANDRA INCISA *'Crispa';* EPIMEDIUM *and* HYDRANGEA PETIOLARIS *under the heavily pruned apple tree, which lends great age and stability to the garden. Ontario Z6B.*

your garden and expect it to be original or even suitable.

Truly creative gardens evolve naturally out of the exigencies of climate, light and local plant culture and move on from there in a highly original fashion. Beware the seductive photograph of something that simply won't work in your area. No matter what I say, it won't discourage you from trying, but that's the way we gardeners learn—the hard way.

Personal style may come in many forms. I've always thought of myself as having an austere style. But a careful look at my possessions, even the colors of the walls, made it apparent that I love soft colors and textures, set in tailored arrangements. Gardening should be an exploration of your own psyche, a matter of getting to know your real self.

The shape and proportion of the rooms of your house should have some bearing on the garden, especially the area closest to the house. Above anything else, keep the style of your plans simpler than that of the house to which the garden is attached. Never get pretentious.

Even if your personal style runs to the formal, in Canada having a huge formal garden based on a plan by Le Notre, the designer of Versailles, makes no sense. It's partly because we don't have the climate. The light is completely different. As are the plants available to us. And we aren't living with such venerable architecture.

If there is no Canadian Garden Style to speak of, it is because we are relatively new to the game. As we develop a style it will not be monolithic or national. It will tend toward various regional styles. And I think that is beginning to happen now as enormous numbers of gardens come into their first maturity. We are responding to both our aesthetic sense and a need for respite in the garden according to what the climate will allow.

In the search for a northern style, we have a lot of visual horrors to work around: garages, driveways, sandboxes, swimming pools, play areas—problems Le Notre never dreamed of. And while most of these items aren't particularly gorgeous, by taking them into account from the beginning, you can blend them gracefully into the whole design of your garden. Just make sure they don't become afterthoughts in your quest for beauty.

What gives the gardens on these pages a special enduring quality are the underlying schematics that went into their creation in the first place. Working on a system or making a scheme is the start of creative gardening.

## THE FUNDAMENTALS OF DESIGN

*"The ultimate goal of a
garden design is that it appear inevitable."*
THOMAS CHURCH

Simplicity is the essence of all great art, and there is no reason why this shouldn't apply to garden design. Simplicity doesn't mean dullness. In fact, dull design tends to be either rigid and formulaic or fussy and over-ornate. In either case the viewer becomes satiated too quickly. Simplicity executed with finesse is far more elegant and interesting.

Simplicity is the most important principle of your planting scheme as well as of the underlying garden design. English garden designer Russell Page, always a man with a good line, once wrote, "Imagine the Parthenon with each column of a different kind of marble! Yet in gardening one is constantly making this mistake."

The foundation of good design is mainly common sense. Common sense with rhythm and style. The principles that apply to good garden design are exactly the same universal principles that govern all works of art: unity, proportion and scale. These fundaments of composition are the principles underlying the design you develop and the plants you choose. When things are out of whack, they make you feel restless. A garden should have a sense of tranquillity. Unity, proportion and scale contribute to that. And through these elements you will find your personal style.

**UNITY** ❧ The first and most important element in gardening, as in art, is unity. Unity is achieved when everything fits perfectly into the whole composition. It is a oneness emanating from the harmonious combinations of the various parts of a design.

Unity can also come from what you emphasize in your garden—a mood or a style—or how you balance your composition with proportion and scale.

In art, unity may come from composition, but in gardening it can start with the quality of soil you have; or the rhythm of the land—whether it is flat or undulating; or even with the kinds of local plants available.

Unity was imposed on my garden because I had to deal with a great deal of shade. There was no way I could move a neighbor's immense weeping willow. And since I wanted hardy perennials, this started me on my way to having hardy shade-loving plants that live together felicitously.

When your design and plant choices are appropriate for the quality of soil in your garden—say, an acid soil filled with acid-loving plants—then the marriage of soil and plants will contribute to the unity of the garden as a whole. Even with such a simple gesture, your garden becomes more sophisticated.

Another way to achieve unity is through the integrity of the materials you use. Transporting stone from southern Italy to northern Saskatchewan is not going to make an integrated whole of your garden. Or to put it another way, if the available material in your area is stone, stick to the local stone.

You can choose a theme to unify your garden—using water, or water-saving techniques, for example. Or you can create unity by repeating certain plant configurations. In England, great gardens such as Hidcote and Sissinghurst have repeating hedges of box and yew.

Experienced gardeners like to talk a lot about the "bones" of a garden. Like having good bone structure in a face. These bones, the skeleton of the garden, can make it a truly magical place. They provide the underlying structure into which all the details fit perfectly. What you don't want in the garden are too many unrelated things—materials, structures, plants that have no bearing on the overall feeling of the garden. You also don't want to bounce from Chinese to Italian renaissance to contemporary Brazilian influences all in one space.

**PROPORTION** ❧ Proportion is next on the list of importance. Sylvia Crowe, the splendid English designer-teacher, says, "Good proportion is the basis of all design and no amount of after treatment and planting can compensate for the lack of it."

Proportion can refer to something as simple as how the length and width of the garden relate to each other, how the horizontal lines relate to the verticals, how the open spaces relate to the planted areas.

The classic definition of proportion is seeing relationships—the relationship of one part to another and the relationship of parts to the whole. Proportion, however, like many other things in design, has to do with the emotions it evokes, with the way you feel about how one thing relates to another. For instance, when something is the same height as a person it feels personal, humane, easily understandable; when larger it might become frightening or inspire awe; if it's smaller it might feel more intimate.

**SCALE** ❧ Scale is another element you have to take into account in your design. Proportion and scale are such potent factors in creating unity that it's impossible to have harmony without them.

Scale refers to the spatial relationships between objects, whether that relationship is between buildings or elements in the landscape. The tension or vibrancy between objects can be almost more important than the objects themselves.

ABOVE: *Marilyn Sale's garden contains this geometric pond. Rear left: lilac 'Katherine Havemeyer' and a climbing Bourbon rose 'Zéphirine Drouhin'. Ontario Z6B.*

LEFT: *This Japanese garden, designed by Torizuka Landscape for the Wiggan family, has a complicated yet calm look.* CELASTRUS ORBICULATUS, *Chinese bittersweet, on the left;* BUXUS, *boxwood;* EUONYMUS. *Ontario Z6.*

PREVIOUS DOUBLE-PAGE SPREAD: *In the garden of Pam and Ray Dalglish the central axis draws the eye to the enchanting summer house. In the background are hybrids of Caroline poplars;* ACER NEGUNDO. CIMICIFUGA RACEMOSA *spikes in the rear right are echoed on the left by delphiniums. Quebec Z4.*

You don't need money to achieve appropriate scale in the well-designed garden. Just a good eye. Fletcher Steele, the great American landscape architect, used to argue that "an old shed and well-proportioned path might possess a kind of charm lacking in the most pretentious parterre."

Your garden has to fit the whole context in which it sits. Undulations of the ground, flat surfaces, background buildings—even how much sky you can see—are important to the scale of your garden. Always keep them in mind.

You do not have to become precious about scale and have everything in your garden so perfectly proportioned that the result is stifling. The ideal placing of one overscaled element can emphasize the rightness of everything else in the design.

One common mistake in scale is to have things too small rather than too large. Most of us are usually intimidated by the grand and so tend to avoid making big statements with large objects or plantings in the garden. Take scale in garden sculpture, for instance. You don't want something dinky. Sculpture should be large enough to be seen, but not so large that it overshadows all the plantings. Very often an incidental sculpture—not always in view from the house—is more satisfying. And it is possible to use a piece of sculpture in the foreground to supply scale for the larger view in the background.

Another caution: don't scale down too far in a very small garden. You still need sensible paths for walking and places to sit. To surround them with nothing but bitty little plants isn't necessarily going to make the garden seem larger. Rather, it will make the whole place feel ditzy.

The intent of good garden design is harmony, and the way you achieve this is through careful use of the principles of unity, proportion and scale. If you can get the geometry in there first, you will find that the design flows more easily and with greater animation.

## GETTING STARTED ON YOUR GARDEN DESIGN

**STEP ONE** ❧ Here's some more reality therapy for you. Gardening can be a black hole for money. That's why it's a good idea to start your design with a blank piece of paper—for a budget. Rather than go crazy being dissatisfied with what you can't have, set yourself a price limit, whether it's three hundred, three thousand or thirty thousand dollars.

Winter is ideal for working out new garden ideas—long enough in most parts of the country to redo plans many times over. The process is therapeutic, and you won't be tormented by the idea that you should be working outside. Of course, you can start any time, just get on with it by following this recipe:

❧ Catalogue everything you have in the garden, from the quality of the soil to the amount of sun it gets in midsummer (and midwinter); the number and size of trees, shrubs and plants already in place; where the shadows fall; the fences and any buildings on the property besides the house.

❧ Look at your garden with absolutely unsullied eyes. Every space has something distinctive about it, no matter where you live. Your site has primordial qualities deep below the surface of the soil. In literature this is called the spirit of the place. It is unique and you must discover that mysterious quality.

❧ List what is most appealing—almost as if you were a real estate agent trying to make a pitch—even if the garden looks abysmal.

❧ Make a parallel list of everything you hate about the site (the noise, the smells, the dreadful garage, a driveway that's too intrusive, even the noisy kids next door).

❧ Make a wish list of everything you'd like to have in the garden, including plants. Gardeners are greedy by nature, so don't feel guilty. I once catalogued everything I'd ever seen in gardens that appealed to me. I wanted them all: a lath house (a shelter for shading plants), benches, sculpture, bird bath, pool, pond, waterfall, patio, gazebo, pergola,

LEFT: *Thomas Hobbs' garden seems almost exotic with* TRA-CHYCARPUS FORTUNEI, *a hardy windmill palm;* CAREX, *striped sedge;* OPHIOPOGON NIGRESCENS; *lavender;* IRIS *'Ecstatic Echo';* YUCCA GLAUCA; *in the rear: yellow blooms of* EUPHORBIA WULFENII. *Looming benignly over this scene is a* BETULA PENDULA *'Youngii', weeping birch. British Columbia Z8.*

BELOW: *Perfect balance in well-designed steps is evident in the garden of Dr. Lee Goossens. Steps are usually recommended for slopes over 25 degrees. To make a leisurely descent have a riser of 4.5 inches (11 cm) and a tread no less than 20 inches (65 cm). Left:* IRIS SIBIRICA; *a swath of* LIRI-OPE SPICATA *under a* CORNUS FLORIDA *'Rubra'. The ferns are* POLYSTICHUM ACROSTICHOIDES. *The flowers in bloom are* GAURA LINDHEIMERI. *Ontario Z6.*

rose arbor, fountain, screens for the compost. I have a garden 19 feet (6 meters) wide and 130 feet (40 meters) deep. The pergola goes over the deck opening on to the garden; the rose (and clematis) arbor leads naturally from one section of the garden to the next; the lath house has turned into a slatted box that can be moved about easily in a small area; the screened area for the compost is there and thriving. Garden furniture is confined to a small stone bench and a bird bath. Alas, everything else belongs in another garden.

❧ Make a list of your essential needs. For instance, if you have a blustery site, immediately plant a windbreak in the path of the prevailing winds.

❧ Screen out local horrors with major trees, shrubs and vines. Start your plans with these verticals.

Children will have to be allowed into the garden, so designate an area for them exclusively (they eventually leave home and you can wrest it back for yourself). Make a sunny sheltered place into a secret garden for kids. Have trees and groups of flowers in scale with kids' heights and with bright colors and interesting textures—children love to touch plants. Choose a square left out of a patio area or a special corner, so there will be as little damage as possible.

It's inevitable that kids will want to be where the adults are, so take this into consideration. Divide the garden with a strip of benches for seating. Make it close to where children will play in the sand. This can become a foliage border in the future. An area for tricycles can become a gravel garden. Any kind of raised platform will make the space flexible and fascinate kids. Make sure you design a storage place for toys and junk—something that fits in with everything else. And remember the animals: a dog will need a place to run.

In a perfect world you'd have the garage designed in the same style as all other outbuildings. If this isn't possible, have the details on the garage coordinate with the cornices of a fence, say, or a particularly good gate. The garage is one place where being swamped by verdure is a virtue, not a vice—plant vines to grow all over the building. Decorate it with fanciful trellis work and plant clematis or other ornamentals.

Then you'll need to account for all the other basics: where to park the car (preferably so it can't be seen); accommodating a swimming pool, present or future; work and storage areas; a place for the compost—absolutely necessary no matter what size garden you have.

This is the stage to decide how you will water the garden. You will save money and resources down the road if you put hoses underground before you put in the infrastructure. Running a xeriphytic garden (one that uses water efficiently) will become increasingly important in the future.

By taking all these elements into account early on in this adventure you will be able to integrate them more easily into your overall design.

PROFESSIONAL GUIDANCE

Sort out what you can do yourself and where you will have to resort to paid help. One of the best investments I ever made was hiring a professional gardener to help me put in a section of checkerboard squares. He understood exactly what I wanted when I said, "Squinch up your eyes—this is how I see the place in five years." It was his idea to reuse the sod from taking up the grass and shape it into a berm. How he placed that rise of earth dictated the direction that section of the

LEFT: *Well-proportioned walks and steps unite the various areas of Elaine Corbet's coastal garden. At the rear:* CEDRUS DEODARA; CRYPTOMERIA JAPONICA; PHYLLOSTACHYS AUREA; *middle storey on the left:* juniper spp.; IRIS X GERMANICA; BERGENIA CORDIFOLIA; CISTUS LAURIFOLIUS; ANTHEMIS CUPANIANA. *Spilling down the hill on the right is* HYPERICUM CALYCINUM. *This garden is filled with lovely foliage and well-coordinated shapes. British Columbia Z8.*

garden would take. Though I didn't know it at the time, it's very, very difficult, if not impossible, to move a berm around. At the time all this seemed like an enormous expense—but it's one I've never regretted.

When hiring a professional, it's crucial to get the right person. Check out at least two gardens the designer has completed. I've seen expensive hard landscaping (lots of stone patios, steps and terraces—the elements that have nothing to do with plants) being perpetrated by people who seemed to have no sense of scale. You'll be able to spot this if you find that your potential designer likes to put tiny little steps into deep terraces. This is the result of bad design. It's hideously expensive work, so you don't want to make *any* mistakes.

It's my experience that people know more about their gardens than they are aware of. They also know more about what they really need and want than perhaps they realize. Don't let anyone impose ideas unless those ideas are so superb that you can't live without them. And don't get bamboozled by someone trying to sell you a lot more than you need or trying to talk you out of what you want. A professional designer should be able to explain to you—thoroughly and expertly—why your idea just won't work.

If you are building walls or getting involved with terraces higher than 3 feet (1 meter), get a professional to do the calculations if not the work.

STEP TWO ❧ Gardening is all about process. The idea of a plan may be anathema to anyone who believes creative gardening is totally spontaneous. But much of the creative process takes place at the planning stage. Don't be put off by people saying, "I just garden, I never make plans." They already have a concept so firmly in mind that they know exactly what they are doing or they have moved very slowly and logically in working out a design over a number of years.

You can make plans in your head or write them out to begin with, but nothing beats having a simple, clear drawing. It will focus your mind incredibly and make you much more organized. You don't have to be a slave to this plan and follow every move. It's a guide to the future, not a dictator.

The most disappointing gardens I've found, even ones chock-a-block with plants, are those with no underlying concept to drive them. Plants plunked into a garden just because they've been brought home from the nursery do not contribute to good design. You might as well do it properly from the beginning and thereby save time and money in the long run.

DESIGN TIPS
❧ As a prelim to making a drawing on paper, take photographs of all the areas of the garden, and from each window. Do this in as many seasons as possible.

❧ Here's a suggestion about starting a design: use powdered chalk to lay down shapes right on the ground. You'll have time enough to look at these two-dimensional lines from every window—until it pours and you lose your drawing. It will give you a good feel for the spaces you want to encompass. And it's cheap to change your mind.

❧ Whenever I plant a new area, I first take bamboo poles and arrange them to demarcate new beds or indicate major plants. If a new shrub is going in, this will give me a good idea of the height (but not the volume) of the plant when it matures. For volume, I use either my imagination or a person to approximate the full size of the plant.

Another device I picked up at a design workshop is useful for designing a contemplative garden. This exercise is to pitch yourself back to your very earliest and happiest place as a child, one that was sacred and secure for you. Draw this magic place. Put in what attracted you so long ago—the trees, a lake, hills, big rocks, secret places to hide in. All these were in my drawing, and I realized that without knowing what I was doing I had incorporated most

ABOVE: *Kathy Leishman designed these well-proportioned steps for her garden. Lower left:* LIGULARIA; PRIMULA JAPONICA; GERANIUM *'Claridge Druce'. Rear right to front:* CEANOTHUS *'Frosty Blue';* ANTIRRHINUM *spp.;* CRAMBE MARITIMA; CLEMATIS *'Miss Bateman';* GERANIUM MACRORRHIZUM *'Ingwersen's Variety';* CENTRANTHUS RUBER; ONOPORDUM ACANTHIUM; LYCHNIS CORONARIA *'Alba';* ARTEMISIA; AQUILEGIA; PHLOMIS RUSSELIANA; GERANIUM PRATENSE. *British Columbia Z8.*

LEFT: *The garden of Mary and Burt Manion, designed by Murray Haigh, shows how good design can disguise a very ordinary garage. Standards of clipped* FAGUS SYLVATICA, *echoed in the conical* TAXUS BACCATA, *yew, underplanted with a hedging of* BUXUS, *boxwood. Ontario Z6.*

of these elements—in miniature—into my garden.

It's an easy step from wild imaginings to interpreting these features in your design. A river could become a river of stones; a tree house, a gazebo; a small bay, the shape of garden beds. Once you've tried an exercise like this to get your mind cleared of all sorts of rubble, you are more than ready to make a simple, clear drawing of your garden.

❧ Using graph paper, make up a convenient scale: for example, 1 inch (2.5 centimeters) equals 5 feet (1.5 meters), or 1 foot (30 centimeters) if you have a small garden. Or use whatever you can work out on the size of paper at hand. Traditional scales are as follows:

⅛ inch:1 foot for a garden 30 x 90 feet (10 x 30 meters); for a smaller garden, ¼ inch:1 foot; for a larger garden, divide it into smaller areas and draw each area ⅛ inch or ¼ inch:1 foot for garden features such as a pergola, and 1 inch:1 foot for detailed construction drawings or sections for walls or fences.

❧ Measure your lot accurately.

❧ Make an outline of the house and indicate where all the windows are (mark how high they are off the ground); where doors are and which way they open. Once you have this basic form done to your satisfaction, copy it about ten times for all the mistakes and changes of mind you will make as you go along.

❧ Start sketching in the contours of the land on the graph paper. If rocks jut out naturally, or if the garden slopes, include this in your garden plan and think of ways to capitalize on these features.

❧ Mark where all the existing plants are, and draw them to scale. Measure the distance from them to each corner of the house. Measure tree canopies from trunk to the edges and check how much shade they make. You probably won't want to move mature trees, so you'll have to work around them. But you can get more sunlight into the garden even on a heavily treed site by trimming out the lower branches of old trees and pruning up as high as possible. This won't cause any damage. You'll end up with a graceful canopy that will also impart dappled shade.

To create a garden design you have to be ruthless. You'll be moving just about everything (other than trees) that doesn't suit. Better to do it at the beginning than change your mind after you've got a few more years of growth on a shrub.

About being ruthless: at this stage you can let out all your hostilities. Don't keep plants just because you've always had them. Now's the time to ask, Why? If there's no good answer, give them away. Intelligent brutality. I will never forget the sense of elation I felt when I realized that I could get rid of a shrub that I'd always hated—someone else loves it now.

❧ Think of your garden design as a whole, organically related to the land around if it's in the country, or let it reverberate with the geometry of the buildings around you in the city.

In all great garden design a sense of tension or opposition is at work. The pull between positive and negative spaces; contrasts between the dark and the light in both buildings and plants. These are important ingredients to get into your design right from the beginning.

## GARDEN ROOMS

This is another one of the those hort-terms you see all the time. And it is a splendid concept. If you look at books about great European gardens you will find that many are divided into sections almost like rooms. These garden rooms provide an underlying pattern that will serve you well—if it looks right in the site. And it doesn't matter how small or how large your garden may be. The English designer Lawrence Johnston, creator of Hidcote, perfected the idea of garden rooms. He took all the good ideas he'd seen in French and Italian formal gardens, incorporated them with the more lavish color borders of his contemporary Gertrude Jekyll, then added in the wild gardens of William Robinson.

Johnston's idea was to alternate between the formal and the looser, more casual. In this way he was able to use a huge variety of plants and still

LEFT: *The redesign of Sheila Paulson's garden is in its early stages in this photograph, but the image shows how the bones of a good design can settle in quickly. Top left: blue spruce and delphiniums; right of the trellis:* PAEONIA *'Tom Eckhard' and* P. *'Fairy's Petticoat'. The tree is* MALUS *'Royalty'. In the right foreground is* CLEMATIS ALPINA RUBRA, *and to its right is* CAMPANULA X *'Birch' hybrid. Alberta Z4.*

BELOW: *Dorothea Lovat Dickson designed layer on layer of plants to create a sense of tranquillity and seclusion in the garden of Marilyn Field-Marsham and Ned Baldwin. Upper left and right:* PRUNUS TRILOBA *'Multiplex', flowering almond tree; left of gazebo:* MISCANTHUS SINENSIS *'Gracillimus', maiden grass; right of gazebo:* M. FLORIDULUS, *giant Chinese silver grass. The dominant grass is* MISCANTHUS SINENSIS *'Zebrinus', zebra grass. Ontario Z6.*

ABOVE: *The sky creates a horizontal line that emphasizes the angles of the paths in the garden of Audrey and John Burrows. Left: blue spruce;* CORNUS SIBIRICA, *dogwood;* FORSYTHIA; SALIX ARCTICA, *Arctic willow; larch. The hedge in front of the border of perennials is* COTONEASTER. *Alberta Z3.*

RIGHT: *This view of Al Zinn's garden, designed by Murray Haigh, shows that one oversized element does not have to overwhelm a small garden. Lower left:* ASTILBE *spp.;* SEDUM SPECTABILE *'Ruby Glow';* PHLOX PANICULATA. *Ontario Z6.*

contain them in an elegant and sophisticated manner. And when one part of the garden was out of season, another was in full flower, giving him a strong architectural feeling in the garden.

The idea of garden rooms has expanded to include rooms with different moods, color schemes or collections of plants, providing an enlarged canvas on which to work. This is also an expansion of the idea of working on the garden a section at a time rather than trying to tackle it all at once.

Russell Page talks of sketching with hedges and paths, adding body by planting trees and shrubs. Then, he suggests, you step back and look "at the whole as a question of decoration." This is where the idea of garden rooms can, once again, come to the rescue. The viewer should never be able to take in the whole garden at once—mystery comes into play when you withhold some of it from first view.

AXIAL DESIGN AND PATHS ᶻᶜ An axis is an imaginary line that runs right through the center of something. The more formal a setting the more traditional it is to have a central axis. You can make a mechanical axis by putting in a garden path. A more subtle approach is to have the axis implied by plantings or by a central focal point. Any hesitation about this is going to weaken the design of a more formal garden and no matter what you do it will be difficult to disguise the fact.

If you are using a central axis with cross axes at right angles, within those axes there should be symmetry and balance. All of the variety is then in the detail. With a main axis the eye needs to travel to a central focus.

Figure out how you want people to get from one place to the next in the garden. This rhythm will be determined by the design and position of the paths. Should people move through slowly, savoring each area, discovering surprises and finding places in which to rest? Or do you want straight and narrow paths that will move the traffic along speedily? If the route is wide and passes through

a bower or pergola, people will inevitably want to linger and contemplate what's here rather than quickly get to what's over there.

Consider how that rhythm will be achieved without formal paths. Will you have stepping stones to get from one section of the garden to another? Or will you use grass as a medium to move around on as well as a design element?

Sketch out on the garden design where paths will go. Obviously they should lead some place. But let's start with where they should *not* be. Don't have a path all around the house—stranding it in a sea of cement or stone. Instead, determine the axes of your garden with paths. They will give shape to the pattern of your design—the simpler the better.

When you design paths make sure that they are wide enough to accommodate two people strolling along if that is your intent. Otherwise have stepping stones that will keep one person at a time moving through the garden. You can make the paths disappear into shrubbery to set up an element of mystery; or use them in forced perspective—narrower at one end than at the other.

FOCAL POINTS ᶻᶜ These are much discussed in garden literature. They can be almost anything you'd like: a fine piece of sculpture or a fountain along a major axis; smaller details such as mirrors or pieces of furniture along side axes. A focal point can be a gorgeous tree with a special shape, or a gazebo.

The eye travels along canals most easily, and that's what the axis will provide—a canal for the eye, whether it's a row of trees, stone work or a hedge directing the eye where you want it to go.

Any repetition in trees, shrubs or colors will also guide the eye to a specific location. Whatever becomes the focus—a gazebo or pond, for example—will gain in importance. You can also create visual side trips by using something like a trellis or small sculpture. But these should not be so significant that they divert from the main journey.

LEFT: *The garden of Lynne Milgram and David H. Kaye indicates just how many plants a small front garden can hold when assembled properly. Clockwise from lower left:* DICENTRA, *bleeding heart;* TAXUS CUSPIDATA, *Japanese yew;* ASTILBE X ARENDSII *'Europa';* RHODODENDRON CATAWBIENSE *'Nova Zembla';* A. X A. *'Bridal Veil';* HOSTA SIEBOLDIANA. *The hedge is* LIGUSTRUM AMURENSE, *privet; in the rear:* ACER PALMATUM *'Dissectum', Japanese cut leaf maple; right front:* ASPERULA ODORATA, *sweet woodruff, and violas. Ontario Z6.*

ABOVE: *Kathy Leishman's garden deals effectively with the spirit of the site. The rocky outcrop becomes a border of* DIGITALIS PURPUREA *'Alba';* CRAMBE CORDIFOLIA; *to the left is* ERIOPHYLLUM LANATUM; ARTEMISIA *'Silver Brocade';* IBERIS AMARA, *annual self-seeding candytuft. Right foreground:* FRAGARIA *'Pink Panda'. British Columbia Z8.*

ABOVE: *Margaret and David Barham have divided their suburban garden into rooms surrounded by a hedge of Chinese elm; the golden delicious apple is cut for shape; divider between the two rooms is a privet hedge fronted by* ACONITUM, *monkshood. Ontario Z5.*

LEFT: *The central axis in Andrew Yeoman's garden makes a direct entrance to the house. The tree dominating this scene is a pin oak and in the rear is a Japanese maple. British Columbia Z8.*

RIGHT: *Tim Saunders' woodland garden has a skillful blurring of boundaries between the grass walkway and the encroaching forest. From the left:* HOSTA *'Royal Standard';* LONICERA CANADENSIS; H. SIEBOLDIANA ELEGANS; H. HALCYON; VINCA MINOR; PAXISTIMA; ARCTOSTAPHYLOS; GALIUM ODORATUM; COTONEASTER DAMMERI. *Ontario Z5.*

ABOVE: *An antique gate frames the view in the garden of John B. Mitchell. The trees cut out of the distance allow a view of a nearby lake. Two rows of hostas edge the path to the gate. Quebec Z4.*

LEFT: *The Goose Allee, as this section of Francis Cabot's splendid garden is called, has a central axis that leads to a sheltered seat. The long border with a background of cedar hedges has* THALICTRUM AQUILEGIFOLIUM, *peonies, centaureas, geraniums,* ALLIUM CAERULEUM *just coming into bud, asters, catmint and* ARUNCUS SYLVESTER. *Quebec Z4.*

RIGHT: *In Francis Cabot's magnificent country garden the eye is channeled toward a striking vista by a break in the cedar hedges. A focal point is created by the statue of Antonia (Claudius' mother) surrounded by* IRIS PSEUDACORUS; I. SIBIRICA; OENOTHERA FRUTICOSA; *and single white peonies. Quebec Z4.*

**THE BORROWED VIEW** ⁊ Look around and see what can be borrowed from the surrounding landscape. Your focal point may become something beyond the garden—a view borrowed by framing it with major plants or trees. This is a time-honored design principle perfected by Japanese gardeners. They take the view of a mountain, cleverly use hedges as a horizontal line—kept at eye level—then frame the view with vertical plants.

## GARDEN TYPES

Garden rooms can be reinterpreted for almost any situation whether in the city or outside it.

**THE COUNTRY GARDEN** ⁊ Because the country garden inevitably spills out into the landscape, you'll need a method to encompass the garden, to make it intimate, to give it a human scale.

TIPS FOR DESIGNING A COUNTRY GARDEN

⁊ Start your design with an existing tree or group of trees. Or a dramatic contour of the land.

⁊ Blur the edges between your garden and the surrounding countryside by allowing plantings to overlap or be integrated with surrounding native plants.

⁊ Use your space the way it's employed in Zen gardens—to set up a bit of uncertainty. Overlap the middleground and the background with hedges, long alleys of trees and meadows of wildflowers.

**SMALL CITY GARDENS** ⁊ City gardens have their own special problems, the most significant of which is that you are surrounded by a lot of things you don't necessarily want to see.

TIPS FOR DESIGNING A SMALL CITY GARDEN

⁊ Privacy is the first thing to consider. A good fence is paramount. If possible, extend it beyond the normal height by adding trellis and covering it with vines for a sense of enclosure.

⁊ To make a small space seem larger, build mirrors (Mylar is weatherproof) into a wall or fence.

⁊ Go back to the ancient practice of trompe l'oeil: a painted-on view or focal point to give width or depth in the garden.

⁊ Emphasize one element in the garden—an oversized pot, a large sculpture, a large tree. A large object in a small space looks even bigger.

⁊ Raise sides and back in a horseshoe shape to give the garden some height.

⁊ Use a rise or berm to break up a dull flat surface and to create surprise and variety.

⁊ In a long narrow space emphasize the narrowness with a straight vista to a special adornment.

**THE KNOT GARDEN** ⁊ Knot gardens have become part of Canadian gardening only in the past decade; they can be adapted to either a city or a country garden. However, they do require an enormous amount of maintenance as well as skill in a planting design.

The original concept of a knot garden was a plant-enclosed courtyard to be seen from windows. Rosemary, lavender, germander, hyssop and thyme filled the spaces between patterned sections of colored gravel and sand. The tradition expanded to include santolina and what has become the most useful plant of all, boxwood. Flowers fill in the spaces of open knot gardens.

To plant a knot garden, you must work out the design very carefully. There are books on traditional designs, but don't get enticed by such a complicated venture without a great deal of research. Just to give you an idea of what goes into a knot garden: a simple small one would occupy 6 square feet (0.5 square meters), with seven plants to each side.

You can create a knot garden in a container (no bigger than one square yard or meter) by taking cuttings of herbs and putting them into the soil in the designated place. Keep damp for a few weeks until roots have formed.

With all knot gardens it's important to decide on a height and keep it clipped constantly. The edges should be snipped low so they don't become leggy, and there should always be a crisp outline to make an effective design.

LEFT: *The startlingly beautiful box hedge knot garden, designed by Torizuka Landscape for the Wiggan family, demonstrates how a well-executed design should look. Rear left: miniature apple; copper beech; Japanese larch; cedar. Ontario Z5.*

BELOW: *Elm trees provide the background in Jackie Dean's garden. A blue spruce finds the proper position beside a hedge of* SYRINGA VILLOSA, *lilac. Front: German bearded iris;* ARTEMISIA *'Silver Mound';* SEDUM SPECTABILE; HEUCHERA, *coralbells; middle: Russell lupines;* ACHILLEA, *yarrow; rear: delphiniums;* LYTHRUM; ACONITUM, *monkshood. Alberta Z4.*

# CHAPTER TWO

# DESIGNING WITH FOLIAGE PLANTS

*"Good design is a matter of good articulation."*
RUSSELL PAGE

*T*he foliage garden is a restful place where beauty unfolds more slowly than in a perennial garden. It's a place where the textures of leaves are far more important than the colors of flowers. Foliage plants can have blossoms and berries, lure butterflies and birds and provide a sanctuary and a shelter.

Establishing a foliage garden means entering a more sophisticated world both aesthetically and visually. There are no easy ways to achieve the great foliage garden. Apart from time, it takes planning—much more so than any other kind of garden. There are many advantages to this. The most important is that the more foliage plants there are in a garden, the less care it will need overall. This does not mean that foliage plants are the no-care solutions for gardeners who are looking for an easy out. Any creative garden is going to take creative maintenance. Trees, shrubs, vines and ground covers do tend, however, to require slightly less attention than your average perennial. And they do require more care in choosing and planting properly in the first place.

What's of prime interest to the perennial gardener—great drifts of color—is transmogrified in the foliage garden into a muted and subtle inclusive picture. Verticals and horizontals; distance and perspective; positive and negative spaces; mass and shape—these become your tools.

To design a garden with foliage plants, you need a special feeling for the plants themselves. No matter how few are added, they will contribute immense energy to your garden design. Once you achieve this visual muscle in the garden, you'll have the underlying structure for the rest of the plants you choose.

There are things to avoid, however. I've seen a foliage garden in which every surface is covered with vines and shrubs, with specimen plants dotted about screaming for attention. It's just as rattling as a yard full of riotous bedding plants. Much as I enjoy wretched excess personally, it has no place in the garden. There must be a balance between foliage and perennial plants. And it would be a poorer place without annuals and biennials added to this potent mix.

Though I've seldom met a plant I didn't like, there are owners who put them together in such a way that they grate. For instance, the lone birch tree on the lawn; the Japanese maple smack dab in the middle of the front garden; a huge stand of pampas grass crammed onto a tiny lot.

The beauty of these plants is often lost if they are always in the same situation. We simply stop seeing them. That doesn't mean you should rush out and chop them down. Redesign the garden around them by adding other plants or superior garden furnishings. Give them a better context and you'll raise the garden above the banal. It can be surprisingly simple.

---

RIGHT: *In a relatively small city garden Peter and Jose Braun have formed a superb design. From back left corner:* BETULA PAPYRIFERA, *paper birch;* JUNIPERUS SCOPULORUM, *spruce 'Blue Haven';* PRUNUS PADUS COMMUTATA, *Mayday tree; another spruce 'Blue Haven';* PINUS MUGO, *mugo pine. In the middle left:* PICEA GLAUCA GLOBOSA, *dwarf globe blue spruce grafted on a stem;* TYPHA, *cattail or bulrush;* JUNIPERUS SABINA, *savon juniper. Bottom left:* FESTUCA OVINA *var.* GLAUCA, *blue fescue grass;* THYMUS VULGARIS, *creeping thyme;* IRIS SIBIRICA; HYDRANGEA ARBORESCENS GRANDIFLORA *'Annabelle';* IRIS X GERMANICA, *bearded iris. Alberta Z3.*

ABOVE: *In her incredible foliage garden, Pamela Frost puts together spiky plants with variegated plants in a graceful style. Background:* THUJA PLICATA *'Fastigiata';* ROSA GLAUCA; MISCANTHUS SINENSIS *'Variegatus', a tall grass;* THALICTRUM AQUILEGIFOLIUM *'Album' (white flowers);* WEIGELA FLORIDA *'Aureovariegata' (pink flowers). Most noticeable in the front row are:* HOSTA *'Frances Williams';* CROCOSMIA MASONIORUM; *and* IRIS PALLIDA *'Variegata'. British Columbia Z8.*

LEFT: *This cool glade in the country garden of Francis Cabot combines the right balance of large-leaved architectural plants and smaller ones with textures that harmonize. The collection of* PRIMULA *contributes many different colors in the foreground; russet shades to the right are* P. FLORINDAE. *The huge plants in the background are* PETASITES JAPONICUS *var.* GIGANTEUS. *Quebec Z2.*

## THE HOUSE

*"The relationship between house and garden is maintained and emphasized by light, air and visual space as it flows freely from one to another."*

THOMAS CHURCH

One object of a garden is to enhance the attractiveness of the house and its property. If you have a dull house, foliage plants can turn it into a place of beauty. And if you are blessed with graceful architecture, you might need only the simple embellishment of a vine rather than a camouflage of plants.

For the visually literate gardener, one of the blights on the landscape is the traditional three-foundation plantings smashed up against a house. This is what passes for "landscaping" in some circles. I've heard too many gardeners bemoan the fact that they hired a professional to improve the front only to have old trees and shrubs ripped out, replaced by one small pointy conifer accompanied by a mounded conifer and another big vertical conifer at the corner of the house. Foundation planting at its worst. And most houses don't even have the obvious foundations that these planting schemes were concocted to disguise.

In order to unite the house and garden, you'll need to look first at the horizontal and vertical forms of your site. Your house is on a horizontal plane. Strong horizontal plants will establish the foreground, the middleground and the background of the garden. Vertical plants can be used both to form a sense of enclosure and to frame a view.

Verticals are crucial to your design. They must be taken into account first, and if you are using vines as verticals get them planted immediately—there are no instant results here; they take several years to be effective.

If one element overwhelms everything else about your site, take full advantage of it. For instance, if you are surrounded by tall buildings your garden is probably shady. Make it even more so—a dramatic and mysterious deep shade. An exotic oasis.

SOME OF THE THINGS FOLIAGE WILL DO

❧ Yellow and variegated foliage plants will provide light where there is none. Almost every species has a yellow or variegated version, so you have an enormous range to choose from.

❧ Create dramatic backgrounds: dark foliage for light plants and light foliage for darker plants.

❧ Provide color for four seasons. We're used to thinking about autumn color and often overbalance gardens in that favor. But even as each season changes foliage will also alter.

If your experience has been mainly with perennials and you've decided to extend your beds to include more foliage plants, spatial considerations become more significant. You can imagine a herbaceous bed in a horizontal plane, but you can't do that with trees and shrubs. Distance becomes especially important. The size of your garden is irrelevant, but the scale of your choices within that context is crucial. You can devise a plan that will work well in a large place and get the same terrific results in a small space by doing it in miniature.

A good foliage garden takes at least five years to settle in and perhaps seven years to look really great. Keep this in mind and be warned—this is not instant gardening.

## TERMS TO KNOW

One of the great pleasures of gardening is becoming familiar with botanical terms. All these terms are graphic, so the more of them you know the more readily you will be able to imagine what a leaf or tree looks like even before you see it.

THE LEAF ❧ Since leaf forms in foliage plants are their most recognizable feature, the botanical descriptions will help you understand the structure of a leaf when studying catalogues and books where these terms are used.

PARTS OF A LEAF: stem, bud, stipule, petiole, midrib, blade and leaf. The bud is usually located at the axil

ABOVE: *Renate and Herb Mayr have chosen striking statuesque plants for a shady border against their house. Rear to front:* FATSIA JAPONICA; CLEMATIS MERIMAWICYIANA *climbs up the wall; the fern is* ADIANTUM PEDATUM; FATSHEDERA LIZEI *is on the wall;* ZANTEDESCHIA AETHIOPICA *(in flower);* HOSTA SIEBOLDIANA *var.* ELEGANS. *British Columbia Z8.*

LEFT: *Rex Murfitt's garden includes a splendid silver foliage border. The edging is* TANACETUM DENSUM AMANI; SANTOLINA CHAMAECYPARISSUS; ACHILLEA *'Coronation Gold' with a* CYNARA CARDUNCULUS, *cardoon;* HELICHRYSUM SEROTINUM, *curry plant;* NEPETA MUSSINII; *big silver leaf is* KIERACEUM WALDSTEINII; LAVANDULA ANGUSTIFOLIA *'Hidcote';* ARTEMISIA *'Powis Castle' by the path. Foreground:* ANTHEMIS PENDUNCULATA TUBERCULATA. *British Columbia Z7.*

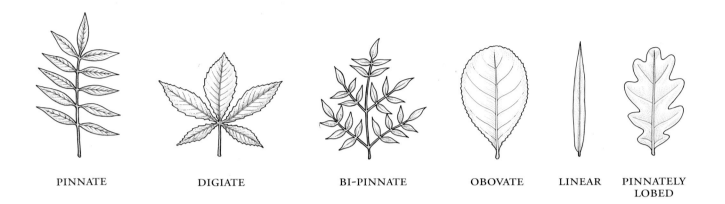

PINNATE     DIGIATE     BI-PINNATE     OBOVATE     LINEAR     PINNATELY LOBED

of the stem and the branch (or twig) of a simple leaf. A compound leaf has more than one leaf emerging from the petiole. The space between these leaflets is known as the rachis.

TYPES OF COMPOUND LEAVES

  Palmate (attached at a common point)
  Odd-pinnate (odd number of leaflets)
  Even-pinnate (even number of leaflets)
  Bipinnate (each pinnae has two leaflets)

DESIGN CAVEATS WITH LEAVES

❧ Don't fill your garden with leaves of the same size. This gives a bland, uniform look.

❧ The shape of the leaf has little to do with the overall shape of a plant—so don't be fooled.

❧ Large size doesn't necessarily make a bold leaf. Mahonias have small leaves but they are bold because they have strong serrated edges with great presence.

❧ Large leaves can add an exotic, sensual feel to a bed. But be careful in siting these plants. They can overwhelm everything else around them.

❧ A leaf's density makes a difference to its appearance. Plant those with the most density in front of those with less density for an ethereal background.

❧ In dense plants use strong shapes: either vertical or horizontal. If you have these shapes with some-

thing that isn't as solid it will look wimpy. Here's an example: CARPINUS BETULUS 'Fastigiata', European hornbeam, has a similar size and shape to QUERCUS ROBUR 'Fastigiata', English oak, but the latter is far more dense.

❧ For accents: the customary way to place plants is to use large foliage as a major accent against a background of smaller massed leaves. But you can experiment for even more dramatic relationships.

❧ A light-colored leaf will always stand out much more vividly against something darker.

## CHOOSING PLANTS

There are some carved-in-stone principles about planting designs and one is to always have the plants related to the site. If you have a wet garden, make it into a refuge for waterfowl by adding a pond. If your garden is dry as a bone, turn it into a xerophytic landscape (one that uses almost no water), or a variation of a maquis or prairie using only native plants. Yearning for a sunny garden when you don't have it, wanting terraces and hills where they are impossible, is a waste of time.

Another important principle is to respect the ecological needs of your plants. By understanding these, you'll be rewarded with healthy, good-looking, long-lived plants. Plants that thrive in a dry atmosphere belong together, as do moisture-loving

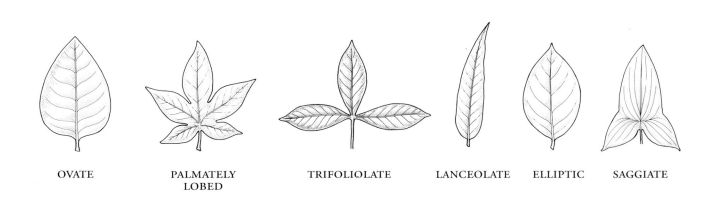

OVATE   PALMATELY   TRIFOLIOLATE   LANCEOLATE   ELLIPTIC   SAGGIATE
        LOBED

plants. Making natural combinations by putting together plants with similar cultural needs (light, soil, water and drainage demands) will provide instant harmony.

❧ Start with the kind of soil you have at hand. If it's a very limy or alkaline soil and you try to force ericaceous or other acid-loving plants to grow, you'll probably end up with rather unhappy-looking plants. If you insist on using plants that don't suit your soil type, be prepared to change the soil in a wide area and to keep on replenishing the minerals for years.

❧ Learn the space requirements of your plants. Trees especially should be given enough room first time round. Let shrubs approach maturity before you start changing your mind. I say this, then go right out and move young shrubs. I may get a more pleasing combination, but the downside is that the poor things take about two years to recover. So apprise yourself of each plant's requirements before making any decisions about placing and moving. It's a great temptation to jam in major plants such as trees and large shrubs to get a finished look quickly. But with crowded planting you run the risk of being cowardly about taking them out when they've matured and you can see the enormity of this mistake. Decent spacing makes healthy plants. Otherwise they become leggy.

❧ Discover everything you can about your microclimate. This means finding out where the prevailing winds come from, how high you are above sea level, when the first and last frosts are expected. The hardiness zone map in my first book, *The Canadian Gardener*, will give you an idea of the frost dates and number of growing days in your zone. But that is very, very general information and many more subtle elements come into play in your own microclimate. Much of this information will come to you quite naturally through observation. And you can always get these vital statistics from the agricultural station nearest you (or the Department of Agriculture).

**PLANT ORIGINS** ❧ Learning where a plant originated can also help you make choices and is a dandy method of achieving harmony. For example, plants from South America are more likely to survive successfully on the west coast of North America than on the east coast. Plants from Japan and China do better in mountainous areas, the central plains and the east of the continent where the conditions echo their origins. If you know that a plant comes from the high Himalayas or Kashmir, you will also know that it is likely to be hardy no matter how fragile it appears to be. The Plant Listings in this book (pages 169–201) give the plant's origin after its name.

ABOVE: *Lilacs form the background in Mr. and Mrs. John P. Fisher's well-balanced foliage border. Left to right:* HOSTA SIEBOLDIANA; ASTILBE; *yellow daylily; sweet woodruff; peonies;* ALCHEMILLA MOLLIS, *lady's-mantle.* VIBURNUM, *dogwood and spirea in background. Quebec Z4B.*

PREVIOUS DOUBLE-PAGE SPREAD: *Marion and Alex Jarvie's brilliantly executed garden proves that the well-designed foliage garden has much color in it, along with the added advantage of shapes that harmonize well with each other. Far left:* DAPHNE *'Somerset';* LARIX X PENDULA, *weeping larch. Top half:* CHAMAECYPARIS PISIFERA *'Lemon Thread', gold threadleaf false cypress. Center rear:* PICEA ABIES *'Reflexa', weeping spruce; far right:* PICEA ALBERTIANA *'Conica', large Alberta spruce; yellow underplanting is* LYSIMACHIA NUMMULARIA *'Aurea' and* LAMIUM MACULATUM *'White Nancy'. Ontario Z5B.*

RIGHT: *Peter and Jose Braun combine talents as plant collectors and designers. Top left corner:* PRUNUS PADUS COMMUTATA, *Mayday tree;* BETULA PAPYRIFERA, *paper birch;* FRAXINUS PENNSYLVANICA SUBINTEGERRIMA, *green ash;* JUNIPERUS SCOPULORUM, *'Blue Haven';* PINUS MUGO, *mugo pine. Ground covers:* SEDUM EWERSII, *pink stonecrop; Siberian cyprus juniper;* HEUCHERA MICRANTHA *'Purple Palace', coralbells.* CARAGANA ARBORESCENS *'Lorbergii', fern-leaved caragana;* PICEA GLAUCA GLOBOSA, *dwarf globe blue spruce grafted on stem. Left ground cover:* THYMUS PSEUDOLANUGINOSUS, *woolly thyme;* T. SERPYLLUM *'Aureum', golden creeping thyme;* H. M. *'Purple Palace';* VIOLA X *'Black Magic', perennial pansy;* SAXIFRAGA PANICULATA, *saxifrage. Alberta Z3.*

ABOVE: *Glen Patterson feels that to imitate a Japanese style would be inappropriate for a Canadian garden. His design reveals the spirit of place and utilizes creative pruning. Lower right:* GAULTHERIA, *salal; upper left:* PINUS GRIF-FITHII, *Bhutan pine. Forward:* CRYPTOMERIA JAPONICA *'Elegans'; to right is* SCIADOPITYS VERTICILLATA, *Japanese umbrella pine; a boxwood pruned with cloud-shaped foliage;* MAGNOLIA X SOULANGIANA. *British Columbia Z8.*

LEFT: *In the garden of Dr. and Mrs. R. M. Peet a collection of Japanese maples blends well with the man-made waterfall and surrounding foliage. Foreground left of wall:* ACER PAL-MATUM *(green);* A. P. *'Bloodgood' (red). Middleground left: dwarf pines; heathers;* JUNIPERUS HORIZONTALIS *'Wiltonii Blue Carpet'; right:* ARCTOSTAPHYLOS, *hairy manzanita;* CHAENOMELES, *red-flowering quince; common sword fern. Foreground bottom left:* CHAMAECYPARIS PISIFERA *'Filifera', red-leaved cypress;* C. HOLLANDIA, *red quince. Right:* COTONEASTER SALICIFOLIUS FLOCCOSUS, *willow-leaved cotoneaster. British Columbia Z8.*

## TIPS ON DESIGNING WITH FOLIAGE PLANTS

Designing with foliage plants is based on simplicity itself—each detail harmoniously relates to the next.

⁊ Hedges, shrubs, perhaps trees, or fences covered with vines will be the outline—the walls, if you will—of your garden rooms. In a very small space you might consider only one room—a partly sub-divided room if necessary.

⁊ Your composition should have underlying patterns associated with each other, and the whole design should relate to the site, the configuration of the ground and your climate.

**HARMONY** ⁊ Along with the suggestions for harmony above, try the following:

⁊ Make a wish list of plants by varieties or in groups for color, texture and so on. If you seem to have too many, throw the list out and start again.

⁊ Use only a couple of plant varieties in the main planting. If you plunk in too many varieties it will confuse the eye, making it dodge about uncomfortably.

⁊ Mirror planting also creates harmony: repeat exactly the same planting on either side of the central axis of the garden. This is an exceptionally good solution in very small gardens.

⁊ Put plants with the same texture or color or plants from the same family together.

⁊ Repeated planting schemes add rhythm as well as harmony to the garden.

**BALANCE** ⁊ Combining plants can contribute to balance almost as effectively as the hard elements in a design.

⁊ Always keep in mind the principle of balancing positive and negative space when you distribute plants. Dark plants represent negative space, light plants positive space. In art, negative space can be just as thrilling as positive space; the same applies to gardening.

⁊ You can achieve balance by using distinct kinds of foliage: large, bold; simple, glossy. Make sure nothing is dominant.

⁊ Combine leaves that repeat each other's shapes —plants with heart-shaped leaves or lance-like leaves, for instance.

⁊ A mass of small-leaved plants needs some strong large ones to bring coherence and interest. If bold leaves are planted in front of little ones, check each side of the planting for balance.

⁊ Always have enough evergreens to act as foils for deciduous plants. Evergreens provide stability and restfulness; deciduous plants light and airiness.

⁊ Don't forget to consider the shape and color of blossoms.

**COLOR** ⁊ It's a big mistake to assume that we have foliage color only in fall. That's of course when we have a *change* in foliage color. But leaf color should be considered in the three seasons (fourth if it's evergreen) whether the changes are subtle or dramatic. ACER PALMATUM, Japanese maple, for example, is a fine green in spring and slowly darkens to its normal burgundy for summer dress. As the days begin to wane this beauty slowly takes on a green mantle again and in the final days of fall it turns flaming scarlet. Every foliage plant has some kind of development like this to take into consideration.

Here's where your sense of rhythm will be most important.

⁊ Don't shove a bunch of different-colored foliages in with others just to get a lot of contrast. Move slowly from one color to the next with strong connecting plants.

⁊ Purple is useful for linking plants set at a distance from one another—a kind of sandwich color. But used too often, the message is destroyed. Gold is another excellent bonding color.

⁊ Be very careful with the color combinations. Delicate spring green may turn into autumnal orange and you won't want that backing up a clashing tone of red or purple.

Color isn't confined just to leaves. Bark can be particularly seductive. Especially in winter when it is more exposed and you can be almost overwhelmed by its beauty. So consider bark when you make a foliage plant selection. I know gardeners who make this the main reason for their choice of a tree or shrub.

When considering color, give serious thought to the background of a major tree. Red maples are beautiful plants, but they are not at their best in front of red brick houses or walls. Just as a birch tree looks better against a dark house rather than a white one.

## VARIEGATED PLANTS

Some people hate them, I love them. The reason most people hate these plants is that they can be overdone so easily. Layer upon layer of variegated plants gives the garden an agitated jerky look. Used with discretion, however, they are marvels. I like to see them up close so that the subtleties in variegation can be better appreciated.

Variegation looks good as a gradation from one strong tone to another or to introduce a lighter accent. If a variegated plant suddenly develops one prominent green branch, it's reverting. Carefully prune the branch back to the collar without cutting into living tissue in the trunk. (See "Creative Pruning" on page 129 for more information.)

Some plants revert more easily than others. ACER NEGUNDO 'Variegatum', box elder, is one example. On the other hand, variegated hydrangeas are stable. But don't, as I have done, put this latter plant up against a variegated dogwood. They look awful together. It was an experiment. The appearance of each improved immediately upon separation.

Sun is a problem with variegation. The plants tend to get scorched when overexposed; they need semishade. And they don't come true from seed, so make cuttings or divisions to propagate.

TEXTURE ❧ Texture is the *feel* of a plant: felted and downy, succulent and squishy, or hard and fixed. One school of thought cautions to keep similar textures together. This creates a seductive, peaceful harmony. But contrasting textures provide a much more fascinating look, I think, giving the garden a subtext.

Whichever you choose, keep in mind that the eye usually goes for finer textures first. If you want this to happen, place finely textured plants as focal points or keep them at eye level.

❧ If you combine coarse- and fine-textured leaves, use about twice as many fine leaves as coarse for a restful feeling. If you use too many fine leaves, you'll get a fussy effect.

❧ Consider the texture in leaves of shrubs—leathery, for instance—then repeat this in the ground cover.

❧ Make contrasts dramatic: fine-textured grasses with the broad architectural leaves of PETASITES JAPONICUS, fuki; PELTIPHYLLUM PELTATUM, umbrella plant, or MACLEAYA, plume poppy.

❧ Plants with extremely dense foliage often look better behind those with looser foliage.

❧ Keep in mind that texture and color change with different light. If you take this into consideration it will improve your planting choices.

## GETTING TO KNOW YOUR PLANTS—INTIMATELY

Looking, feeling, even smelling a plant will help you become horticulturally literate. To really understand foliage plants, do your own planting. This is a very important part of gardening. You'll learn more and learn more quickly about the actual nature of gardening by close contact.

You'll also save a bundle of money and end up with an intimate sense of the plants themselves—their textures, foliage, shape of the root—and, in turn, this will help you place them in choice positions. As the scents of roots and leaves become more familiar, you'll establish a greater sensitivity to the plants.

LEFT: *Janet and Trevor Ashbee have organized foliage to good advantage in their garden. Clockwise from back left:* CORNUS KOUSA CHINENSIS; LARIX X PENDULA; JUNIPERUS *'Blue Haven';* THUJA HOLMSTRUP; ECHINACEA PURPUREA; PETASITES JAPONICUS. *Ontario Z5.*

BELOW: *Pamela Frost's garden is designed with an artist's eye for carefully chosen combinations of shape and form. Left:* CORNUS KOUSA; *right:* AUCUBA JAPONICA *'Variegata'; front middle:* HYDRANGEA; *to the left:* KIRENGESHOMA PALMATA *just showing behind* HOSTA *'Cynthia'. Bottom right:* IRIS FOETIDISSIMA *'Citrina';* LAMIUM MACULATUM *'White Nancy'. British Columbia Z8.*

ABOVE: *Glen Patterson designs each section of his garden so that the subtleties of plants can be appreciated. Clockwise from rear left:* RHODODENDRON *'Wilgen's Ruby';* PRIMULA BEESIANA; CORNUS NUTTALLII *spp., native dogwood;* R. *'Moonstone';* R. BUREAVII; R. *'Lem's Monarch' (in flower); the climbing vine is* AKEBIA QUINATA. *Large-leaved* R. MACABEANUM × *'Promise of Spring'. British Columbia Z8.*

LEFT: *Foliage plants are the most important feature in the garden of the late Barbara Frum and Murray Frum. Left:* FORSYTHIA × INTERMEDIA; SALIX *(large tree); ground cover is* HEDERA HELIX *with moss near path; lower right: assorted ferns with* LIGULARIA DENTATA ' *Desdemona'; top right:* PINUS SYLVESTRIS. *Ontario Z6.*

ABOVE: *The late Dr. Henry J. Landis had a talent for assembling plants for their architectural shapes. From left to right:* PICEA PUNGENS *'Globosa'; deciduous tree behind is* ACER GRISEUM; PAEONIA SUFFRUTICOSA, *tree peony cultivars, in bloom;* PICEA GLAUCA *'Albertiana Conica';* CHAMAECYPARIS NOOTKATENSIS *'Pendula';* ACER PALMATUM *'Bloodgood';* FAGUS SYLVATICA *'Tricolor';* PINUS STROBUS; PICEA ABIES *cvs.;* PICEA ABIES; PINUS DENSIFLORA *'Umbraculifera', Tanyosho pine;* PINUS STROBUS *'Nana'. Ontario Z6.*

LEFT: *The steep path down Columba Fuller's garden is graced with* AESCULUS HIPPOCASTANUM, *horse chestnut; a hanging basket of Boston fern;* PACHYSANDRA; *blue carpet juniper; a variety of rhododendrons; ostrich ferns;* EUONYMUS; *yew;* HOSTA FORTUNEI. *Ontario Z6.*

## TREES IN A GARDEN DESIGN

Back in the 1930s, American landscape architect Thomas Church urged us to save trees and to build houses, gardens and garden compositions around them. We should have been listening more carefully.

Instead we've virtually denuded our suburban areas of trees. One suburban gardener I know has planted three trees in his backyard to give both shade and seasonal color. "If everybody in the area did the same thing and planted different trees, we'd have a gorgeous forest here in a few years." He sighed wistfully, knowing that it won't happen.

Trees in the city don't fare much better. Somewhere in the misty past politicians prescribed that most Canadian cities should have maple trees lining all streets. Not necessarily the best tree (shallow roots that aim straight for sewer systems). But the worst part is having one species blanket an entire city, all planted at the same time. They will all probably die at the same time. And there is no program to cull the weak ones now and put in new trees to replace what will be terrible gaping holes a few years down the road.

Biodiversity means having as many different communities of plants as possible in a region, and it will increasingly become an important buzzword. Monoculture is its opposite. This is unfortunately what we've condemned many of our streets to.

This reflects our often baffling approach to trees. We have so many forests, we take trees for granted.

A general attitude is that trees are dirty (fallen leaves, I suppose), inconvenient (ditto) or take up too much space (all the more for cars). We need serious re-education. Trees are the lungs of the planet and they are the best hope we have of breathing properly as our cities choke on their own car fumes. They are more effective as air conditioners than any machine. And as the ultraviolet rays become more dangerous to people because of ozone depletion, trees (if they survive) and their shade will become even more important.

With the right kind of care, trees can carry our history with them—hundreds of years into the future. Trees are the symbol of life; we should keep as many as possible in our gardens.

If you have an old tree that's healthy enough to keep, do it a favor. Build a safety deck around it so that air can reach the roots and to provide protection to the root system. Have it pruned expertly. Feed it occasionally.

You'll find all sorts of hidden beauties in the most ordinary of trees if they are pruned properly. Removing lower branches allows as much light as possible into the garden and makes a more airy, graceful canopy. I've seen a garden change completely as a vista is opened up. But leave this chore to competent professionals.

Once you have the trees thinned out, you can see how well or badly the verticals serve you and whether you should add more trees to your garden. A very large specimen tree can act as a focal point and will probably indicate what logically needs to be planted around it. If you can't remove a tree that's blocking the view, or overshadowing the house, work with it—adjust your design plans.

**TREE FORM** Shape or form is so crucial to large trees that it is a good idea to spend a long time pondering your choice of what trees to plant. In fact, the bigger the tree is in maturity, the longer you should take to make a decision. Head to the nearest cemetery. It's here that you'll find mature examples of trees to compare with the striplings found in nurseries.

The shape of trees will give your garden a profile. They provide the verticality you'll need and set up tension with the more horizontal shapes. Even the words to describe tree forms are beautiful and self-descriptive:

 *Vase-shaped:* ULMUS, elm; CELTIS, hackberry; SOPHORA JAPONICA, Japanese pagoda tree

 *Broad and spreading:* QUERCUS, oak (white, red, black); JUGLANS NIGRA, black walnut; FRAXINUS AMERICANA, white ash

❧ *Oval:* CRATAEGUS, hawthorn; CATALPA, catalpa; FAGUS, beech; AESCULUS, horse chestnut

❧ *Columnar:* CARPINUS BETULUS 'Fastigiata'; POPULUS NIGRA 'Italica', lombardy poplar; BETULA PAPYRIFERA, paper birch; TAXODIUM DISTICHUM, bald cypress

❧ *Picturesque or irregular:* GYMNOCLADUS DIOICA, Kentucky coffee tree; GINKGO BILOBA, maidenhair tree; KOELREUTERIA PANICULATA, golden-rain tree; ARALIA SPINOSA, devil's-walking-stick

❧ *Pyramidal:* LIRIODENDRON TULIPIFERA, American tulip tree; LIQUIDAMBAR, sweet gum

❧ *Drooping:* SALIX BABYLONICA, Babylon weeping willow; PRUNUS, cherry

Then there are the variations including the following:

❧ *Round:* some CRATAEGUS, hawthorns; PRUNUS SARGENTII, sargent cherry; ELAEAGNUS ANGUSTIFOLIA, Russian olive; ACER PALMATUM, Japanese maple

❧ *Fan-shaped:* CLADRASTIS LUTEA, yellowwood

❧ *Clumped or multiple stemmed:* CERCIS CANADENSIS, redbud; AMELANCHIER, serviceberry; COTINUS COGGYGRIA, smoke tree

❧ *Horizontal branching:* VIBURNUM PLICATUM, Japan snowball; CORNUS ALTERNIFOLIA, pagoda dogwood; ROBINIA PSEUDOACACIA, black locust; CRATAEGUS CRUS-GALLI, cockspur thorn

**THE FRAMEWORK** ❧ The framework of trees will set the mood of your garden and the context for the details of your design. A row of trees can form the edges of the garden; be a windbreak; interweave to act as a hedge (pleaching). If the lower limbs are cleared out, a higher canopy can be a shelter for a whole host of new plants. If you do this all along a fence line you can add an extra height to the garden while keeping the area below for other plants.

Trees provide respite in the middle of the city and shelter for wildlife. You can use trees to screen out an ugly unwanted view. You can use them to frame a beautiful borrowed view. But don't over-plant trees. Six trees in a small garden are enough to give it character.

❧ Big trees create atmosphere: open and airy, close and damp, or woodsy and protective.

❧ Always compare young specimens you're considering planting with mature ones. That dull-looking little twig in your hand might become a 30-foot (10-meter) giant in a few years. I've mentioned going to cemeteries; arboreta and botanic gardens also have trees going back more than a century. You'll find out what grows well in your area—a major consideration in an expensive plant.

❧ Plants that echo or agree with each other should be placed relatively close to one another; the farther apart related plantings are, the more links will be needed in between.

❧ For good basic planting combinations, use only one or two varieties. By putting in too many dissimilar trees you run the risk of ending up with discord.

❧ Grow two species that are unrelated but have a similar shape.

❧ Make sure there is a balance between evergreen and deciduous trees and shrubs; too many evergreens look static and create a chilly atmosphere. By having only deciduous trees, you'll end up with a bleak winter scene. A personal guide is to have almost half evergreen plants, the rest deciduous plants.

❧ Think of both summer and winter effectiveness of trees—the shapes when they are full and when they are empty of leaves.

❧ Think about foliage color from season to season. This needs careful observation because there are subtle gradations.

❧ Use false perspective to highlight dramatic foliage effects: for instance, place a medium-sized red maple at the end of an avenue of tall columnar trees. Or plant large trees close at hand and smaller trees in the distance to give a feeling of greater distance in a tight space.

❧ If you have a formal garden consider using

LEFT: *The dignified 125 year-old apple tree was part of the original farm where the Wiggan family now has their city garden. Trimmed to a bonsai-like shape, it forms a perfect focal point. At the foot of the tree:* EUONYMUS, *quince and a magnolia. Ontario Z6.*

BELOW: *This is the splendid entrance to Andrew Yeoman's Ravenhill Herb Farm. Clockwise from left:* LAVANDULA ANGUSTIFOLIA, *English lavender; Irish yew and a Douglas fir in the far distance;* SENECIO GREYI; *a bank of ivy; various species of thymes; at the front is Baltic thyme. British Columbia Z8.*

standards (trees grafted on a single stem) in one or two rows instead of a conventional hedging.

᭞ But don't have too many sharp vertical accents or you will have a pointy forest that's an affront to the eye rather than a place of harmony.

Carefully consider how you will unite the different storeys of the trees. In a few years the middle storey will be occupied by large shrubs up to 15 feet (4.5 meters) and small trees 15 to 20 feet (4.5 to 6 meters). So consider certain trees from the start as effective links. GINKGO BILOBA, maidenhair tree, for example, is a marvelous connector between upper and lower storeys because of its color and size and because it grows slowly to medium height.

The texture found in trees' trunks, twigs and branches also contributes to the foliage garden:

᭞ Coarse texture is for drama—one only has to look at GYMNOCLADUS DIOICA, Kentucky coffee tree, or RHUS TYPHINA, staghorn sumac, to know that they are all good specimen plants (they can stand alone as a highlight in the garden).

᭞ Fine texture is for delicacy: any BETULA, birch; ELAEAGNUS ANGUSTIFOLIA, Russian olive; or SALIX, willow.

᭞ Thick trunks give a sense of solidity and age; a gnarled form can add a picturesque quality to a garden.

᭞ Dense trees include the following: CRATAEGUS, hawthorn; FAGUS, beech; ACER SACCHARUM, sugar maple; QUERCUS PALUSTRIS, pin oak; LIQUIDAMBAR, sweet gum; CARPINUS, hornbeam.

᭞ Trees for beautiful shadows and patterns include: CERCIS CANADENSIS, redbud; CORNUS FLORIDA, flowering dogwood; CARYA OVATA, shagbark hickory; CATALPA; GINGKO; ULMUS AMERICANA, American elm; KOELREUTERIA PANICULATA, golden-rain tree.

᭞ Experiment with textural contrast by combining needled with broad-leaved plants and then repeating them on the ground to make a fascinating pattern.

TREES AS WINDBREAKS ᭞ Trees used as hedges make a stunning division in the garden or lining for a path. They even work well along a wall. This kind of design is best either in a formal garden or in a large country garden. But if you are subject to prevailing winds that sweep across your property every day, consider using trees as a windbreak—to moderate the force of the wind. On the prairies they are called shelterbelts and protect not only buildings but also crops. A windbreak reduces the force of the wind by at least a half.

᭞ Windbreaks should be a minimum of 6.5 feet (2 meters) high.

᭞ If the site is extremely windy, consider a double hedge as a windbreak. A row of fastigiate (without spreading branches) trees such as yews, junipers or cypress will give you a strong vertical presence. Then plant a lower hedge inside the garden. This creates a softened line and gives twice as much protection.

᭞ Other plants for windbreaks: ALNUS CORDATA, Italian alder, grows fairly quickly; ILEX AQUIFOLIUM, holly, gives a dark dramatic background as well as protection; AMELANCHIER ALNIFOLIA, Saskatoon serviceberry; CARAGANA ARBORESCENS, pea tree; SYRINGA spp, lilacs; THUJA, arborvitae.

᭞ A windbreak creates a moist background for evergreen plants such as rhododendrons. Plant at least 2 feet (60 centimeters) away from the roots.

## SHRUBS IN A GARDEN DESIGN

The value of shrubs in any garden is incalculable. They provide an internal framework in borders and act as coverup for perennials that have faded away. Large shrubs provide the eye with succeeding storeys down from the trees and so connect the garden's various levels. As well, shrubs don't need staking or dividing and have such a wide variety of textures and leaf forms. They can, in fact, perform almost any design function you think up.

Shrubs range in height from a few inches or centimeters to 20 feet (6 meters). The foliage garden will

ABOVE: *The combinations in the garden of Carmen Varcoe and Ed Kowalyk include, from back left to right: phlox foliage;* EREMURUS ROBUSTUS *(spikes);* DICTAMNUS ALBUS. *Foreground left to right:* STACHYS LANATA; ARTEMISIA *'Blue Mound';* PHALARIS; IRIS TECTORUM *(foliage);* AGROPYRON SPICATUM, *blue grass. British Columbia Z8.*

ABOVE: *A glorious early morning view in the garden of Barbara and Murray Frum. Left:* PINUS STROBUS *'Pendula'; lower right:* DAPHNE X BURKWOODII *'Carol Mackie'. Ontario Z6.*

RIGHT: *Glen Patterson works beautifully with the magnificent rocks on his land. In the background:* JUNIPERUS CHINENSIS; *from the left: rare* RHODODENDRON CONCATENANS *'Orange Bill';* R. *'Cinnamon Bear';* POTENTILLA NEPALENSIS; R. TATSIENENSI. *Coming forward:* IRIS KAEMPFERI; PINUS BUNGEANA, *lace-bark pine;* CEDRUS DEODARA *'Sprite'. Foreground left:* R. *'Ptarmigan' and* R. *'Razorbill';* R. PSEUDOCHRYSANTHUM; R. *'Crimson Pippin'. British Columbia Z8.*

have spring-blooming beauties, summer flowering, fall opulence and winter greenery in its shrubs.

The right combinations or associations of shrubs can demand attention in ways they would never do by themselves. By putting completely different kinds of shrubs together, you will add a wide variety of textures and leaf forms to your garden and create a lively transition between changes in color.

To make up exciting and original combinations of these plants is a passion with obsessed gardeners. The secret in meshing a shrub with perennials is to relate the shrub to as many of the plants around it as possible. This can be done by echoing some of the shrub's characteristics—color, leaf texture or size—in the surrounding plants.

Since the middle storey of the garden is just above eye level, this is where the most intimate relationship with the viewer is established. It is in the middle storey that the viewer first makes discoveries about the shapes and sizes of leaves. This is also the level at which blossoms are most prominent. When putting in new shrubs, make sure the colors don't clash with surrounding perennials. If they do, put the shrub somewhere else—or move the perennials. You don't want a clashing error to come back for an annual haunting.

Catalogue whatever shrubs you have in the garden and get rid of anything that looks unhealthy or just plain terrible. Give overgrown or shapeless shrubs a creative pruning to see if they still justify their existence. You'll be amazed at how quickly they perk up with decent handling.

⁂ Shrubs will cast shade over the plants around them, so keep that in mind when you devise combinations.

⁂ Feathery leaves break up light and bring a sense of buoyancy to dark or dull areas.

⁂ Shrubs with small leaves are great little space fillers. For instance: RHODODENDRON IMPEDITUM or R. 'Ramapo'; SPIRAEA 'Pink Princess'.

⁂ Resist the temptation to always place simple-leaved plants with compound—this inevitably turns into a visual cliché.

⁂ It's effective to display two kinds of pinnate foliage with something more static such as a conifer.

⁂ Some shrubs belong to the fringe of the garden—ones that mix well and blur the line of surrounding natural growth. This is especially important in the country, where the garden may merge into a woods. Using native plants rather than something exotic is sensible for this area. CORNUS ALBA 'Sibirica', Siberian dogwood; KERRIA JAPONICA, Japanese kerria; and other varieties with colorful twigs look wonderful massed in the distance.

Some shrubs have become the mainstay in many gardens. As though a magic wand is waved, a new garden acquires a weigela, a mock orange and a big floppy hydrangea. There is nothing intrinsically wrong with these shrubs. They just need a new way of being used.

I have an ancient CHAENOMELES, quince, that is a particularly vile orange, but it's been espaliered and fronted by other shrubs and doesn't look too bad once the blooming season is over. It's been there for such a long time that the glorious new cultivars available now weren't around when it was planted.

If you do have these overused plants, try moving something innovative next to them to make them sparkle once again. Or search for a different variety. Hydrangea, for instance. That great floppy-headed creature so beloved of most gardeners isn't the only one around. There are some magnificent ones such as H. PANICULATA 'Grandiflora', commonly known as Peegee. H. QUERCIFOLIA is one of the all-time garden greats with oak-leaved form that turns a burnished bronze in autumn—fantastic.

**SHRUBS AND THE LOWER STOREY** ⁂ One of my favorite ways to use shrubs is to treat them, especially the smaller ones, almost like perennials—in borders, as edging, as well as specimens. Having the surprise element of a shrub in any border, but particularly at the front, slows the eye before it can move on too quickly.

To gracefully merge the middle and lower storeys

of the garden it's necessary to mix up shrubs and perennials. Perennials with important or dramatic foliage should have places of honor in any bed: KIRENGESHOMA PALMATA; CRAMBE CORDIFOLIA, colewort; RODGERSIA; PETASITES JAPONICUS, fuki; GUNNERA; PELTIPHYLLUM PELTATUM, umbrella plant. The last three are great gobblers of moisture, so if you have them in an ideal situation, they will take over. In harsh climates, dappled shade and minimum moisture will keep them well behaved.

⁂ The secret with shrub-like conifers is in mixing up the shapes and colors as well as the sizes. Dwarf and slow-growing conifers always work well together.

⁂ Roses go beautifully with almost any shrub, yet we still insist on having a square patch designated for the Rose Garden. The alternative is to plant roses all through the garden, with shrubs that thrive in the same conditions, to avoid those long naked legs.

⁂ Gray and silver plants are my favorites and there are many in the shrub category: BUDDLEIA, butterfly bush; CARYOPTERIS, bluebeard; PEROVSKIA; lavender; hebes; sage; gray and green SANTOLINA; ARTEMISIA ABROTANUM, southernwood; shrubby potentillas, to name a few.

⁂ Gray plants and grasses go together as if by magic.

⁂ Planting at the skirts of shrubs should be considered very carefully. Visually this practice is a good idea, but you don't want to interfere with the root system of the taller plant. Heaths and heathers are examples of non-competitors. They are shallow-rooting and also provide a cool spot for other roots.

## HEDGES IN A GARDEN DESIGN

Hedges have been called the living bones of the garden. They certainly are a tool for defining the space. They can be used to create a visual pause, or for privacy. Two parallel hedges become a corridor. A single hedge set out by itself can be a striking element in a design. Or a hole cut in the hedge—a clairvoyance—creates a view through to another area.

Of all its virtues the greatest contribution a hedge can make to a garden is the instant calming effect. A dark hedge is the most beautiful background possible for almost all plants and certainly for statuary.

Hedges can be used to make a garden appear larger or smaller—forced perspective. If a double row of hedges converges slightly, it makes the horizon seem more distant. The tradition is to use an avenue of hedges not only as a windbreak but as a corridor to a focal point such as a piece of sculpture, fountain or bench at the end.

In a country garden, hedges can be used to define the end of garden and the beginning of countryside without blocking the view. In city gardens they can outline garden rooms. In both cases they provide useful horizontal planes.

All hedges, however, take up space from other plants and suck up nearby nutrients. Keep this in mind if you decide to plant one. As well, it takes about 10 years for a hedge to mature.

For planting instructions, see page 132.

A gorgeous informal hedge can be made with shrub roses, but you must be prepared to let them grow more or less at will. No clipping into neat shapes here, just deadheading. I can't think of a better way to screen a swimming pool in the country. Or to keep the neighborhood children from hell away from the garden.

Hedges recommended by Trevor Cole, director of the National Arboretum, in Ottawa: THUJA OCCIDENTALIS 'Brandon', white cedar, 'Robusta', Siberian cedar, and 'Techney'.

Other hedges that I like:

⁂ VIBURNUM DENTATUM, arrowwood, has glossy leaves and a good red color in fall.

⁂ CRATAEGUS MONOGYNA, English hawthorn, is both a good boundary and a background.

⁂ FAGUS SYLVATICA, European beech, keeps some brownish leaves in winter.

LEFT: *Thomas Hobbs' patio is sheltered by the golden cypress hedge that creates an appropriate background for* PHORMIUM, *New Zealand flax, in the urn, with* HELICHRYSUM PETIOLATUM *trailing about. Front left:* HOSTA SIEBOLDIANA *var.* ELEGANS; RODGERSIA TABULARIS *with ferns coming naturally out of the stone wall. British Columbia Z8.*

BELOW: *Francisca Darts' extraordinary garden has whimsical touches such as this free-standing hedge. Left:* YUCCA GLORIOSA *var.* NOBILIS. *Background:* VIBURNUM TOMENTOSUM; V. MARIESII *and* V. PLICATUM *'Pink Beauty'; the tree is* MORUS ALBA *next to* RHODODENDRON X PRAECOX. *The rounded evergreen is* CRYPTOMERIA JAPONICA *'Vilmoriniana'. British Columbia Z8.*

ABOVE: *Glen Patterson uses a boxwood hedge,* BUXUS SEM-
PERVIRENS, *as punctuation between two garden areas.
The background trees are* PSEUDOTSUGA MENZIESII,
*native Douglas firs. Middle storey from left:* CRYPTOMERIA
JAPONICA *'Elegans';* CHAMAECYPARIS PISIFERA *'Filifera
Aurea';* KALMIOPSIS LEACHIANA; ACER PALMATUM *'Cripp-
sii', Japanese maple. Through the opening: rock surround-
ed by* RHODODENDRON RADICANS; R. SERPYLLIFOLIUM;
R. IMPERATOR; R. TSARIENSE. *British Columbia Z8.*

LEFT: *Hedges are used as background and to lead the eye
down the* tapis vert *in Francis Cabot's country garden.
They appear to extend the raised beds. Right to left:* ROSA
RUGOSA *'Alba';* FILIPENDULA *'Alba';* HEUCHERA SAN-
GUINEA *'Ava';* ACHILLEA PTARMICA *'Boule de Neige';*
PHLOX MACULATA *'Miss Lingard'; single white peonies; in
and above the wall:* GYPSOPHILA REPENS; CAMPANULA
COCHLEARIIFOLIA *and white-flowered alpines. Quebec Z4.*

ꙮ CARPINUS BETULUS, European hornbeam, keeps its dead leaves in winter, stands up to winds and has strong architectural presence. Easy to make into a good shape.

ꙮ ILEX AQUIFOLIUM, holly, evergreen, creates an impenetrable hedge; can be clipped into shapes.

ꙮ BERBERIS, barberry, is a beautiful plant and I envy anyone who got it before its sale was banned in parts of Canada where wheat rust (a virulent disease) is a problem.

ꙮ PRUNUS LUSITANICA, Portugal laurel. A lovely shiny surface for an informal garden.

ꙮ TAXUS BACCATA, English yew, hates wind and water-logged conditions but needs clipping only once a year. Space at 3 feet (1 meter). It will turn brown if planted ½ inch (1 centimeter) deeper than it was at the nursery.

ꙮ PRUNUS NIGRA, Canada or purple-leaved plum, makes hedges 6 to 8 feet (2 to 2.5 meters).

ꙮ COTONEASTER HORIZONTALIS, rock cotoneaster, can be trained as a hedge or screen.

ꙮ X CUPRESSOCYPARIS LEYLANDII, cypress, creates a protective background with a strong vertical element.

ꙮ For very low ornamental hedges: RUTA GRAVEOLENS 'Jackman's Blue', common rue, and SANTOLINA CHAMAECYPARISUS, lavender cotton; ARTEMISIA ABROTANUM, southernwood; or BUXUS MICROPHYLLA KOREANA, Korean boxwood.

## VINES IN A GARDEN DESIGN

The verticals, the walls, of a garden are as important here as they are to a house. Using vines creatively can stretch the number of plants you can grow. They will decorate your fences, shrubs and trees. Vines can run rampant along the ground, and give a finished look to the garden. I've mentioned this before and it bears repeating—plant vines as soon as you possibly can once you've come up with your design since they will, with some exceptions, take at least three years to properly fill in spaces.

Vines soften the hard outline of a conifer if you allow them to ramp through its branches. Make sure they have small flowers instead of obvious ones that create a rather vulgar effect.

Vines climb to the light, so you can start many in shade. Some are twiners that grab on to anything they touch; others drape themselves over other plants or fences; others have aerial rootlets that attach themselves to any surface and use them for clinging without any other support.

Use vines to frame windows and doors and diminish the effect of hard edges on fences and buildings. Or use them to clad the dreariest of buildings and make their forms so riveting that any dullness is disguised. But make sure whatever building you allow them to grow over is in good condition. If brick is chipped, vine tendrils will work their way into the material and break it apart even more. However, vines protect sturdy walls from the ravages of weather and add another layer of insulation.

TIPS ON PLACING VINES

ꙮ Vines are invaluable at disguising ghastly views or framing beautiful ones.

ꙮ Use vines to flank special garden features such as mirrors, wall sculptures or fountains.

ꙮ Cover that empty wall you've been staring at for years. It will lift your spirits as well.

ꙮ Think about what you'll put at the feet of your vines. Some look gorgeous, gnarled and exposed, but others need something to keep the root run cool and make them look anchored in place. One good companion plant for vines is ALCHEMILLA MOLLIS, lady's-mantle. The soft green velvety texture is pure sensuality. Bulbs also look good at the feet of vines.

ꙮ If you need sun on your vine, stretch a wall or fence upwards with a trellis. This will allow light to hit the vine on both sides.

ꙮ In dry shade consider using HEDERA, ivy. H. HELIX, English ivy, or PARTHENOCISSUS TRICUSPIDATA, Boston ivy, both put up with dreadful conditions.

ABOVE: *Maureen and Brian Bixley divided their country garden into separate rooms and created intimacy in each area. In this section a clematis collection is grown in raised beds among perennials such as* CORE-OPSIS VERTICILLATA *'Moonbeam';* HYPER-ICUM OLYMPICUM; ERIOPHYLLUM LANATUM. *Ontario Z5.*

LEFT: *Susan Ryley's potting shed takes on glamour when it's covered with* HYDRANGEA ANOMALA PETIOLARIS, *climbing hydrangea. White flower heads are* CENTRANTHUS ALBUS. *Left to right in front:* BALLOTA; *large leaves of* HELLEBORUS ORIENTALIS; GERANI-UM *'Johnson's Blue';* SALVIA ARGENTEA, *this-tle;* ASTER TONGOLENSIS *'Bergartern'. British Columbia Z9.*

MY FAVORITE VINES

❧ SCHIZOPHRAGMA HYDRANGEOIDES, Japanese hydrangea vine: looks like HYDRANGEA PETIOLARIS but it blooms earlier in the plant's life. The blooms last for months and the leaves turn bronze in autumn.

❧ HYDRANGEA PETIOLARIS, climbing hydrangea: this was my favorite until I discovered the one above. It's another self-clinger and will eventually take over any surface you put it near. It's the waiting that counts. Because of its density this is a great plant for a really ugly fence.

❧ CLEMATIS: Any clematis in any season. There is a color for every possible combination; and once they've taken hold they spread quite happily up trellises or through trees. Make sure you don't plant them in with greedy plants. The roots like to be shaded, but if they are in a rain shadow under other plants they will shrivel up and die. They like lots of food and drink.

❧ CAMPSIS RADICANS, trumpet vine: has attractive red or yellow flowers that hummingbirds love. It will grow in the shade but tends to become rampant.

❧ WISTERIA SINENSIS 'Alba': I wouldn't be without a wisteria climbing over the pergola. This one has an intoxicating perfume and it's the only one I've ever been able to get to flower.

❧ AMPELOPSIS BREVIPEDUNCULATA 'Elegans' is the variegated cultivar of the porcelain vine. The cobalt blue berries alone are magnificent.

❧ PARTHENOCISSUS QUINQUEFOLIA, Virginia creeper: has poisonous blue-black berries but the amazing scarlet it turns in fall makes it a splendid covering plant. Be careful what you put it on, though—it will grow over anything, including windows.

❧ Climbing roses of any color combined with ivy. This is a sensational effect and does wonders for a sterile blank wall.

## GROUND COVERS IN A GARDEN DESIGN

A ground cover is any invasive plant that is more or less low to the ground. A community of creepers of all sorts, low-growing shrubs and grass are all considered ground covers.

Grass is the most common ground cover partly because we don't use enough imagination in what we choose to blanket the soil with. I'm not a great fan of grass. It's overused and the machines that keep it perfect are smelly. Grass is costly to put in, takes time to maintain, and we tend to dump chemicals all over it to keep it green.

There are some places where grass is an ideal ground cover—areas where there's a lot of traffic, for example. Grass makes a wonderful garden path and provides a cool retreat, a respite, a place for seating. As just one element rather than the whole of the ground carpet, grass is wonderful. Grass needs some sort of coherence as well. It can't just be plunked down and dribble off at the edges. Used as a shaped ground pattern, grass can be gorgeous. Closely mown grass will create a channel through rougher, wilder swards of grass in a natural garden or meadow.

Another reason we are drawn to grass is that it is refreshing. It is a calming background for more assertive plants. But you can achieve this same effect from any of the glorious ivies available and establish ground patterns that have more intensity. In your garden composition you want a ground cover to provide a background on which you can build the rest of your design. Think of how tranquil a stretch of ivy can be. Then imagine further that same ivy

RIGHT: *Kathy Leishman gardens on a ravine with rock outcroppings that determine to some degree the plants she chooses to fit into the landscape. From lower left (on the rock):* ERICA; AJUGA; CORYLOPSIS PAUCIFLORA; RHODODENDRON THOMSOMII; CAMELLIA JAPONICA; ARRHENATHERUM BULBOSUM; HELLEBORUS CORSICUS; EUPHORBIA MYRSINITES; ADIANTUM VENUSTUM; SAXIFRAGA X URBIUM; EUPHORBIA CHARACIAS *(with yellow flower heads); to the right:* ACER *foliage. British Columbia Z8.*

with very carefully placed plants woven into it like a tapestry. You add a dimension, a frontal plane, and the excitement of your design increases dramatically.

If you have a boring ground cover, boringly placed, everything else is going to have a tough time in the interest department. Yet an exciting ground cover will pull your total composition together, adding depth to texture.

Hostas and ferns are two families of plants that are so versatile you can work them in with shrubs and under trees, providing you add lots of humus and water regularly if it's dry shade. These two perennials are among my favorites and I've tried to incorporate plenty of them. I'm torn here between collecting as many varieties as I can and making conscious design decisions. Usually my collecting instinct comes first.

### MY FAVORITE GROUND COVERS

❧ I would not live without as many of the thymes as possible. They range from THYMUS PSEU-DOLANUGINOSUS, woolly thyme, a ground-hugging crawler, to T. X CITRIODORUS 'Aureus' and T. C. 'Silver Posie', evergreen shrubby forms; to T. SERPYLLUM 'Coccineus', mother-of-thyme, T. VULGARIS 'Argenteus', T. V. 'Gold Edge', T. MONTANUS 'Alba' and T. M. 'Rosea'.

❧ ALCHEMILLA MOLLIS, lady's-mantle, is one of those plants I love to use as both an edger and a ground cover.

❧ Spiky plants can provide drama as well as verticality in combination with ground covers: consider YUCCA FILAMENTOSA, Adam's needle yucca; ERYNGIUM; PHORMIUM TENAX, New Zealand flax; CORDYLINE AUSTRALIS, giant dracaena, and any SISYRINCHIUM, blue-eyed grass.

❧ CERATOSTIGMA PLUMBAGINOIDES, blue ceratostigma, is a beautiful shrubby plant with brilliant blue flowers.

❧ Moss makes a wonderful ground cover for a damp shady place. You can establish it by mixing live moss, a bit of sugar and a cup of beer in a blender. Then spread it over the surface you want to cover.

# CHAPTER THREE

# THE GARDEN IN WINTER

$W$inter arrives just as most of us are gardened-out. But while nature is resting up for the following year's renewal it's the time to contemplate the "bones"—the infrastructure or underpinnings—of the garden. They're most conspicuous at this time of year.

Wandering through the winter garden I am, again and again, taken with surprise by the captivating beauty of certain barks, the color in twigs, the lushness of conifers. Forms and textures are revealed intimately. Whatever axis you decided to put in your garden is obvious. No other season displays these basics so well.

It is also one of the most joyous times for a gardener even though you spend more time looking at the garden than being in it. This is a typical principle of all winter gardens: what you lose in one aspect you gain in another. It is the season to reflect on garden fantasies—thinking up new combinations, making lists in your garden diary and contemplating a new start.

Since I have no grass in my garden there are no depressing sheets of brown. The garden is filled with color: the deep greens of MAHONIA AQUIFOLIUM, Oregon holly-grape; PIERIS JAPONICA, lily-of-the-valley bush; KALMIA LATIFOLIA, mountain-laurel. The blue in grasses such as FESTUCA OVINA 'Glauca', blue fescue; HELICTOTRICHON SEMPERVIRENS, blue oat grass; CHAMAECYPARIS PISIFERA SQUARROSA 'Intermedia', false cypress; JUNIPERUS spp. Golden bronze in grasses such as CAREX BUCHANANII, sedge; the silver of artemisias that haven't faded yet. And all the colors found in twigs stripped of leaves: red, yellow and green.

In winter the garden is like a stage setting—focused and dramatic. Everything is in relief. In this elemental state, look carefully at how you can eliminate the worst features of the surrounding landscape. This is also the time to deliberate on how paths should be moved. Do they serve you well? Can they be transformed and be part of a whole new garden design?

## PLANTS AND THE WEATHER

Plants have fascinating strategies for adapting to rotten weather. In the Arctic you can see twig-like black spruces that are thousands of years old. These trees survive in areas where there is barely any soil and what there is is very acid. Ice crystals form between the cell walls rather than inside the cell where they'd cause damage, and thus allow the tree to withstand dehydration.

The extra-cellular freezing/viscous binding is a plant tissue's antifreeze mechanism. There is a decrease in pressure when water freezes between cells of plant tissue, which causes water inside the cell to flow out by osmosis. The water outside the cell freezes and forms a barrier between inner cells and the external stem tissue. The moisture left in the cell is just enough to ensure survival. This viscous liquid has an incredibly low freezing point.

In the fall, trees undergo a metabolic and chemical change brought on by lower temperatures and diminishing daylight. Typical of any plant adapted

RIGHT: *The late Murray Haigh's garden was a place of enchantment. Each year he came up with an idea of how to make his garden more salubrious in winter. This installation is simple to make (the instructions are on the following page), and recycles leaves into circles that look like giant pomanders. Properly placed furniture becomes sculptural under a layer of snow. In the background is a faux temple entrance to the carport, which adds a touch of whimsy. Ontario Z6.*

to winter temperatures, they accumulate a dense concentration of sugar for much-needed energy and protection.

Proper conditions—such as the right kind of soil—will also help a plant's adaptability. Here's a striking example used by plantsman John Sabuco: A Zone 2 plant that thrives in dry, poor soil will die in wet, fertile soils in areas as warm as Zone 4.

In some plants the margin between injury and death might be as little as 1°F to 3°F (0.5°C to 1.5°C). For instance, a plant adaptable to −20°F (−29°C) is damaged at two hours of exposure to −22°F (−30°C) and killed at four hours of exposure to −25°F (−32°C).

Photosynthesis continues in winter, albeit slowly; using the sun's energy, the plant turns carbon dioxide into oxygen and carbohydrates.

Transpiration takes place all the time in all plants. In winter, coniferous, broad-leaf and narrow-leaf evergreens transpire faster than deciduous plants and are more susceptible to drying out or desiccation. But they are less harmed by low and sudden changes in temperature. One strategy of these plants is to hug or lie close to the ground. The small surface of a needle or scale on a conifer is a form of protection against desiccation in keeping water in woody tissues from freezing.

Desiccation—the evaporation of moisture from the plant's tissue—also persists in winter. More moisture evaporates than the plant can replace. Thus, as a plant gets ready for winter (called hardening off) its ability to survive depends on how much water it gets. If it is dry going into winter, the plant will suffer even more as transpiration increases on warm winter days.

Wind speeds up evaporation of moisture from plant tissue. The winter sun is also a problem: it raises the surface tissue temperature and increases the rate of transpiration. Winter burn causes broad-leaved evergreens to turn brown unless they have some protection. Use cuttings from Christmas trees or other evergreen prunings and lash them to the

south sides of vulnerable plants. Or fashion more handsome screens out of bamboo stakes woven together—these are easy to store as well. The traditional method is to use burlap: drive four stakes into the ground 3 feet (1 meter) away from roots and wrap burlap around the stakes like an open-topped tent. Don't remove too early in the year; wait until you are sure that the sun won't scald plants.

Rapid changes in temperature can also cause moisture in the bark to expand then contract, causing it to split. This is another reason to protect plants with mulch or by wrapping them with burlap or pine boughs.

## WINTER INSTALLATIONS

Landscape architect Murray Haigh designed his garden in winter with humor and with a sense of metaphor. The robust form of his summer garden lost some of its edge in winter. To overcome this, he created an installation that captured the things he loved in his garden: hard symbolic forms, elemental configurations, all designed to be environmentally sound.

TO MAKE A WINTER INSTALLATION

❧ Pyramid: Use a 2 x 2 foot x 1 inch (60 x 60 x 2.5 centimeter) piece of plywood as the base. Drill holes in it so moisture will flow through. Nail a 2 x 2 inch (5 x 5 centimeter) lip around the edge. Then take four 1 x 1 inch (2.5 x 2.5 centimeter) strips of wood 3 feet (1 meter) long and hammer one into each corner and join all at a point. Use chicken wire to mold into a pyramid shape, keeping the wire in place with two-sided carpet tacks.

❧ Finials: The small 2 x 2 inch (5 x 5 centimeter) finial on top is chicken wire formed around an old milk bottle and held in place with the carpet tacks.

❧ Round forms: Chicken wire is very malleable and can be used to create a great number of shapes. One idea is to mold the wire to the shape of an urn that you'd like to use in the garden, and then fill

ABOVE: *In the Wiggan garden a* BUXUS SEMPERVIRENS, *boxwood, hedge becomes sculptural in its own right. Left foreground:* JUNIPERUS CHINESIS *'Pfitzerana'; small white pine. Ontario Z6.*

RIGHT: *Mary Anne Brinkman designed her heavily shaded front garden to make a formal entrance to her house and a strong winter statement. The garden is in its second year here with* BUXUS MICROPHYLLA *'Green Gem'; the two standards are* EUONYMUS FORTUNEI *'Canadale Gold'. Ontario Z6.*

the wire with as many leaves as you can jam in with the end of a broom. (Leaves are amazingly dense, and the wire form will take far more than you can imagine.) Hold the edges together with carpet tacks and then turn the wire form upside down and place on top of your urn. This is a great way to recycle leaves as well as create a winter sculpture.

Other suggestions for refurbishing the winter garden:

⁊ Use lichen-covered evergreen branches and red CORNUS, dogwood, twigs to create a winter bouquet in a large stone vessel.

⁊ Leave artemisias and annual dusty miller in the ground to form pale shadows on a dark background.

⁊ Move furniture, pots, urns and other *objets* so you can see them more clearly from windows.

## PLANTS FOR THE WINTER GARDEN

When choosing plants for winter appeal make sure they have a distinctive shape, color or texture.

⁊ CATALPA has a marvelous shape and interesting long beans; STACHYS and lavenders stay silver gray; santolinas darken; THYMUS PSEUDOLANUGINOSUS, woolly thyme, looks ravaged but wonderful.

⁊ For winter shape: SALIX MATSUDANA 'Tortuosa', corkscrew or dragon-claw willow.

⁊ CORYLUS AVELLANA 'Contorta', European filbert, with its weird shape, looks better in winter than in summer.

⁊ Trees with gorgeous bark: ACER PENSYLVANICUM, striped maple; PRUNUS MAACKII, amur chokeberry; P. SERRULATA, Japanese flowering cherry (this is my favorite); ACER GRISEUM, paperbark maple; A. PALMATUM SENKAKI, coral bark maple; PARROTIA PERSICA, parrotia; PINUS BUNGEANA, lace-bark pine; STEWARTIA PSEUDOCAMELLIA, Japanese stewartia.

⁊ BETULA, birch trees, for the white bark, and in some varieties for pendulous shapes.

⁊ Arbutus has a very limited West Coast range but it is one of the most beautiful trees in form and

has fascinating peeling bark in winter.

⁊ In warm areas consider: JASMINUM NUDIFLORUM, winter jasmine, which can be used on a trellis, as a ground cover or in a planter.

⁊ Plants for winter interest anywhere: MAHONIA JAPONICA, M. AQUIFOLIUM, Oregon holly-grape; HELLEBORUS FOETIDUS, stinking hellebore, H. LIVIDUS CORSICUS, H. NIGER, Christmas rose; lavenders and sage.

⁊ PYRACANTHA, firethorn: I have this vine espaliered on a fence, and the intense orange berries are like clusters of jewels.

⁊ SYMPHORICARPOS, snowberry, with pure white berries and CALLICARPA BODINIERI var. GIRALDII, beautyberry, with lilac berries, both deciduous; the berries are incredibly lovely in winter.

⁊ We should never forget the beauty of ornamental grasses in this season: MISCANTHUS SINENSIS 'Gracillimus', eulalia grass, and other majestic bronze grasses such as CAREX BUCHANANII, sedge, are dramatic foils for more static plants such as ILEX CRENATA, Japanese holly, and ILEX GLABRA, inkberry; or JUNIPERUS spp.

⁊ CHAMAECYPARIS PISIFERA 'Aurea', false cypress, is a shower of gold all year round and looks particularly good in the winter garden.

⁊ C. P. 'Boulevard' is a soft steely blue.

⁊ RHODODENDRON 'P.J.M.' turns red to purple. Be sure to protect from winter burn.

⁊ All viburnums are great plants and the following perform well in winter: VIBURNUM TINUS, laurustinus, is evergreen; V. X BURKWOODII has semi-evergreen leaves. In warmer areas, V. X BODNANTENSE has clusters of small fragrant pink or white flowers; V. X CARLCEPHALUM has dense flower heads up to 6 inches (15 centimeters) across. Use V. FARRERI or V. FRAGRANS for scent.

⁊ Other plants for winter scent: CHIMONANTHUS PRAECOX, wintersweet; LONICERA FRAGRANTISSIMA, winter honeysuckle; HAMAMELIS MOLLIS, Chinese witch-hazel; DAPHNE MEZEREUM, February daphne. Artemisias hold scent all year round.

ABOVE: *Barbara Wilkins' winter garden is filled with color: the pear tree is surrounded by* DEUTZIA GRACILIS; *behind is* PICEA GLAUCA *'Conica'; in front is a dwarf* TSUGA; *top right:* CHAMAECYPARIS NOOTKATENSIS *'Pendula'. Ontario Z6.*

BELOW: *The influence of Japanese pruning is evident in the Wiggan garden:* TAXUS CUSPIDATA, *Japanese yews; behind the tall tree is* TSUGA CANADENSIS, *Canadian hemlock; the deciduous shrubs are* POTENTILLA FRUTICOSA. *Ontario Z6.*

ABOVE: *In this garden designed by Christopher Campbell the elegant trellis stands out dramatically against the snow. From left: crabapple;* RHODODENDRON *'P.J.M.';* ROSA GLAUCA; R. *'Fairfield Blaze';* R. *'America';* VIBURNUM; WISTERIA *'Laurence';* SYRINGA VULGARIS; SPIRAEA SHIROBANA. *Ontario Z6.*

LEFT: *Wendy Cook's garden was designed early in this century and now stretches across three gardens.* EUONYMOUS *spp. edge the central axis, which leads to a rose garden. The sweep of the steps and the terracing show exactly the kind of scale and proportion that makes a great design. Ontario Z6.*

ABOVE: *Neil Turnbull designed this garden for David and Ronny Fingold. On the right:* RHODODENDRON CATAWBIENSE *'Bousault'; background: Colorado blue spruce. Ontario Z6.*

LEFT: *Another view of the Fingold garden. In the foreground: weeping mulberry; boxwood 'Green Velvet';* BETULA JACQUEMONTII, *Himalayan birch. In the background: Colorado blue spruce mask nearby houses. Left:* PICEA ABIES *'Ohlendorffii', spruce. Ontario Z6.*

## VINES WITH WINTER INTEREST

The verticals in your garden become terribly vulnerable to scrutiny in winter. There aren't many evergreen vines except for HEDERA HELIX, English ivy, that will survive winter in Canada. Remember the old saying: "The first year it sleeps, the second year it creeps, the third year it leaps." When you are putting ivy up against walls and fences, make sure it's protected from burning winter sun.

❧ Combine PARTHENOCISSUS QUINQUEFOLIA, Virginia creeper, with ivy. Once it starts to look ragged after the spectacular fall display, the ivy will be there to look good all winter.

❧ EUONYMUS FORTUNEI, wintercreeper, is a deep green glossy addition to the winter garden. E. F. 'Sarcoxie', E. F. VAR. RADICANS, E. F. 'Emerald Beauty', 'Emerald Charm' and 'Emerald Gaiety' are incredibly tough as well as beautiful.

❧ COTONEASTER HORIZONTALIS, rock cotoneaster, has scarlet berries as well as small round leaves; C. APICULATUS, cranberry cotoneaster, can be trained without wires; and C. DAMMERI turns a lovely red in winter.

❧ JUNIPERUS HORIZONTALIS 'Blue Wilton', creeping juniper, is wonderful draped over low walls or trained up stakes and along wires.

## EVERGREEN GROUND COVERS

Evergreen ground covers provide winter interest as well as tying sections of the garden together handsomely.

❧ ARUM ITALICUM, Italian arum; BERGENIA CORDIFOLIA, heartleaf bergenia; HEDERA HELIX 'Baltica', Baltic ivy; PACHYSANDRA TERMINALIS, Japanese spurge. Add in a POLYSTICHUM ACROSTICHOIDES, Christmas fern, one of the few evergreen ferns in northern climates.

❧ ARCTOSTAPHYLOS UVA-URSI, bearberry or kinnikinick, likes exposed sandy rocky places, or use in a woodland under pines.

❧ For spiky contrasts use YUCCA FILAMENTOSA, Adam's needle yucca. This has never been one of my favorite plants but it is so versatile and ironically sensual with a dusting of snow over its sharp lance-like leaves, that I melt. It is gorgeous in winter.

❧ In warm climates, PRUNUS SUBHIRTELLA 'Autumnalis', Higan cherry, has white flowers from November to April.

❧ Other winter pleasures: the joy of seeing broad-leaved evergreens and conifers together; dwarf conifers combined with ivies; heathers with prostrate junipers; MAHONIA AQUIFOLIUM, Oregon holly-grape, with its dark burgundy leaves up against the bare red twigs of CORNUS ALBA 'Sibirica', Siberian dogwood; the beauty of the low-lying twigs of ACER PALMATUM, Japanese maple, with a ground cover of ASARUM EUROPAEUM and A. HARTWEGII, wild ginger.

❧ In the woodland combine hellebores and ivies with bergenias and ARUM near PIERIS JAPONICA, lily-of-the-valley bush, and a KALMIA LATIFOLIA, mountain-laurel.

❧ A great old sage plant, lavender, EUPHORBIA MYRSINITES, spurge, and STACHYS BYZANTINA, lamb's-ears, look wonderful together.

❧ All the artemisias look shaggy and droopy but still felted a lovely gray in winter.

❧ The graceful arches of COTONEASTER DIELSIANUS MAJOR with its incredible red berries up against a fence with wintersweet all over it is glorious.

The plants in my winter garden work for most other seasons as well, backing up the principle that one should never use anything unless it has at least three seasons of interest.

# CHAPTER FOUR

# THE GARDEN IN SPRING

Spring—ethereal as gossamer with sunlight streaming through flowering shrubs. How could anyone not feel an incredible surge of joy in this season? The sight of an ERICA HERBACEA, spring heath, flush with magenta blooms makes my heart leap, eager for a glimpse of that first snowdrop. It brings a swell of hope into my life like nothing else.

Apart from deeply romantic thoughts, spring is when I start making lists for trips to the nursery. It's also the time I uncover plants too early and then have to cover them right up again. It's the time to find out what didn't make it through the winter. And to determine what has to be separated and moved.

## BULBS

All manner of shrubs and trees can be underplanted with masses and masses of bulbs—there's no such thing as too many. The shrubs in their turn will cover up most of the mess bulbs leave behind as their foliage ripens.

In a woodland garden, plant bulbs to naturalize: NARCISSUS, CROCUS, ACONITES, ERYTHRONIUM, MUSCARI and SCILLA just as starters.

**DESIGNING WITH BULBS** ⚜ Think in terms of rivers of bulbs when you plant around shrubs and trees. Little, even big, clumps don't look quite natural. I usually cast my bulbs out in streams, mixing NARCISSUS with MUSCARI, SCILLA, CROCUS and FRITILLARIA. I dig them in at different levels so they will come up at different times and blooms will carry on for months.

I think it's especially pleasing to have a color theme when choosing bulbs. Color dotted here and there without any logic makes the eyes fidgety. Some years, the emphasis may be on blue and white and cream. Other years it might be lilac, yellow and blue.

I'm not keen on a whole bunch of different varieties of the same bulb mixed up together. I plant NARCISSUS 'Thalia' along with N. 'Jack Snipe' and N. 'Minnow' because they mingle well but am careful about other combinations of varieties. Adding something in harsher yellow tones would throw off the whole balance.

⚜ Put the earliest little bulbs such as GALANTHUS, snowdrops, along the driveway or a path so that you'll catch a glimpse of spring as you dash from car to door.

⚜ Plant bulbs—preferably something with fragrance—at either side of the front door. Start with daffodils and then later on lilies.

An important principle is to tuck bulbs around established clumps of perennials. When you lift overgrown plants for dividing in fall, plant bulbs beneath them to grow up through and around the perennial. "If they hit a root base," says Laura Rapp, "they'll make a sharp turn to the left and carry right on."

Around the perimeter of peonies, she suggests CROCUS, SCILLA, MUSCARI, species tulips and tiny daffodils. Or, perhaps, a stream of tulips moving close to and out behind a peony. As the peony grows, its foliage will hide the dying bulbs.

---

RIGHT: *Early morning light bathes the garden of Barbara Wilkins. It is built down the side of a ravine with no sense of encroachment whatsoever. Rear left:* ROBINIA PSEUDOACACIA, *black locust; right:* CERCIS CANADENSIS, *eastern redbud. Left top to bottom:* RHODODENDRON *'Janet Blair';* AZALEA *'Pride's Pride';* R. ANWHEIENSE, *a hardy plant covered with pink flowers;* AZALEA *'Phyllis Moore';* A. *'Linda' fronted by an unknown azalea. Right top to bottom:* R. BRACHYCARPUM *spp. tigerstedtii;* R. *'Pinnacle';* R. *'Yaku Prince';* R. YAKUSIMANUM; R. BUREAVII. *Ontario Z6B.*

ABOVE: *Tim Tanz's small courtyard garden is a refuge from the city:* EUONYMUS FORTUNEI *'Sarcoxie' runs up the wall;* TULIPA PURISSIMA *'White Emperor' interplanted with* ALLIUM GIGANTEUM; VINCA MINOR, *periwinkle, spills over the edge of raised beds.* PELARGONIUM X DOMESTICUM, *Mary geranium, in containers. Ontario Z6B.*

LEFT: *Laura Rapp constructed a folly in what might have been lost space in her city garden. Under the huge* FRAXINUS, *ash trees, there are thousands of bulbs; from left:* NARCISSUS *'Mount Hood' and* N. *'Stainless';* N. *'Jack Snipe';* TULIPA PURISSIMA *'White Emperor'; in the background is a yellow* NARCISSUS *'Honeybird'; far back:* N. *'Romance';* AMELANCHIER; CORNUS ALTERNIFOLIA, *pagoda dogwood, and bottlebrush buckey run rampant. Ontario Z6.*

The intense reddish-plum color in the new foliage of roses goes especially well with the classic blues of MUSCARI and SCILLA. Add a few tulips drifting away just behind the clump of roses.

Here are some other plants Laura Rapp likes to tuck spring bulbs around both as good combinations and as a way of disguising the dying foliage: Put MUSCARI LATIFOLIUM, grape hyacinth, along with DICENTRA, bleeding heart, or use them as an edging along a hedge of dwarf lilacs. Another edging is the pure white of ANEMONE BLANDA. Around hostas, LEUCOJUM, snowflakes, or white tulips look the best. With ferns use TULIPA 'Spring Green'. And add lilies to clumps of daylilies.

To me the most obvious and easiest coverup for dying bulb foliage comes from a collection of hostas. It doesn't matter that slugs like them as much as I do. I consider the slug patrol part of the daily routine, and handpicking these slimy devils gives me a weird sort of pleasure. Of the hundreds of hostas here are some of the loveliest: HOSTA LANCIFOLIA; H. 'Hadspen Blue'; H. 'Frances Williams'; H. 'Krossa Regal'; H. 'Ginko Craig'; H. PLANTAGINEA 'Honeybells'; H. 'Halcyon'; H. 'Snow Cap'; H. SIEBOLDII 'Kabitan'; H. 'Sum and Substance'; and H. TOKUDAMA. Plant early bulbs and narcissi around and under hostas and they will live happily together for many years.

Watch where the sun falls in the garden during spring thaws. Fences and walls facing south absorb heat during the day and radiate it at night, so this area will be warmer than others. Any bare soil in the garden will heat up first, and that's where to place such early bulbs as SCILLA; GALANTHUS, snowdrops, IRIS DANFORDIAE; ANEMONE BLANDA; PUSCHKINIA; CHIONODOXA, glory-of-the-snow; ERANTHIS, winter aconite, and, of course, CROCUS.

In mid-bulb season, late March and April in most parts of the country, plant for a display of daffodils and FRITILLARIA—preferably together for effect.

May marks the end of the daffodil season and the beginning of the tulips. Species tulips, such as FOSTERANA, GREIGII and KAUFMANNIANA, are among my own favorites. Then there are CROCUS TOMASINIANUS; ERANTHIS HYEMALIS, winter aconite; GALANTHUS NIVALIS, snowdrop, for all shady spots; add IRIS RETICULATA for early spring color along with dwarf daffodils.

## TREES FOR THE SPRING GARDEN

Here's when I want flash: great bountiful loads of blossoms. The following are among the finest I know:

All of the magnolias have something good to say for themselves. MAGNOLIA STELLATA, star magnolia, flowers before its leaves unfurl and combines superbly with bulbs. It is the smallest of a family that can grow to 20 feet (6 meters), so magnolias fit in almost anywhere.

CERCIS CANADENSIS is the eastern redbud (it's a native plant); the pink flowers shine against leafless deep brown branches. In fall, it's a blaze of color with delicate fruit hanging below its branches. It's a good gap filler between early and late-flowering fruit trees. C. OCCIDENTALIS, western redbud (native to California): in spring magenta flowers are followed by shiny blue-green heart-shaped leaves; turns gold in fall and in winter has sienna-colored hanging seed pods.

CORYLUS AVELLANA 'Pendula', weeping filbert, has enchanting pale yellow catkins to grace the arching branches.

AMELANCHIER LAEVIS, Allegany serviceberry, PRUNUS SUBHIRTELLA 'Pendula' and 'Rosea', Higan cherry, and MALUS X ARNOLDIANA, crab apple, all provide showers of blossoms.

RIGHT: *Barbara Wilkins is a collector of plants who places them with a real sense of style. Top to bottom left:* AZALEA POUKHANENSIS; DEUTZIA GRACILIS; TSUGA, *dwarf hemlock;* CORYDALIS LUTEA. *Top to bottom right:* A. *'Cascade';* PICEA GLAUCA *'Conica', dwarf Alberta spruce. Ontario Z6B.*

**ABOVE:** *Don Armstrong's complicated garden holds thousands of plants. Upper left:* PAEONIA LUTEA *fronts a* MAGNOLIA GRANDIFLORA; *on the fence:* DRYOPTERIS FILIX-MAS; CAMELLIA JAPONICA; RHODODENDRON AUGUSTINII. *Far right:* KIRENGESHOMA PALMATAM. *Far left:* SMILACINA RACEMOSA, *false Solomon's-seal;* IRIS SIBIRICA; RODGERSIA AESCULIFOLIA; R. PODOPHYLLA; R. PINNATA. *Pool:* EPIMEDIUM; ABIES LASIOCARPA. *British Columbia Z8.*

**LEFT:** *In Kathy Leishman's garden the old stone bridge is flanked by* PRUNUS *and* ACER. *Left:* SASA VEITCHII, *Kuma bamboo grass;* JUNIPERUS CHINENSIS *'Pfitzeriana Old Gold'. Right:* COTONEASTER MICROPHYLLUS *in bloom. British Columbia Z8.*

ABOVE: *The central focus of this area of Audrey and Glenn Mellish's garden is* CORNUS KOUSA CHINENSIS, *Chinese dogwood. To the left is* VIBURNUM PLICATUM *'Shasta', double file viburnum; smaller shrub to the right is* V. FARRERI *'Nanum', dwarf fragrant viburnum. The overhanging branches are from* ACER PALMATUM *'Blood-good'. Ontario Z6B.*

## SHRUBS FOR THE SPRING GARDEN

Apart from absolutely ravishing blossoms, scent is what the spring garden is all about. HAMAMELIS, witch-hazel, was one of Gertrude Jekyll's favorites and it's become one of mine. Put it near a path where its delicious odor will draw you along.

Viburnums are among my favorite shrubs. There is one for every season, and most of them have four seasons worth of value: spring flowers, beautiful foliage, fall color and gorgeous form and often evergreen leaves. Hardly anything else could be asked for. VIBURNUM PLICATUM 'Mariesii' and V. P. 'Shasta' have a horizontal branching form and splendid white flowers; V. X JUDDII has a glorious scent as well.

❧ OSMANTHUS DELAVAYI, devilweed, has white flowers from mid- to late spring. One of the most profuse white-flowering shrubs is MALUS SARGENTII, Sargent crabapple.

❧ AMELANCHIER, serviceberries, have showers of almost ghostly white flowers in very early spring. In cold areas these plants are a godsend. They make an admirable transparent edging to a garden room and seem immune to almost any abuse. A. ALNIFOLIA, A. ARBOREA, A. CANADENSIS and A. LAEVIS (this one has flaming red autumn color) are great varieties.

❧ ENKIANTHUS CAMPANULATUS is a superb shrub for the mixed border. The little pink-veined campanula-like bells come along in late spring.

❧ DAPHNE CNEORUM, rose daphne or garland flower, has a glorious scent. Another fragrant shrub is CHOISYA TERNATA, Mexican orange, which needs acid soil in a sheltered area.

❧ FOTHERGILLA MAJOR has almost bluish foliage and white flowers in later spring; PIERIS JAPONICA, lily-of-the-valley bush, is evergreen and has sprays of white or pink flowers depending on the species.

❧ In the warmest parts of the country camellias are a magnificent addition to spring: the blossoms range from simple to double to peony forms in colors from pure white through pale pinks to deep almost reddish pink.

❧ For the warmer parts of the country: CEANOTHUS, California lilac. C. THYRSIFLORUS is one of the best.

❧ Lilacs don't have to be ordinary to thrive: SYRINGA VULGARIS 'Charles Joly' is double wine red; S. V. 'Lavender Lady'; S.V. 'Ludwig Spaeth' deep purple; 'Katherine Havemeyer' mauve pink; 'Michel Buchner' double lavender; 'Sensation' purple red; 'Ellen Wilmott' huge white double flowers; S. X PERSICA 'Donald Wyman' wine red single flowers; S. PATULA 'Miss Kim' is a dwarf lilac.

**RHODODENDRONS AND AZALEAS** ❧ These broad-leaved evergreen shrubs with a marvelous variety of shape and color are the most popular and certainly among the most important of all foliage plants. They are endlessly useful.

In some parts of the country there are so many rhodos blooming in a mad variety of clashing colors that it's easy to get rhodied-out. Too many of them were plunked down without thought years ago. Now they've assumed monstrous proportions. In carelessly combined plantings one can find stands of mature orange and magenta and red plants that are grotesque. In bright light they look plastic. It's too bad because the more subtle varieties and the species plants are sublime. A great many of the stronger-colored rhodos and azaleas look good only with each other—especially the mauve and pink varieties—so don't try to match them up with anything else except evergreens.

To start adding these ericaceous plants to your garden, try some iron-clad azaleas. Deciduous azaleas are hardy to −25°F (−32°C). Here are some of the loveliest rhododendrons and azaleas for both flower and foliage:

❧ R. YAKUSIMANUM: tolerant of harsh conditions and has one of the most beautiful pink flowers. It has long elliptical leaves and beautiful felted underbellies (indumentum).

❧ R. 'P.J.M.' blooms heavily in April with lavender-pink flowers. Evergreen leaves turn purple in fall.

ABOVE: *Heather and Richard Mossakowski's garden perches on a steep slope that leads down to the sea. The garden contains over one thousand rhododendrons, but the excellent design ensures that the site is not overwhelmed by this largesse:* AZALEA *'Sakidara' in front;* RHODODENDRON *'Anna Rose Whitney' (pink in background); in the center is a group of rhododendrons. British Columbia Z8.*

RIGHT: *In Francisca Darts' densely planted garden this* RHODODENDRON OCCIDENTALE *stands out;* CORNUS KOUSA CHINENSIS *'Milky Way' is behind;* EUPHORBIA PALUSTRIS *is at the base in the background. British Columbia Z7.*

LEFT: *Richard Birkett designed and constructed this enchanting waterfall to appear as though it had been there forever. It is surrounded by* RHODODENDRON X FRASERI; R. SCINTILLANS *in pink;* R. *'Nova Zembla' in red. Ontario Z6B.*

❧ Among the azaleas: R. SCHLIPPENBACHII, royal azalea, has pale pink mid-May blossoms.

❧ R. CINNABARINUM is evergreen and has a scent.

❧ R. 'Ramapo' is a tiny purple-flowered rhodo. Leaves have felted underbelly. Like most of the small-leaved rhodos, leaves turn rusty brown in winter and then turn slowly back to steely gray in spring.

❧ Check out R. MACABEANUM for sensual woolly white underbelly.

Most rhododendrons need part shade but some, such as R. 'P.J.M.', can take a lot more exposure to sun. Large-leaved evergreen plants need shelter from the wind, which dries them out. They should be mulched with pine needles or finely shredded bark to keep roots moist and soil temperatures even. They will need shelter from the bright March sun.

Most rhododendrons won't need fertilizer and, unless they are poorly sited, are pretty carefree. They prefer an acid soil, but if you have clay, make raised beds with lots and lots of sphagnum moss dug in. This improves drainage as well, which is important for all ericaceous plants. Again add pine needles and shredded bark for mulch.

## VINES FOR THE SPRING GARDEN

If you make the right choices you can have vines blooming all three seasons. Here are my favorites for their spring bloom:

❧ Clematis is the natural selection for the spring garden. The following spring winners are beautiful species with small elegant flowers: C. ALPINA, C. ARMANDII, C. MACROPETALA.

❧ AKEBIA QUINATA has lovely-shaped leaves and seed pods that show up in late summer.

❧ HUMULUS LUPULUS 'Aureus', yellow-leaved hop.

## SPRING GROUND COVERS

Ground covers can do just about anything demanded of them: provide a background for other plants, knit the garden together, add color and warmth. But in spring they seem particularly to shine. Shrubs will only partly cover up the dying foliage of spring bulbs; ground covers complete the job. OMPHALODES, to my mind, is one of the best covering-up plants there is. Tulips engulfed by forget-me-nots, alas, has become a cliché, but it's still a lovely way to disguise dying leaves.

GROUND COVERS WITH SPRING BEAUTY

❧ CORNUS CANADENSIS, bunchberry, has oval leaves and white flowers. It's a very tidy plant.

❧ VIOLA LABRADORICA, Labrador violet, with its deep purple leaves flourishes in woodland settings or in sunlight.

❧ LAMIUM, dead nettle, has many lovely forms; I like the luminous quality of L. MACULATUM 'White Nancy', and L. M. 'Sissinghurst White'.

❧ STACHYS BYZANTINA, lamb's-ears, and EUPHORBIA MYRSINITES, myrtle euphorbia, are great gray carpeters.

❧ For the woodland: small bulbs such as snowdrops, wood anemones, cyclamen, SCILLA and winter aconites work beautifully when there are no leaves in the trees and you can appreciate their fragile beauty. Plant with GAULTHERIA, ivy, BERGENIA, LAMIUM, EPIMEDIUM and ASARUM EUROPEUM, European ginger, for a year-round green ground covering.

❧ Heaths and heathers used sparingly are great assets since they are shallow-rooted, aren't aggressively competitive and provide a cool root run for other plants.

# CHAPTER FIVE

# THE GARDEN IN SUMMER

*I*n summer the foliage garden needs strong plantings of herbaceous perennials that look their most glorious best when backed or framed by foliage plants. Almost any blossom is displayed to greater advantage when it has a complementary or contrasting background. Blobs of flowers here and there tend to have a scattered look. But with foliage plants to bind or weave disparate elements together, the garden can become cohesive.

The foliage garden without perennials would be a sorry place. Though my garden doesn't run in the perennial riot-of-color league, it's colorful enough for me. I like to have flowers somewhere about for both sight and scent from the start of spring to the end of fall. I would be bereft without them. So in this I may not have the purist's attitude to the foliage garden.

Mine is a mixed garden, eclectic I'd say, and it works especially well in our country since we have such long winters. Herbaceous perennials vanish and leave bare spots everywhere; therefore, a blend of foliage and perennial plants makes great sense.

One of the most enchanting things about gardening is working out vibrant new plant combinations. Pick up ideas on garden tours, visiting neighbors' gardens or just by looking, reading and dreaming.

To originate combinations, think in terms of constructing garden pictures. Start by moving plants—constantly. Most books warn you to do this only in spring and fall. But I keep things in motion as long as I can. I do follow two carved-in-stone rules, though: stop moving plants about six weeks before hard frost is expected, and never move plants before the soil warms up in spring. The specific dates are different in every area, indeed in every garden across the country. And of course no one counts on the weather.

Putting plants together brings out the creativity in any gardener. Take into consideration points already discussed: the shape and architectural quality of the plant, the texture of a leaf, the color of a blossom. Some successful combinations are due to serendipity, others come from taking risks. Still others evolve from careful thought.

Even with a good imagination, not everything is successful. I've put together some real howlers: LYCHNIS CORONARIA, rose campion (magenta), nestled right up against a lily of particularly livid orange hue. Or the GEUM COCCINEUM 'Mrs. Bradshaw' against a background of THYMUS SERPYLLUM 'Coccineus'. These are herbaceous disasters. My follies with foliage plants tend to be fewer because I'm much more cautious. But one poor MAHONIA was in two different spots before the perfect place was found. A PIERIS JAPONICA 'Variegata' died during a change of mind. You have to accept this if you are going to be an adventurous gardener.

Once you decide to be a mover and shaker, take some precautions. The following tips are for perennials (tree and shrub information can be found in Chapter 7):

❧ Don't move plants at midday. I lean toward late afternoon on the theory that the heat of the day is mostly past and it will soon be cooler for the plant in its new home.

---

RIGHT: *Marion and Alex Jarvie have designed a foliage border with dazzling color. Top center from left:* DAPHNE *'Somerset';* LARIX *'Pendula'; far right back:* PICEA ABIES *'Reflexa'; left center:* ALLIUM AFLATUNENSE *'Purple Sensation'; below:* THUJA OCCIDENTALIS *'Rheingold'. Lower left to right: seedheads of* PULSATILLA VULGARIS, *pasqueflower;* JUNIPERUS SQUAMATA *'Blue Star';* FESTUCA GLAUCA, *blue grass. Ontario Z5.*

᯽ Make sure you take as much local soil with the plant when you shift it and give it as much space as you can allow in the new location.

᯽ Water deeply and regularly for a couple of weeks. After this period of grace, it's do or die in my garden.

᯽ Make sure there is good drainage. And apply a heavy dose of top dressing. I find this is much more effective than digging compost in with the new plant.

᯽ Be prepared to put up with blossoms dropping off and not coming back until next year if you move a perennial in full bloom.

As one of my hortgurus, Susan Ryley, says, "A new plant is a treasure. You put it in a place where you can see it to get used to it. Then once you know it, start moving it around."

## SUMMER PLANT COMBINATIONS

These are some of my own combinations and others observed in favorite gardens that are pleasing:

᯽ Purple sage with wallflowers behind it.

᯽ PHYSOCARPUS OPULIFOLIUS 'Luteus', golden ninebark, with purple sage.

᯽ Golden LONICERA, honeysuckle, with ILEX CRENATA, Japanese holly, in a pot.

᯽ Variegated SCROPHULARIA, figwort, backed by CRAMBE CORDIFOLIA, colewort.

᯽ CLEMATIS and CIMICIFUGA, bugbane.

᯽ ARTEMISIA X 'Powis Castle' with SEDUM TELEPHIUM 'Vera Jameson'.

᯽ DESCHAMPSIA CAESPITOSA, tufted hair grass, with RODGERSIA PINNATA ELEGANS 'Rosea'.

᯽ ROSA RUGOSA (or R. GLAUCA as it's being called once again) with ARTEMISIA ABSINTHIUM, wormwood.

᯽ Hortguru Marion Jarvie's elegant combination for a very small garden: A gray upright juniper, JUNIPERUS COMMUNIS 'Pencil Point' (after 10 years 4 feet/1.3 meters high by 1 foot/30 centimeters wide), with a dark bottle green CHAMAECYPARIS OBTUSA 'Nana Gracilis', one of the Hinoki cypresses (this dwarf variety will grow to 3 feet/1 meter in 10 years). Then add a small spreading dwarf yellow-green plant such as TSUGA CANADENSIS 'Jeddelah', Canada hemlock, which is prostrate and can be mounded over a rock. It will take 10 years to grow 2 feet (60 centimeters) across.

## TREES WITH SUMMER INTEREST

᯽ FAGUS SYLVATICA 'Tricolor', tricolored European beech, and F. S. 'Pendula', weeping European beech.

᯽ LIRIODENDRON TULIPIFERA 'Aureo-marginatum', tulip tree, with yellow edges to the deep green leaves.

᯽ STYRAX JAPONICUS, Japanese snowbell, has a gorgeous display of white flowers on polished green leaves.

᯽ DAVIDIA INVOLUCRATA, dove or handkerchief tree, is quite amazing—the large white bracts hang like hankies from the bright green leaves.

᯽ CATALPA SPECIOSA, northern catalpa, has huge white flowers backed by even bigger leaves.

᯽ STEWARTIA PSEUDOCAMELLIA, Japanese stewartia, has peeling bark and white flowers in midsummer.

᯽ CORNUS KOUSA CHINENSIS, Chinese dogwood, is a great beauty any time but especially when its blooms smother the spreading branches in early summer.

᯽ AESCULUS GLABRA, Ohio buckeye, has dark green leaves that back up yellow-green flowers in early summer.

᯽ ROBINIA PSEUDOACACIA, false acacia or locust, has pendulous clusters of pea-like white flowers in early summer.

᯽ LABURNUM ALPINUM, Scotch laburnum, has glossy leaves and long chains of gorgeous, utterly poisonous flowers.

RIGHT: *The potting shed in Susan Ryley's garden makes a serendipitous background for architectural plants. From left: single climbing rose 'Dainty Bess' and the pink-splashed leaves of* ACTINIDIA KOLOMIKTA; *white* THALICTRUM AQUILEGIFOLIUM. *Forward from left:* IRIS PALLIDA *'Variegata';* ARTEMISIA *'Lambrook Silver';* SALVIA ARGENTEA *and* HELICTOTRICHON SEMPERVIRENS, *blue oat grass. British Columbia Z8.*

ABOVE: *In Susan Ryley's courtyard you can see the changes in garden levels. A clipped box hedge frames the low cement wall above the pond. Left to right: the straplike leaves of* CRINUM X POWELLII; EUPHORBIA CHARACIAS WULFENII *is in flower;* RODGERSIA PINNATA *'Superba' makes a dramatic contrast with blue oat grass. The softness of* DICTAMNUS ALBUS, *white gas plant, fits in behind a white lavender.* DESCHAMPSIA LEXUOSA *'Aurea' and* DIANTHUS. ILEX CRENATA *'Golden Gem' is in the gray pot; clipped* SANTOLINA *and* LONICERA *'Baggensen's Gold' are also in pots—a marvelous way to introduce flexibility to any area. British Columbia Z8.*

LEFT: *Susan Ryley's cottage mix of foliage and color creates a poetic concoction. Left to right: the lettuce-green leaves of* CLETHRA ALNIFOLIA, *sweet pepperbush; spikes of delphinium and digitalis back up the purple smoke bush;* ARTEMISIA *'Huntington';* LILIUM REGALE; *borage;* ASTRANTIA MAJOR; PENSTEMON *and* ARTEMISIA X *'Powis Castle'. British Columbia Z8.*

## SUMMER-FLOWERING SHRUBS

Summer-flowering shrubs are great bonuses. In spring they provide background for bulbs and blossoms and then in summer they bloom when most other flowers are beginning to look a bit sad.

❧ EXOCHORDA X MACRANTHA 'The Bride'—I love the arching form of this shrub and of course the shower of white blooms.

❧ PHILADELPHUS X LEMOINEI 'Belle Etoile' and P. X LEMOINEI 'Avalanche' have fragrant white flowers early to midsummer.

❧ DEUTZIA SCABRA has oval deep green leaves with white blossoms in early summer.

❧ HYDRANGEA QUERCIFOLIA, oakleaf hydrangea, has white flowers in late summer; turns almost purple in fall. H. MACROPHYLLA 'Veitchii' is an oval glossy-leaved shrub with pale blue flowers in late summer.

❧ STYRAX WILSONII, Wilson snowbell, has white flowers with yellow centers against dark green slender leaves.

❧ ARONIA MELANOCARPA, black chokeberry, has white flowers in late spring, black fruit, and glossy leaves that turn red in fall.

❧ SORBARIA SORBIFOLIA, false spiraea, has ecru flowers in summer. Since it suckers profusely, plant it where you need a useful, handsome filler.

❧ CHIONANTHUS VIRGINICUS, fringe tree or old-man's-beard, has white flowers in early summer, blue berries, and turns yellow in fall.

❧ KOLKWITZIA AMABILIS 'Pink Cloud', beauty-bush, has an arching shape, with bell-like flowers in June.

❧ TAMARIX RAMOSISSIMA, tamarisk, has feathery plumes of pink in late summer.

❧ CYTISUS BATTANDIERI, Moroccan broom, has silvery leaves with yellow flowers in early to midsummer.

## ANNUALS

It's impossible to imagine a summer garden without annuals. You don't need many to make a profound impact. Even a foliage garden will be spruced up during the dog days of summer with the lambent beauty of annuals. Leave space to punch in these plants for an instant lift. I don't have much room for them but I put them where they are needed: in holes left by bulbs; in areas where I know the blooms will be off other plants and I will need a hit of color in a month or so. I use them in pots for moving around.

I had no idea I was a collector of pots until one year when bringing them indoors I found they filled most of my dining area and left me without a place to eat.

I always plant one pot with white impatiens because they glow at night. I like them to lighten up murky places on the deck. Poor impatiens have been overused—a major disservice. I've seen them constitute entire gardens.

❧ Fill pots with annuals for glorious splashes of color: begonias; impatiens; pansies; NICOTIANA ALATA (the scented kind, not the hybrids, which have no scent at all).

❧ Window boxes: I like the combination of blue and white or blue and silver: CERASTIUM TOMENTOSUM, snow-in-summer, and LOBELIA ERINUS 'Crystal Palace'; BROWALLIA, bush violet, with ARTEMISIA, wormwood; DELPHINIUM, larkspur, and SENECIO.

---

PREVIOUS DOUBLE-PAGE SPREAD: *The mixed border in Susan Ryley's garden features the gray leaves of* CYTISUS BATTANDIERI *with the gray foliage of* THALICTRUM FLAVUM GLAUCUM; *large white flowers of* HYDRANGEA PETIOLARIS *in back row. Middle left to right: foliage of* GERANIUM *'Magnificum';* BALLOTA PSEUDODICTAMNUS; RHAZYA ORIENTALIS *(blue);* ARTEMISIA *'Huntington';* HELIANTHEMUM *'Wisley Pink';* ARRHENATHERUM ELATIUS *'Variegatum', bulbous grass;* CENTRANTHUS ALBUS; NEPETA TUBEROSA; *the small* BALLOTA ACETABALOSA; *and a gray-leaved* BUDDLEIA FALLOWIANA. *British Columbia Z8.*

LEFT: *This exquisite front garden was designed by Murray Haigh for Aileen Wolff to capitalize on the formal aspects of her house. Clockwise from left:* RHODODENDRON *'P.J.M.';* AZALEA *'Herbert';* ACER PALMATUM *'Bloodgood';* PACHYSANDRA TERMINALIS; EUONYMUS *'Sarcoxie';* TAXUS CUSPIDATA. *Ontario Z6.*

BELOW: *In this tranquil city garden a collection of bonsais creates an oasis. Behind the fence is a* CRATAEGUS; *in front is* RHODODENDRON LAURELLI SANCTON *and* PIERIS JAPONICA. R. GUMPO *is in the front center and to the right is* R. CILPINENSE *flanked by* HELLEBORUS ORIENTALIS; TRILLIUM OVATUM *and* ADIANTUM PEDATUM. *British Columbia Z8.*

ABOVE: *The serene inner courtyard of Gerald Straley's patio garden includes a variety of perennials in pots around a small pond. Left foreground:* ALLIUM MOLY *fronted by* CAREX CONICA; ASPHODELUS FISTULOSUS; HOSTA LANCIFOLIA *and* HELLEBORUS FOETIDUS *'Westerflick';* HEMEROCALLIS *'Sunday Gloves'. In the background:* FATSIA JAPONICA *gives a lush look to the garden. In middle behind the pond is* BETULA PENDULA *'Youngii'; on the right is* ACER CIRCINATUM. British Columbia Z8.

ABOVE: *In Gary White and John Veillette's magic retreat, the lady stands among a* ROSA *'Nevada' and a pyrus, which supports* HYDRANGEA PETIOLARIS, *climbing hydrangea; background:* MALUS BACCATA, *Siberian crab;* ACER PLATANOIDES *'Crimson King' is borrowed from the neighbors. Right:* LAVATERA OLBIA; MISCANTHUS *seedling;* ELYMUS GLAUCUS, *giant rye grass;* PHLOMIS RUSSELIANA; GERANIUM ENDRESSII; *self-sown California poppies. The pots create a miniature landscape. British Columbia Z9.*

LEFT: *In Janet and Trevor Ashbee's garden* VIBURNUM X BURKWOODII; MAHONIA AQUIFOLIUM; JUNIPERUS *'Skyrocket' provide a background for their collection of pots. The trough includes alpines and some bonsai. Ontario Z5.*

❧ Ballotas, senecios and hebes are too tender for all but the warmest climate zones, but try them in pots for beautiful foliage effects.

❧ Gray foliage plants: HELICHRYSUM, everlasting; SANTOLINA, ARTEMISIA, silver-lace; FESTUCA OVINA, sheep fescue; sedums, tectorums, sempervivums. All of these plants look magnificent in pots and used as links between plants in borders.

**CONTAINER FLEXIBILITY** ❧ It's a good idea to put plants that you can't accommodate anywhere else in the garden in containers. I stick containers right into borders, moving them around to change the mood or look of the garden.

In our cold climate it's impossible to leave beautiful clay pots outside, but that's a minor inconvenience compared to how adaptable they are. You can experiment with plant combinations in miniature. And a planted container adds a wonderful bit of punctuation to any border.

If you can afford them and they fit in with your garden style, get stone urns or copies of old ones. Make sure they have the right context—a pair on each side of a walkway; a single one to announce the entrance to a different part of the garden; or put into the center of a bower.

❧ The tops of containers should be as wide as or wider than the base.

❧ Go for the big picture and group pots of different sizes in large numbers. One or two may look just a tad lonely. A good combination might be plain terra cotta pots with flowers and square wooden tubs for trees and shrubs or perennials with architectural foliage.

❧ A metal plant stand, even without any pots or plants on it, can be moved into another part of the garden to make a vertical line in the midst of horizontals.

❧ To have a permanent planting in our cold winters, the container will have to be a minimum of 14 inches (35 centimeters) in all dimensions. Most dwarf evergreens will be happy in this size container, as will BUXUS, boxwood.

❧ As a loose rule I keep my choices for pots confined to two types of plants. If you jam in more, keep the style of pot as simple as possible.

❧ Use an overscaled pot as a sculptural element by not planting in it at all.

❧ I have one enormous Chinese pot that stays out all winter. I fill it with huge piles of red dogwood twigs for a winter bouquet.

## SUMMER-FLOWERING VINES

This is the season for the vertical garden. Keep the blossoms of summer-flowering vines foremost in your mind as they will have lots of competition from perennials coming into flower at the same time.

❧ Here's a combination from my garden that I think is sensational: AMPELOPSIS BREVIPEDUNCU-LATA 'Variegata', porcelain berry, with GALEGA OFFICINALIS, goat's-rue, a white-flowered herb. The variegation of the vine and the white blossoms blend perfectly.

❧ LATHYRUS SYLVESTRIS, the perennial sweetpea, makes lovely cut flowers. There are two versions: one in pink and the other in white. There is also the annual sweetpea vine, L. ODORATUS, which grows quickly and comes in many colors.

❧ The following clematis are all noteworthy ornamental vines: CLEMATIS X JACKMANII is the popular purple vine—it will keep going for weeks with deadheading; C. 'Perle d'Azur', C. 'Ville de Lyon'. Species clematis: C. COMPANIFLORA, C. FLAMMULA, C. MAXIMOWICZIANA, C. MONTANA.

❧ LONICERA, honeysuckle, comes in many forms, often scented with blooms that range from yellows through to dark reds.

❧ CELASTRUS SCANDENS, American bittersweet: the summer flowers are small but the berries last through the winter.

❧ And of course the gorgeous climbing roses: ROSA 'New Dawn' is splendid flung over a bower; R. 'Albertine' and R. FILIPES 'Kifsgate' are both vigorous climbers.

❧ ACTINIDIA KOLOMIKTA, kiwi vine. This twining vine with cream, white and pink leaves has white flowers in summer.

❧ ARISTOLOCHIA MACROPHYLLA (also called A. DURIOR), dutchman's-pipe. It's not the little flowers so much as the large heart-shaped leaves that are of interest.

❧ ACONITUM VOLUBILE is the climbing form of monkshood. It threads through shrubs nicely.

❧ HYDRANGEA PETIOLARIS (also called H. ANOMALA) has glorious white flowers backed by glossy green leaves.

❧ WISTERIA SINENSIS 'Alba' not only has gorgeous panicles of white flowers but the scent is intoxicating.

❧ SCHIZOPHRAGMA HYDRANGEOIDES, Japanese hydrangea vine, has glorious large creamy white flowers with heart-shaped sepals.

## SUMMER GROUND COVERS

It's surprising what works as ground covers, as the following list attests:

❧ GERANIUM MACRORRHIZUM has magenta flowers in summer, and turns bright red and yellow in fall. It grows in shade too.

❧ SAXIFRAGA X URBIUM, London-pride, in great swathes is an incredible sweep of pink and white, which works well in light shade and moist soil.

❧ STACHYS BYZANTINA, lamb's-ears, goes well with the prettiest of hardy geraniums, G. ENDRESSII 'Wargrave Pink'; the pink and gray blend beautifully together.

❧ Herbs massed in as ground covers are among my favorites for both sight and scent: lavenders (LAVANDULA ANGUSTIFOLIA 'Hidcote' and 'Munstead Blue' are the hardiest); sages, thymes, ballota and hyssop, hebes, and especially euphorbias, sedums and calmintha.

❧ CERATOSTIGMA PLUMBAGINOIDES has brilliant blue flowers in late summer and its foliage slowly changes to brilliant carmine in fall.

❧ VIOLA CORNUTA blooms almost all summer.

❧ I love carpeting perennials such as CAMPANULA PORTENSCHLAGIANA, C. CARPATICA and C. PORSCHARSKYANA, which grow slowly but surely in shade and provide a gem-like glow.

❧ MAZUS REPTANS tolerates shade and damp soil and has lovely lilac-colored flowers.

❧ ERICA TETRALIX, bog heather, with silvery foliage and white flowers.

❧ PAXISTIMA CANBYI, rat-stripper, likes shade and is a beautiful evergreen ground cover.

❧ SAGINA SUBULATA 'Aurea', pearlwort, isn't really moss but it's a terrific ground cover, especially to fill in spaces between bricks or stones.

# CHAPTER SIX

# THE GARDEN IN AUTUMN

*R*ight from the beginning I concentrated on autumn in my garden, so it is close to my heart. This is the richest, most beautiful time of year. I love subdued colors in all other seasons, but in this one, the autumnal blaze of color fits my mood. The scent, the touch and the feel of this season is as though nature must give us its last magnificent burst of energy before quietly retiring. Foliage, of course, comes into its own in autumn. Fiery colors of trees and shrubs are the background for the radiant blooms of long-lasting perennials.

What else can compete with the brilliant tones of ECHINICEAE, purple coneflower; ECHINOPS, thistle; HELENIUM, all the asters or Michaelmas daisies, chrysanthemums, CIMICIFUGA, ACONITUM, phlox and gaura? Foliage plants of course. They act as foils for all that color. By selecting the appropriate foliage plants you can tone down brilliant colors or make a passage from one bright color to the next so that the eye doesn't become exhausted.

This is a good season to get as much work done as possible. The soil is still warm, the nights a bit cooler. And there's always a chance for a last surge of warmth after the first frost. Woody plants are usually happiest being planted at this time of year since growth will be greatly reduced and flowering long since over.

This is also the season to divide plants, to replant, to move things around. Calculate about six weeks back from the usual first hard frost in your garden and use this as a guide to your last plant/transplanting date for most woody plants. Personal knowledge of your garden's microclimate will give you a much more precise idea of which plants will thrive. In my garden hard frost usually happens around mid- to late November. So I carry on blithely transplanting perennials and shrubs into October. The farther north you are the longer the days are. But after the autumn equinox, the light falls off quickly and you have to work fast. Don't touch grasses, sedums, shrubs such as hydrangea, or any other plant with beautiful seed heads. They will look decorative all winter, especially against the snow. Over zealous cleaning up is detrimental to the garden's health and looks stiff and less aesthetically pleasing.

## AUTUMN COLOR

What happens in fall is a shift in development of chlorophyll, which transforms the sun's energy through photosynthesis. Chlorophyll combines with water and carbon dioxide to manufacture sugars to provide food for growth. The formation of chlorophyll depends on bright light. When chlorophyll is in full supply the leaf is green. As daylight hours wane, photosynthesis slows down, depleting chlorophyll and slowing down the production of sap. Once chlorophyll disappears other pigments always present in the plant become obvious.

Colors are brighter when it's been a warm sunny summer with lots of rain. An early frost will destroy leaf cells and there's no chance for carotenoids to

---

RIGHT: *Autumn is a favorite time in my own garden. Strong colors come into play combined with silver foliage. Along the fence: wisteria and lathyrus with assorted clematis and beauty berry vine; major shrub is* COTONEASTER DIELSIANUS; *from left foreground:* ARTEMISIA X *'Powis Castle';* ASTER *'Harrington's Pink';* CHELONE; SEDUM SPECTABILE *'Autumn Joy';* BUDDLEIA DAVIDII; *center row:* CERATOSTIGMA PLUMBAGINOIDES *backed by the silvery* CARYOPTERIS X CLADONENSIS; A. X *'Powis Castle'. Ontario Z6.*

show or anthocyanins to be made. With an early fall of sunny cool days, the presence of anthocyanin increases, turning oak, red maple, sweetgum and dogwood their brilliant colors.

The very opulence of the season makes it difficult to design the autumn garden. We are almost overblessed with foliage colors—too many demanding attention. It's a time for some caution.

The first principle of designing the autumn garden is to keep in mind how strong autumn colors can be. When you put anything next to a plant that will change radically, the combinations can be truly eye-crunching. Others merely clash. But some colors reach an almost neon intensity.

❧ The glory of the autumn garden should include any form of ACER PALMATUM, Japanese maple, but take care with an orangy-red ACER and any purple plant. This is not a happy combination.

❧ Keep perennial colors in mind as well. I put a late-blooming flashy lingerie-pink phlox next to a viburnum that turns almost burgundy. They fought. The phlox was moved.

❧ To make things easier, many late-flowering trees and shrubs have white blooms, which leaven the hot shades of fall. PRUNUS SUBHIRTELLA 'Autumnalis', Higan cherry, and CLETHRA ALNIFOLIA, summer-sweet, are two examples.

❧ CEANOTHUS X DELILIANUS 'Autumnal Blue' is an evergreen shrub with lovely pale blue flowers that go on into fall.

❧ ELSHOLTZIA STAUNTONII, mint shrub, deciduous with long slender purple flowers; the dark green leaves turn red later on.

❧ Because evergreens—conifers and broad-leaved —will be more obvious in fall, think in terms of static and fluid combinations. Evergreens are static, so put them with something that sways, such as ornamental grasses.

## AUTUMN PLANT COMBINATIONS

My hortguru, Marion Jarvie, is an expert on conifers, therefore she thinks a lot about the fall and winter garden. Here's one of her most dramatic autumn combinations: ILEX VERTICILLATA, winterberry; PICEA GLAUCA 'Montgomery', dwarf blue spruce; HEUCHERA MICRANTHA 'Montrose Ruby' underplanted with COLCHICUM and LIRIOPE.

❧ Among my favorite plants are the CIMICIFUGA, bugbanes. They are magnificent plants with deeply notched branches and a shower of white flowers from August to frost. C. RACEMOSA, black snakeroot, or C. SIMPLEX combined with THALICTRUM, meadow rue, and Japanese anemones are a glorious sight in and out of bloom. C. R. 'Atropurpurea' is smaller with darker foliage, and I have it combined with a light frothy plant, GAURA LINDHEIMERI, for a gorgeous heart-stopping effect. The latter is a great plant that blooms for months in Zone 5.

❧ ACER PALMATUM 'Atropurpureum', Japanese maple; LIGUSTRUM X VICARYI, golden privet, and a variegated CORNUS, dogwood, look good in a group.

❧ Viburnums are fragrant shrubs in spring and brilliant in fall. I have VIBURNUM PLICATUM 'Shasta' with ELAEAGNUS ANGUSTIFOLIA, Russian olive: the deep russet of the shrub and gnarled gray of the tree combine shape and texture impeccably.

## PLANTS FOR MAGNIFICENT FALL COLOR

Woody foliage plants will survive most early frosts unscathed, giving great value since they last right through to winter.

I keep emphasizing my great passion for all artemisias. These grand gray-to-silver plants fit companionably with just about anything in the garden. In fall they seem even more gorgeous than during the rest of the year and they perfume the air indelibly. ARTEMISIA ARBORESCENS and A. X 'Powis Castle' are a bit tender and look rather limp after the first hit of cold weather, but there's something wonderfully decadent about plants tattered at the edges in fall. Don't cut them back until spring. They may look a little sad, but in most parts of the country the plant will need all the protection it can get.

ABOVE: *The garden of Mary and Terry Mills capitalizes on every square inch in a relatively small space. In the central border:* MALUS *'Red Jade' below* VIBURNUM FARRERI; BERGENIA CORDIFOLIA *'Evening Glow'. In the background:* AMELANCHIER ALNIFOLIA *underplanted with* SEDUM *'Autumn Joy' and* IRIS FLORENTINA. *Front steps are flanked by* PICEA GLAUCA *underplanted with* ALCHEMILLA MOLLIS; AUBRETIA DELTOIDEA. *Ontario Z6.*

ABOVE: *Louise Weekes designed this glorious garden with thousands of plants. From rear left:* JUNIPERUS VIRGINIANA; DAPHNE *'Carol Mackie';* CROCOSMIA *'Lucifer'; in the middle:* PENNISETUM *'Hamelin'; Siberian iris 'Silver Edge';* LIGULARIA *'Desdemona';* PAEONIA *'Constance Spry'; right:* EUPATORIUM PURPUREUM *'Gateway'. Ontario Z6.*

LEFT: *Murray Haigh designed the ideal fall garden for Beverley Burge. Over the wall:* STEPHANANDRA INCISA *and* COTONEASTER DAMMERI; VERBENA *sp. in urn;* PICEA GLAUCA *'Albertina Conica'. Across center wall:* JUNIPERUS PROCUMBENS *'Nana';* CERASTIUM TOMENTOSUM *(gray); far right:* COTONEASTER HORIZONTALIS. *Left to right in upper bed:* JUNIPERUS *'Blue Haven';* ECHINACEA PURPUREA; ACHILLEA *hybrid (pink);* HYDRANGEA *'Annabelle' (green);* SEDUM SPECTABILE *'Carmen'. Ontario Z6.*

❧ HAMAMELIS VIRGINIANA, autumn witch-hazel—gold flowers open when the plant still has gold leaves. The bloom continues after the foliage has gone.

❧ For a spectacular shrubby ground cover with good color you cannot go wrong with CERATOSTIGMA PLUMBAGINOIDES. It has blue blossoms and in autumn the foliage turns a sumptuous red. This plant will probably succumb to partial winterkill, but don't worry; it will faithfully come back, if a bit slowly.

❧ PEROVSKIA, with gray foliage and blue blossoms, continues to look good well into the cold weather. CARYOPTERIS X CLANDONENSIS, bluebeard, blooms for at least five weeks. I've found that it's much safer to wait until spring to cut either of these plants back. Do it by about two-thirds. They bloom on new wood.

❧ MYRICA PENSYLVANICA, northern bayberry, grows as a hedge to 12 feet (3.5 meters) in the right situation. It has glossy green leaves right through autumn. Turns bronze in winter.

Other plants with good fall color: ACER SACCHARUM, sugar maple, A. RUBRUM, red maple; BETULA PAPYRIFERA, white birch; LARIX, larch, turns golden and drops its needles—one of the few conifers to do so.

❧ ILEX DECIDUA and I. VERTICILLATA, winterberry, have brilliant red fruit in fall.

❧ HIPPOPHAE RHAMNOIDES, sea-buckthorn, is almost a small tree and has silver leaves and dazzling orange berries in fall.

❧ NANDINA DOMESTICA, heavenly bamboo, is a barberry that has crimson berries in fall.

❧ CORNUS FLORIDA 'Cherokee Chief', flowering dogwood, has deep rosy bracts in autumn (white flowers in spring); foliage turns red.

❧ C. KOUSA CHINENSIS, Chinese dogwood, is an elegant large shrub that leans to one side at the top. Birds like the fruit. It's resistant to the blight that has affected C. FLORIDA.

❧ ELAEAGNUS COMMUTATA, silverberry, is an evergreen shrub and an excellent screen or espalier. E. PUNGENS 'Marginata' has silver edges.

❧ COTINUS COGGYGRIA 'Purpureus', 'Velvet Cloak', 'Royal Purple', smoke plant. I love this plant, and it works well in a border if you keep it pruned from the start. These purple-leaved cultivars harmonize well with other colors. Like many of their ilk, color will fade in higher temperatures.

❧ VIBURNUM RHYTIDOPHYLLUM, leatherleaf viburnum, stays evergreen in warm areas in a wind-sheltered site. Superb screen. Has almost black berries.

❧ BUDDLEIA DAVIDII 'Black Knight', butterfly bush, really does attract butterflies and birds to add to the colors and sounds of late summer and early fall. The deep silver-blue foliage lasts well into the fall and the bright blue flowers last until the end of September if you deadhead regularly.

❧ METASEQUOIA GLYPTOSTROBOIDES, dawn redwood: this unusual deciduous conifer turns yellow, pink and red in autumn. It's a spectacular tree that should be grown more often.

❧ GINKGO BILOBA, maidenhair tree, is one of my favorite trees. The glorious golden color in the fan-shaped leaves glows in autumn.

## VINES FOR THE AUTUMN GARDEN

❧ CLEMATIS PANICULATA, sweet autumn clematis, has white flowers in early autumn.

❧ C. TANGUTICA and C. ORIENTALIS both have yellow blossoms.

❧ C. TEXENSIS 'Duchess of Albany' has rose-colored flowers in early autumn.

❧ POLYGONUM AUBERTII, silver lace vine, is called the mile-a-minute plant for good reason; it's rampant beyond belief. The pretty white fall flowers attract masses of bees and wasps. It should only be used as a fast coverup.

❧ HUMULUS LUPULUS 'Aureus', the yellow form of the hop vine, is much less rampant than other varieties and is almost luminous.

❧ PARTHENOCISSUS QUINQUEFOLIA, Virginia creeper, makes a spectacular autumn display, particularly when combined with HEDERA HELIX, English ivy.

ABOVE: *John Thompson designed this border with foliage color and texture for Marilyn Lightstone and Moses Znaimer. Upper left:* ACER PALMATUM *'Oshio Beni'. Coming forward:* A. P. *'Bloodgood' fronted by* RHODODENDRON *'Roseum Elegans';* R. *'P.J.M.';* PINUS MUGO; *next layer left:* TAXUS BACCATA; BUXUS KOREANA *and* PICEA OMORIKA *'Nana';* R. X WILSONII; R. PUNCTATUM; VIBURNUM FARRERI *'Nanum';* DAPHNE X BURKWOODII *'Somerset'; Ontario Z6.*

LEFT: *The small city garden of Adrienne Clarkson and John Ralston Saul holds a wealth of sensual plants. Top row left to right:* CLEOME *'Purple Queen';* EUONYMUS FORTUNEI; CARAGANA ARBORESCENS PENDULA; FAGUS SYLVATICA; SYRINGA X HYACINTHIFLORA; CERCIDIPHYLLUM, *Katsura tree. Center left:* PHLOX PANICULATA; RUDBECKIA *(purple);* ACIDANTHERA; ASTER *'Little Blue Boy';* P. PANICULATA; PICEA PUNGENS. *Bottom left:* ANEMONE JAPONICA; LILIUM; CHRYSANTHEMUM GRENADINE; IRIS RETICULATA; ARTEMISIA DRACUNCULUS, *tarragon;* CRYPTOMERIA JAPONICA *'Compressa'. Ontario Z6.*

LEFT: *A stunning entrance to a private garden designed by Tom Sparling. Hedge is* BUXUS MICROPHYLLA KOEANA *'Winter Beauty'; tree is* BETULA PAPYRIFERA. *Ontario Z6.*

RIGHT: *The front garden of Dr. Glenn Renecker was designed by Lois Lister to make a formal entrance to the house. Left:* LABURNUM; *next is a flowering crab. Clipped boxwood make splendid evergreen hummocks. Ontario Z6.*

BELOW: *In William J. Hurren's garden the back wall is smothered in* PARTHENOCISSUS TRICUSPIDATA *'Veitchii', Boston ivy; lower right:* HYDRANGEA PETIOLARIS, *climbing hydrangea. Ontario Z6.*

ABOVE: *Humber Nurseries, the leading grower of ornamental grasses in Canada, also has a gorgeous exhibition garden. The major grass is Japanese plum 'shire'; left to right:* DESCHAMPSIA CAESPITOSA, *tufted hair grass;* PENNISETUM ALOPECUROIDES, *fountain grass;* ANDROPOGON GERARDII; HYSTRIX PATULA, *bottle brush grass;* BOUTELOUA GRACILIS, *mosquito grass. Ontario Z6B.*

LEFT: *In this garden designed by Paul Hamer native trees and shrubs keep the integrity of the landscape and attract birds. Saskatoons, crab apples and choke cherries are among the aspens, ponderosa pine, native sage and cragana. Left: Kinners Gold Broom grass; right: mugo pine, rhubarb and Siberian iris. Alberta Z3A.*

## ORNAMENTAL GRASSES

By fall, grasses come into their own with long luminous inflorescence (flowers on a stem) that become incandescent. If you decide to add grasses to your garden make sure the variety doesn't spread by stolons—stems that grow along the ground —unless you want to use it as a ground cover.

I never really appreciated the beauty of conifers until I put a wonderful grass, PENNISETUM ALOPECUROIDES, Chinese fountain grass, next to one. The movement of the grass against the static background of the conifer is enchanting. *Voilà*, a new passion was born. That meant tearing out the whole bed and adding more of the same.

These grasses all ripen and tend to look their best as they come into autumn:

CAREX ELATA 'Aurea', Bowles' golden sedge, tolerates some shade, as does OPHIOPOGON PLANISCAPUS 'Nigrescens'. The latter has grass-like purple-black leaves. It's great in pots as well.

MISCANTHUS SINENSIS, eulalia grass. The fall foliage is a breathtaking mix of burgundy and gold.

FESTUCA OVINA 'Glauca', blue fescue, has mounds of steel blue that looks good with any of the small blue conifers. It's small and well behaved enough for the rock garden.

HELICTOTRICHON SEMPERVIRENS, blue oat grass, like most grasses prefers well-drained soil. I have it next to CLEMATIS STANS, a small shrubby plant with blue flowers and interesting seed heads.

CAREX MORROWII 'Variegata', sedge, has swirls of striped leaves, and I have it near CLEMATIS TANGUTICA and a ground cover called SHORTIA GALACIFOLIA, which has glossy green leaves a little like GALAX.

PENNISETUM ALOPECUROIDES, Chinese fountain grass, has giant pink feathery heads.

IMPERATA CYLINDRICA RUBRA 'Red Baron', Japanese blood grass. The red becomes a more intense almost flame color in fall.

CALAMAGROSTIS BRACHYTRICHA (also called ACANATHERUM BRACHYTRICHA), feather reed grass. This lovely grass can take some shade and has a rosy inflorescence. I have it with sedums and conifers, and it meshes well with other ornamental grasses.

MOLINIA CAERULEA ARUNDINACEA, purple moor grass. The seed stalk shoots up 3 feet (1 meter) above the green foliage and it all turns a mellow gold in autumn. Use for a striking vertical accent.

## THE FRUITS OF FALL

I'm referring here not to the usual fruits you harvest, but to the berries that appear in autumn. They can be found on ground covers, shrubs and vines and will add more interest to a garden because most hang on through the winter—a great boon for foraging birds.

CORNUS CANADENSIS, bunchberry, has creamy white bracts. This ground cover likes cool, moist, acidic soil.

ARUM ITALICUM, Italian arum, produces arrow-shaped leaves in fall and red-orange berries. A. I. 'Pictum' has gray-cream leaves.

AMPELOPSIS BREVIPEDUNCULATA 'Variegata' is one of my favorite vines, a stunner. The common name, porcelain vine, is a perfect description. When frost kills off the leaves, the china-blue berries remain.

CALLICARPA JAPONICA 'Leucocarpa', beautyberry, has small white berries; C. BODINIERI VAR. GIRALDII has blue-purple berries.

GAULTHERIA is an ericaceous evergreen shrublet with dark green foliage and deep, deep blue berries.

ROSA MOYESII is a shrub with dark green leaflets and bright red clusters of hips in fall.

VIBURNUM SARGENTII turns yellow to red in autumn with red fruit.

SYMPLOCOS PANICULATA, sapphire berry, has brilliant cobalt-colored berries.

EUONYMUS EUROPAEA, European euonymus, has reddy-pink fruit capsules that open above orange berries.

ILEX X ALTACLARENSIS 'Golden King', holly, produces red fruit in fall.

SORBUS HUPEHENSIS 'Pink Pagoda', mountain ash, is covered with pink berries in autumn. Another University of British Columbia Botanical Garden introduction.

# CHAPTER SEVEN

# THE MAINTENANCE OF FOLIAGE PLANTS

The more we try to understand nature and how it operates, the better gardeners we make. To impose order on nature is one thing—we call that garden design. But to try to improve on nature is probably foolhardy. In most of human history, we've seldom improved on natural processes.

To appreciate how foliage plants function, imagine a forest. The forest floor is covered with litter that no little gremlin nips about and sweeps up during the autumn. So why do we do it in our gardens? When I think of the time I've wasted in the past twenty-five years cultivating around plants, I wonder if I really ever thought things through. No one is out in the forest scratching around the edges of trees and shrubs cultivating, adding fertilizer.

The path to creative maintenance is to have more understanding of the nature of the soil and ecological process and to generally leave things alone. Assuming you do the planting right in the first place. The following ideas on how to get the best value out of your foliage garden work just as well for perennials.

## SOIL

Soil is an amazingly complex medium. Every time we tinker with it, even in our own small parcels of land, we usually upset the fine balance that has evolved over millennia.

Soil is, in fact, so complex that we are only beginning to understand its true nature. The more we learn, the more reckless it seems to saturate it with pesticides and herbicides and other synthetic chemicals that interfere with its vitality.

Soil is divided into layers: on the surface is humus, consisting of organic matter, which is constantly being broken down. This layer feeds the soil beneath and the plants on top. Then comes topsoil: here's where the majority of life in the soil resides. Its liveliness depends on organic matter, which breaks down into nutrients. Below that is subsoil: here the soil is poorer, rockier, with fewer nutrients than the other layers. Finally there is the almost impermeable layer of hardpan. This is where there is no activity, no soil life. And where you'll get into trouble with drainage. Each of these layers varies in depth depending on where you live. Topsoil is usually no more than 1 foot (30 centimeters) deep. And hardpan can be as close to the surface as a few inches or centimeters.

That's about all that soils have in common. In every region in the country, in every backyard in the country, soil has different characteristics. Apart from differing textures, there are differing pHs, for example. The pH means potential hydroxyl (an alkaline ion of hydrogen). This is expressed in numbers from 0 to 14. The lower the number the more acidic the soil. The higher the number the more alkaline the soil. A neutral soil, where most plants like to live, has a pH of around 6.5 to 7.5.

RIGHT: *Andrew Yeoman has a dramatic raised-bed entrance to his garden. In the background: wild plum; Douglas firs. In the raised bed left to right:* SENECIO GREYI *(gray mound); red- and white-flowered oregano; golden oregano; variegated marjoram; silver thyme;* ARTEMISIA *'Silver Mound'; peppermint. Far right: the leaves of* MAGNOLIA X SOULANGIANA. *Against the storage house is a winter jasmine on the left; pink and white flowers of* DIGITALIS *and a gray columnar juniper species on the right; hardy marjoram; the yellow flowers are Jerusalem sage. British Columbia Z8.*

Learn what kind of soil the plants you choose will be most happy in. If the plants have a special need, you will find this indicated in the Plant Listings (pages 169–201). You can get your soil tested by taking samples from different parts of the garden, mixing it up and sending it to your local Department of Agriculture. Some garden centers provide this service as well.

It's a lot easier and, in the long run, wiser to choose plants that suit the soil you already have at hand. But if you do want to change the soil to accommodate certain plants, be sure to do it over a wide area (as wide as the plants' roots will stretch to in maturity) and to a depth of at least 1 foot (30 centimeters).

Texture of soil is important as well. It can be light and sandy, or it can be heavy clay soil. You'll be able to tell by rubbing it in your hands and squeezing it. Clay soil makes a shape; sandy soil falls apart; anything in between is loamy—the kind of soil you can grow almost anything in.

**WHAT'S IN THE SOIL?** ᷂ There is drama underground. Stuart B. Hill, the Canadian soil guru, writes: "In a square metre of soil there can be more than ten million nematodes and protozoa, one million mites and springtails, and thousands of other invertebrates."

All life in the soil depends on the nutrients freed up as organic matter breaks down. Average soil is made up half of mineral particles and half of water and air. As earthworms burrow through the soil, mite-sized animals live in the air spaces left behind and protozoan-sized organisms live in the water film.

The right balance of water, oxygen and organic matter is crucial to the health of soil organisms, and as a gardener part of your job is to keep this balance.

TIPS ON SOIL MANAGEMENT
᷂ A dark soil absorbs more heat than a sandy or light-colored soil and therefore heats up faster in spring.

᷂ Drainage is very important. Almost all plants do better in well-drained soil. You can tell if your drainage is terrible by pouring water on the soil and seeing how long it takes to be absorbed. If it sits for several minutes, your drainage is poor and you should modify the soil. Start digging, and when you hit hardpan you will know just how much space you have to deal with. You may have to add a coarse material like gravel or weeping tiles so that water has a chance to run off. And if your drainage problem is really serious you may have to put in drainage tiles.

᷂ If you decide to amend the soil, to make it more absorbent or to have faster drainage, be sure to thoroughly mix the new soil or materials in with the original soil. Lumping a whole lot of new stuff on top of the old is going to restrict the movement of water, oxygen, nutrients and animal life.

It seems terrifically simple-minded to say that's all there is to looking after the soil. You may of course have other problems with your soil that require amending it. For instance, the texture of the soil might be less than desirable. Adding sand, compost, manure and peat moss will lighten up heavy clay soil. Peat moss will also make very sandy soil more absorbent. Compost will improve any kind of soil because it continues to decompose, adding nutrients in the process. Any other moves we make tend to upset the delicate balance that the soil reaches naturally.

Plants might turn yellow if you've added raw humus to the root zone—a bit of shock there. That's another reason I don't bother digging anything into the soil; instead, I just add organic material to the top of the soil. Plants will straighten themselves out without a lot of help on your part except to give them a hit of compost or manure and mulch.

LEFT: *Columba Fuller's steeply sloped lot has stone terracing to maximize the amount of space for planting. Above the stonework:* HOSTA FORTUNEI; H. F. *'Variegata'; miniature rhododendron;* EUONYMUS *and* HYDRANGEA *'Hills of Snow';* POTENTILLA *'Sutter's Gold';* P. *'Mount Everest'. Foreground:* ALCHEMILLA MOLLIS *backed by Korean boxwood. Ontario Z6.*

BELOW: *The garden of Katherine and Philip MacKenzie has a graceful separation between sections with* PARTHENOCISSUS QUINQUEFOLIA, *Virginia creeper, draped along cedar arches. In front of the arches from the left:* IRIS KAEMPFERI, *Japanese iris;* DIGITALIS, *foxglove; daisies. Ground cover:* AEGOPODIUM *'Variegatum'. In front of statue: Chinese delphinium. Foreground:* LAVANDULA ANGUSTIFOLIA. *Quebec Z4.*

## FOLIAGE PLANTING

Long-revered habits in planting are challenged as more and more research is done on the structure and requirements of plants. For instance, I grew up with the notion that a 50 cent plant should have a $5 hole—upgraded regularly to account for inflation. Conventional wisdom held that to dig down deep meant strong and healthy root growth. But this is not necessarily true.

The new wisdom says, don't change the quality of the soil you're filling the hole with. For years I've been merrily adding compost or sheep manure to amend the soil, thinking I was doing the plant a big favor. But I should have been using the soil I dug out as is. The problem with alien soil is that in about three or four years the tree or shrub will get into trouble when roots begin to stretch into new territory. Don't mollycoddle and the plant will then know what it has to deal with. Tough-love gardening.

The following information is based on my own experience plus two books that have made a major difference in my life. They are so full of the common sense often neglected in talking about trees and shrubs that I cannot recommend them highly enough to anyone who becomes fascinated by foliage plants. I have leaned heavily on the wisdom contained in these books by Alex Shigo and John Sabuco; the books are listed in the Bibliography.

PLANTING TREES ⁊ The new common sense information contradicts another old saw. The roots of trees do not mirror the tree canopy as most of us envision. It has long been presumed that root systems extend only as far as the dripline—the tip of the branches or what we *think* of as the edge of the tree. However, roots may extend from twice to almost three times farther out than the dripline.

From these main roots spreading outward in all directions, there are little feeder roots. These fine rootlets run from 3 to 6 inches (8 to 15 centimeters) just below the surface. Anyone who has ever dealt with the virulent root system of a silver maple will be able to attest to this. Roots want to stay in that top bit of soil where humus is adding minerals. The new planting information tells us that the best action is to dig a hole that's very wide instead of being deep.

⁊ **For balled and burlapped plants**, make the hole the same depth as the root ball and at least five times the width (or a minimum of 3 feet/ 1 meter across). Back-fill with soil. Then tamp down so that the top of the root system is level with the ground.

⁊ Here is a caveat about balled and burlapped plants: do you know what's inside that burlap? There could be girdled roots (ones that turn on themselves in a strangulating way), or unwanted insects and fungus. You'll have to get rid of all this. Don't include burlap in the planting hole as is often recommended. Anything sticking out on the surface acts like a wick for water. Remove the burlap and examine the roots carefully. Cut out anything that looks diseased.

⁊ **For container plants**, make the hole five times as wide as the container, and dig down deep enough so that the top of the plant's root system will be just above the surface of the soil. Back-fill with soil and tamp down.

All of this is based on the premise that you have good drainage. This is essential, especially in fall

---

RIGHT: *The garden of Dr. and Mrs. R. M. Peet has a small bridge over a man-made watercourse. From the left:* PHOTINIA X FRASERI *hedge;* ACER PALMATUM; AZALEA *foliage; dwarf pine;* A. P. *'Dissectum Viride';* A. P. *'Atropurpureum Bloodgood'; bamboo. The big stump is covered with climbing ivy, scrub maple and salal. Behind stump:* VACCINIUM PARVIFOLIUM, *wild huckleberry. To the right of the bridge:* ACER PALMATUM; CORNUS FLORIDA *'Welchii', tricolor dogwood; yellow-caned and green-caned bamboo with ferns. British Columbia Z8.*

planting, since you don't want the plant sitting around all winter with slowly rotting wet feet. And you must be sure you are putting the plant in soil that is right for its needs. If not, then either get a different kind of plant or change all the soil in a very large area and improve the drainage.

The symbiosis between root and leaves is critical. As leaves are destroyed so are the roots below. Without the nutrients from roots, leaves can't complete photosynthesis. Without photosynthesis, essential elements won't get to the roots. Think about that the next time you hack away at a tree or shrub—or watch anyone else do the same.

Soil around trees should not be compacted. Soil should be kept porous to allow oxygen to get at the roots. Though worms and all the other burrowing creatures do a great job of aerating the soil, if it does become compacted, press a spading fork gently into the soil and move it back and forth.

Fall is the ideal time to get foliage plants into the ground—if you have at least six weeks before a killing frost. The soil is still warm and the potential for retaining oxygen is at its highest, thus encouraging root growth.

If you buy local field-grown plants that are dug out bare root or balled and burlapped, it's best to transplant in dormancy (when there are no leaves on them). Plants will establish themselves quickly in the new site. Container-grown plants can most successfully be planted in fall; but, they also can be transplanted any time since the root system is intact.

Trees store energy for winter in the form of carbohydrates and fats. In moderate climates, even though tops of plants are dormant, roots are regenerating themselves. In warm coastal regions the high oxygen levels in the soil encourage roots to continue rapid growth in the fall. Cooler air temperatures reduce moisture loss, reducing demand for water from roots and freeing up energy for growth.

No matter what your regional climate, make sure transplanting is done long before frost or leaf drop—both times of stress for the plant.

DRAINAGE ❧ As water drains through the soil, it displaces oxygen. Therefore, a soggy soil retains very little oxygen and contributes to root rot.

❧ Dig a hole as deep as you can before hitting hardpan and fill it with water several times during the day and in the evening; if it is still draining 12 hours later, improve drainage or put in bog-loving plants.

❧ To improve drainage: plant on a berm—a strip of soil 6 to 9 feet (2 to 3 meters) long raised 12 to 18 inches (30 to 40 centimeters) above ground level. Raised beds automatically have better drainage.

❧ To lay tiles means you have to have a place where the water can be drained to because the tiles slope away from the site. They should be laid below the depth that frost penetrates into the soil.

## LAISSEZ-FAIRE GARDENING

It bears repeating that looking after the soil is the first job of stewardship in the garden. The more I garden the more I'm convinced that by top dressing the soil with compost and other organic matter such as leaf mold and manure and by adding mulch as thick as I can, I'm doing just about the best I can to improve the soil. As organic matter on top of the soil breaks down, it feeds the soil, *ergo* any plants living in that soil.

As more and more research is done on the nature of soil, this doesn't seem like a bad interim activity. For the past three years, I've done nothing to my plants except top dress with compost and manure when I plant. I don't fiddle about with the soil when I put plants into the ground and I don't do any cultivating at all the rest of the year. I'm pretty faithful about watering. I also handpick pests for at least half an hour a day at the height of their various cycles. I don't scrape my garden clean in autumn, but once the ground is frozen, I add a thick layer of mulch.

One of the many virtues of mulching and top

dressing is that it's almost unnecessary to add any other fertilizers. You won't confuse yourself or the plants.

The problem with an excess of soil fertility is that too much soft growth in plants is produced and plants will lack vigor. By laissez-faire gardening you will avoid excess and plants will absorb what they need when they need it.

MULCHING ❧ The reason I add mulch, and then some more mulch, to my garden twice a year is that I'm lazy. Instead of cultivating between plants, I fill all spaces with mulch, which protects the soil and, as it breaks down, contributes nutrients. The mulch does the work of amending the soil for me. That's what happens in the forest. That's what happens in my backyard.

Fans of mulching extol its virtues to the point where you're convinced that that's pretty much all you have to do to garden successfully. Almost.

We are entering an era in which water conservation is going to be a prime factor in making and maintaining a garden. We'll probably have water rationing and be on water meters some day soon. In the meantime, it's important for gardeners to use water efficiently. Mulch conserves moisture from rain water in the soil. You won't have to water as much, and you won't be using water that's dosed with chemicals.

Ultraviolet rays are very damaging to the earth, and mulch protects the soil just as a good sunblock protects your skin.

Mulching has to be done only twice a year: in late spring, and again in the fall after the ground has frozen hard. Mulch must be applied to a minimum of 2 inches (5 centimeters). Anything less is useless. Remove fall mulch in spring when any danger of a last frost is over and toss it into the compost to finish breaking down. Allow the soil to warm up, and once plants have started showing new growth, add a thick layer of fresh mulch around them.

Spring mulch keeps the soil cool, helps stamp out weeds, retains moisture and, as it slowly breaks down, adds nutrients to the soil.

Fall mulching has a different purpose. It protects plants by keeping the temperature of the soil even. What devastates plants more than cold weather or howling winds are freeze-thaw cycles. Ground freezes are fine with the plant, but when a thaw comes along, the ice melts and water pushes oxygen out of the soil. The plant wakes up again and starts to function as though spring has arrived. Then comes a drop in temperature that makes the water in the soil expand as it freezes and this can force the plant right out of the ground. Roots will then be exposed to raw winter temperatures. A protective layer of mulch will prevent root damage and disturbance. Winter mulch also helps guard against a plant's exposure to one of the most devastating experiences—the killer spring frost.

Mulching imitates nature by adding a layer of protection, and this organic material breaks down to continue feeding the soil. Just let most leaf litter stay where it falls under trees and shrubs. Or store all those leaves you rake up every fall in bags with a little soil. They can be distributed around the garden after they've partially decomposed, adding to the level of humus in the soil.

There is a myth I keep hearing about mulch— one you must be on guard for. It's the so-called nitrogen pull theory, which suggests you add some form of nitrogen supplement to woody or carbon-rich mulches (such as cocoa beans or leaves) to keep them from depleting nitrogen already in the soil. It sounds kind of crazy when you look at any healthy forest. It does not suffer from nitrogen depletion when there is a layer of duff or litter on the ground. So why would this happen in gardens? ❧ My favorite mulches are ground-up cocoa bean hulls and finely shredded bark. See my book *Ecological Gardening* for a complete list of mulches. ❧ If you use finely shredded bark, make sure it is from trees native to your area—they have grown in soil of the same pH.

A good mulch has an aesthetic benefit as well since it provides a background on which you grow plants. This can contribute to the unity of a garden.

Nature created the perfect mulch—snow. A good deep blanket of snow protects the plant from wind and all the other ravages of winter. If there's enough snow cover to withstand sudden thaws, it will keep plants safely dormant.

The downside of mulching is that the mulch material becomes home to slugs and earwigs, among other pests. Since a great deal of gardening is about attitude, just view mulch as a trap for pests. It makes handpicking the little devils easier because you know where they are during the day.

**FERTILIZING** The only slow-release fertilizer I use is something called Mussel Mud Plus. It comes from Prince Edward Island and is composed of ground-up shells, fish meal and rock phosphate that accrue along the bays and estuaries of the Island.

Since Mussel Mud breaks down so slowly, it can be added at any time, so it's perfect for someone who keeps forgetting to do certain basic chores. This sharp powder *seems* to keep squirrels away from newly dug areas, but it has to be reapplied after each rainfall. It also helps speed up activity in the compost.

Other favorite fertilizers include most of the seaweed concoctions you can buy commercially; a combination of manure and compost; blood meal and compost (for nitrogen); or bone meal and compost (for potassium). Rock phosphate, occasionally applied over a wide area, also breaks down slowly.

**CREATIVE PRUNING**

My hortbuddy Trevor Ashbee says that creative pruning is any pruning that looks like nothing has been touched. This means that when you trim trees or shrubs, don't take out any more than one third and do it over a couple of years.

Creative pruning is a skill every gardener should acquire. A good course is invaluable. Read as many books as possible on the subject. A vague axiom is to prune about once a year or whenever the shrub or vine looks scraggly.

I never go into the garden without a pair of secateurs to keep me company. A little snip here, another there to keep out the dead and the dying. It's the major pruning jobs you have to think about seriously. Foliage plants should respond beautifully to pruning; you can shape them the way you want to for the most part.

Begin pruning right after planting by removing any dead branches. Prune out fungal diseases as soon as you notice them. Cut behind the infected area immediately if plants have problems such as black knot, fire blight or any bacterial diseases.

Always remove weakened branches, anything dead or any plant that looks like it's dying, no matter the season or condition. Take out water shoots—the thin vertical branches coming from horizontal branches. In summer, after flowering, remove anything at odd angles or growing back toward the center, and any branches crossing or rubbing one another.

Prune for shape and to let light into the plant. This also improves the size and quality of blossoms.

Trim for beautiful side effects: to expose bark on plants such as STEWARTIA; CORNUS, dogwood; ACER GRISEUM, paperbark maple; PRUNUS SERRULATA,

LEFT: *Foliage plants in the garden of Barbara and Murray Frum almost seem to engulf the house, making this a cool oasis. From the top:* GLEDITSIA TRIACANTHOS *'Sunburst'; to the left: a collection of rhododendrons. Left center:* LARIX DECIDUA *'Pendula';* PRIMULA JAPONICA; SANGUINARIA CANADENSIS *(in front of the primula); lower right:* DEUTZIA GRACILIS; *center right:* RODGERSIA SAMBUCIFOLIA. *Ontario Z6.*

Japanese flowering cherry; for multiple trunks; or for an interesting asymmetrical form.

⅋ Avoid perfect symmetry for the most part.

**STYLES OF PRUNING** ⅋ You can *stool* a plant, which means cutting back hard each spring to encourage larger leaves. You see this done with catalpas and London plane trees.

⅋ *Topping* means taking out the leader trunk (the main branch growing out of the top of a tree) at a node in order to keep the tree smaller than its genetic code dictates. This should be done from the start in a tree's life. If you wait until a tree is too old and start lopping off the top, you might as well remove the whole tree and get something that's the right size. Right plant, right place is never more appropriate than with siting a tree. Topping should be done over three or four years. There is always a risk of infection because there's no zone of protection at the base of these stems.

⅋ *Pollarding* is the practice of pruning to keep a tree ball-shaped: the tree is topped when young and the new sprouts (shoots) form. The shoots are cut back to the bud every year once the leaves have fallen off.

⅋ *Pleaching* is a method of training trees into forms by intertwining branches, then clipping them smooth. The lower trunks are usually kept bare. The whole effect is architectural and quite distinctive. An alley, arch or separation of garden rooms can be created with pleaching. Plant a line of standard trees at least 5 to 6 feet (1.5 to 2 meters) high and 10 feet (3 meters) apart. Keep the branches bared to 4 feet (1.2 meters) and remove any growth from between the laterals. Spread wires horizontally between the trees at this level. Then train the branches along the wires. When the trees grow naturally in this direction, remove the wires.

PRUNING TIPS

⅋ Before pruning, clean off the cutting edges of secateurs with household bleach. Dirty tools can spread infections all over the garden.

⅋ Try to remember if your trees, shrubs and vines bloom on new or old wood. I constantly have to look things up—this information penetrates slowly. Tagging helps. Put a small piece of twist tie—something that will show up—around the lower part of the plant, using, say red (fall) or green (spring) to indicate what time of year to prune. Many shrubs will rebloom and are improved by pruning right after flowering. Some plants can't wait. Check in the Plant Listings (pages 169–201) whether a plant blooms on a new wood or on an old wood before you prune.

**PRUNING TREES** ⅋ Most trees can be left alone quite successfully. But if you have a tree that is threatening to turn your garden into a dank dark space, get a professional to come in and take all the lower branches out. The idea is to leave a refreshing tall canopy to give dappled light and leave the lower storey for other plants.

When young, most trees take kindly to a light annual prune. But don't fall into the ultimate anthropomorphic fallacy that a tree will "heal" itself once it has been cut into. It doesn't. Once wounded, always wounded. A tree doesn't regenerate; it compartmentalizes its growth. When it's cut, the entire tree rushes to protect itself against the injury. The area is walled off to prevent infection. The isolated area—the cut section—dies and the rest carries on.

The same applies when we say a tree "bleeds" — maples and birches, for instance. We're told not to let a tree bleed. Well, the sap that runs after they've been cut is necessary to protect them against possible infection by disease.

When a tree is properly pruned, a protective barrier in the form of a ring of callus forms around the wound. Never apply tree wound dressing. This is useless at best and, at worst, will hold in rot or insects.

A tree's energy comes and goes in cycles. Prune

when the energy reserves are high and the plant can withstand the assault. For instance, in spring when leaves unfold and new wood begins to form, the tree is drawing heavily on its stored reserves. But once leaves open and draw in the sun's rays, energy builds up again.

With deciduous trees, the best times to prune are during the winter or late dormancy before buds swell and there are vast reserves of energy, or after leaf formation. In warm areas prune when trees break dormancy in very early spring, not when going into dormancy in winter. With evergreens, prune in late winter or early spring when you can see what winter damage has taken place.

Never prune too close to the end of autumn—new growth might develop and won't have time to harden off before winter's onslaught. Never prune when things are wet; this will only encourage diseases to spread throughout the garden.

The worst times to prune are when a tree has been through a period of great stress:

❧ When leaves are forming or when they are about to drop off.

❧ During or after a season of drought.

❧ When a tree has lost a great many leaves to disease or pests.

## CARVED-IN-STONE RULES

❧ Start pruning early in a tree's life. All the experts agree that you can't prune a big tree down to small-tree size and keep it healthy. But you can help keep a small tree healthy by proper pruning.

❧ Remove branches for safety: when things are likely to whap you in the eye, or they're about to fall off, or are interfering with wires.

❧ Remove branches to control the size and shape of a tree.

❧ Remember that when more than one-third of leaf-bearing twigs are removed you run the risk of killing large branches.

## PROPER TREE-PRUNING TECHNIQUES

Proper pruning is both art and science. The science is in understanding the role of the collar in pruning. This is the distinct bulge at the base of a branch. The base is made up of a series of collars. Each year a layer of tissue is added to this collar until it has a definite bulge. This amazing structure holds the branch securely against the tree. The art comes in always leaving the branch collar intact but cutting as close to it as possible.

❧ To start, cut the limb back by about two-thirds (A) so it won't break away and risk tearing the trunk (E).

❧ Closer to the trunk, saw the stub from the bottom to about one-third of the way through the branch (B).

❧ Start a second cut from the top, about ¼ inch (1 centimeter) away (C). The branch will break near the first, bottom cut. Then make a final smooth cut (D) at the branch collar and remove the stub. The angle at which you do this will have to be calculated by eye—there is no handy formula. It should be from the outside top of the branch collar to the outside bottom. You want to cut as close to living wood in the trunk as possible without cutting into it.

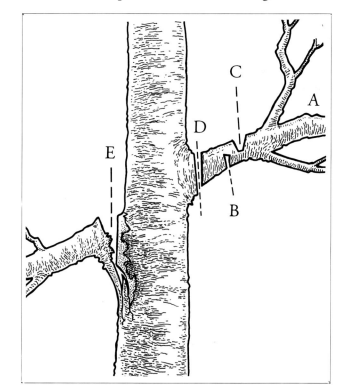

The most common mistake in pruning is to lop off a branch flush with the trunk or the branch it emanates from. This is called a flush cut. A flush cut exposes the trunk to infection; rot could set in above and below; and an internal crack might develop and split in temperature extremes. And don't leave a stub—it will allow infestation to enter the tree. Be especially careful with young trees—branch collars aren't obvious.

❧ Never shear trees and shrubs with machinery. Get an expert to do it properly or learn how yourself.

❧ To shape a tree, remove tips of branches—make a slanted cut above a bud. Cutting off the end buds encourages more lateral buds to develop.

PRUNING CONIFERS

Very few plants can stand shearing. This practice—so beloved by those owning machinery—is the indiscriminate removal of branches. Yews are one of the few species to respond to this treatment.

Branch collars in conifers are flat against the trunk, so you will need a flat cut against the collar rather than one on an angle.

❧ Remove some branches on conifers to allow open places where branches and trunk may be seen. This contrasts dense foliage with open woody structure.

❧ With old low-growing conifers, prune out lower and side branches to show off the old wood.

❧ In spring take the dead needles off conifers— just rub them gently so that anything brown comes off. This not only improves their look in winter but allows more air and light into the interior of the tree.

❧ Cut off part of the candles—the new green shoots—in early spring to control growth.

PRUNING SHRUBS ❧ Creative pruning is time-consuming. Those gardeners who hack away at shrubs with heavy-duty machines are not doing the plants any favors at all. Never take out more than one-third and do it subtly enough that you can't notice it's been done. In shrubs, you are mainly pruning for shape and beauty.

❧ Start by working from within. To thin, remove any branch right back to the source.

❧ Remove any crossed, misshapen or dead branches and twigs.

When to prune:

❧ Spring-flowering shrubs, such as forsythia, azaleas, spiraea, viburnum, lilac, dogwood and redbud, and vines should be left alone until after the blooms have dropped.

❧ Summer- and fall-flowering shrubs such as CLETHRA, BUDDLEIA, CARYOPTERIS and PEROVSKIA should be pruned in early spring in colder parts of the country or late in fall in warm areas.

❧ Don't take out low branches from large-leaved shrubs or they'll look top-heavy.

❧ Start pruning when plants are young and do it lightly in the first few years.

❧ Prune the following for artistic shapes: azaleas, hawthorn, PRUNUS, shrubby cotoneaster, PITTOSPORUM and lilacs.

❧ Non-flowering shrubs improved by judicious pruning are boxwood, pines, hemlocks, spruces, hollies and hedges. They tend to look messy, and pruning will create beautiful shapes.

HEDGE MAINTENANCE ❧ Evergreen hedges can be planted as late as December in warmer parts of the country. But everywhere, they must be well watered before freezing sets in. And keep watering once a week during the following year.

Trevor Cole, director of the National Arboretum in Ottawa, which has a superb collection of hedges, recommends the following:

❧ Formal hedges: a dwarf formal hedge should be under 3 feet (1 meter); plant 18 inches (50 centimeters) apart. Plant two per yard (meter) for all hedges up to 7 feet (2 meters) tall; three for every 7 feet (2 meters) for hedges over this height.

ABOVE: *This delightful garden includes a splendid specimen of* METASEQUOIA GLYPTOSTROBOIDA *on the right. On the left:* HELIOPSIS *'Summersun';* MISCANTHUS SINENSIS *'Zebrinus'; center:* BAMBOOSA SASA VEITCHII. *Quebec Z5.*

RIGHT: *Landscape architect Janet Rosenberg's garden has* ROSA *'Golden Wings' and morning glories rambling over this beautifully designed wooden fence. Ontario Z6.*

ABOVE: *In Elaine Corbet's garden* PYRACANTHA, *fire thorn, is espaliered along this handsome old cedar fence. The underplanting is* HELLEBORUS ORIENTALIS. *British Columbia Z8.*

LEFT: *In the food garden at the University of British Columbia Botanical Garden, a Gravenstein apple is espaliered along a Belgian fence. British Columbia Z8.*

❧ Informal hedges: plant apart at half the final height of the hedge. For instance, if you want the hedge to grow to 36 inches (1 meter) tall, plant 18 inches (50 centimeters) apart. The width should be about half the height you want to end up with. That is, if the height you want is 8 feet (2.5 meters), the width should be 4 feet (1.25 meters).

❧ All hedges should be planted a minimum of 2 feet (60 centimeters) inside the property line so you don't trespass on your neighbor's land. Allow more room for hedges wider than 2 feet (60 centimeters).

❧ If you want to create a thick informal cedar hedge quickly, plant cedars in a staggered double row.

❧ To plant a hedge, dig a trench 3 feet (1 meter) wide and 2 feet (60 centimeters) deep. Run a string down the center as a plant guide. Hold the plant in place against the string, fill in and tamp firm. Water deeply.

❧ A trick in initial pruning is to choose the shortest plant in the hedge and prune off one-tenth the height of this one. Then lop off the others at the same height. This will produce side shoots. Water regularly the first year and keep the top cut hard. Shear the sides lightly the second year, but again cut the top hard.

❧ If a hedge gets too tall, you can prune off one-third of the height without bumping it off.

❧ **Very important:** Make the bottom of the hedge wider than the top so that light can get into the center and snow won't weigh heavily on it—prune out 2 to 4 inches (5 to 10 centimeters) for every foot (30 centimeters) of height. A 6-foot (2-meter) high hedge 30 inches (75 centimeters) at its base should be 6 to 18 inches (15 to 45 centimeters) across the top.

❧ With deciduous hedges, after planting cut back to about 1 foot (30 centimeters) from the ground even if they have no branches on them. This will force lateral growth. Deciduous hedges won't need pruning the following year and only pinching back

to keep them bushy. From the third year on, use normal trimming during the growing season—late June and early July.

❧ You cannot cut back all the branches of evergreen hedges. If you chop them back to bare wood—that's all you'll have forever.

❧ Every time you trim your hedges give them a good feed of compost or well-rotted manure.

❧ A trick to keep animals away from a young hedge is to run two taut rows of heavy fishing line through it.

**PRUNING ROSES** ❧ Prune lightly when you plant —take out any crossed or dead branches. Cut back the central leader by less than one-third to compensate for root damage. What it can't support will die and you can chop off the dead parts. One of the goals in pruning roses is to open spaces to allow for better air circulation. Remove suckers from base.

❧ Always prune roses hard the first spring after planting; shrub and climbing roses don't need much pruning after that.

❧ For rambling and climbing roses, keep three to five of the strongest canes and prune out the rest.

❧ For all roses, take out any diseased canes—about 4 inches (10 centimeters) below canker or other diseased area.

❧ On perpetual or repeat bloomers, prune back to an outward-pointing bud.

❧ On horizontally trained climbers and trailing ground covers, prune to an upward-pointing bud.

❧ Shrub roses need careful pruning after summer flowering; cut out weak growth if shrubs become too rampant; in spring reduce strong short stems to two-thirds of their length.

❧ With grandifloras and floribundas, prune to a simple shrub shape; remove most of the older wood. In cold winter areas, prune in spring before buds burst; in mild winter areas, prune in fall.

❧ With hybrid tea roses, nip back tips of year-old canes; remove two-year-old canes. Do this in late fall when it's cold and no new growth will be encouraged.

LEFT: *This harmonious lathe house provides protection for shade-loving plants in Louise Weekes' garden. Top left:* HOSTA *'Snowden';* OPHIOPOGON NIGRESCENS; LILIUM HANSONII *and* L. X DALHANSONII; HAKONECHLOA MACRA AUREOLA. *To the right:* JUNIPERUS VIRGINIANA *and* ASARUM EUROPAEUM. *Middle storey:* HELLEBORUS ATRORUBENS; PAEONIA *'Leda', tree peony. Foreground left:* BRUNNERA *'Varigata';* B. *'Hadspen Cream';* LIRIOPE MUSCARI, *big blue lilyturf. Ontario Z6B.*

BELOW: *Harmony is achieved in this very old lattice screen in Francis Cabot's garden. A very good example of how to connect a small outbuilding with a hedge and fence. The shrubs are* CORNUS SIBIRICA, *dogwood. Quebec Z4.*

⅋ Old roses in jammed-up beds should be pruned once a year in very early spring after you see what's been winter-damaged.

⅋ For roses that bloom once, wait until bloom is over, then remove any tangled stems and cut back halfway.

**PRUNING VINES** ⅋ Prune vines growing on buildings after frost is well into the ground in late fall. Do this only to keep the vine under control—out of gutters and away from windows, for instance.

⅋ Espaliered vines: remove the top when the desired height is reached. Select framework from lateral branches and keep pruning out anything that doesn't follow the pattern you've chosen. If you do this from planting time on, the roots will adjust.

⅋ Grapes and wisteria will grow from a pollarded head: cut off the top portion of the leader stem. This will encourage sprouts. Remove sprouts back to the collar at the end of the season. A knob will form. From then on prune back to the pollard head.

⅋ Wisteria accepts particularly harsh treatment. Let the leader sprout and grow to the length needed. Pinch the ends of all six or seven branches—these will send out side shoots; cut these back to four leaf nodes from the main covering branches. This will probably force the vine to produce flowers in a year. I have one that has not responded to any treatment for twenty-five years, but I love the leaves anyway.

⅋ Clematis: The flowering and pruning times are contained in the Plant Listings on page 175-76.

**PRUNING GROUND COVERS** ⅋ Ground covers usually don't need pruning. With most ground covers, remove any dead-looking sections and you'll get shiny new growth. Cutting back once a year usually rejuvenates growth, but check the Plant Listings (pages 169–201) to make sure. The important thing is to keep looking underneath plants to see that no diseases or pests are thriving.

Since it's difficult to improve the soil after a ground cover has taken over, make sure you've put the plants into a well-prepared site with plenty of compost or well-rotted manure. Then mulch in between plants. A regular hit of manure tea (manure and water mixed and left to stand for a day) will help fertilize established plots.

# CHAPTER EIGHT

# FURNISHING THE GARDEN

*F*urnishing the garden is like exposing your soul—revealing some of your innermost secrets and creativity. But to ornament the garden is to give it special character. Go at this with a great deal of caution.

I'm not against humor in the garden—most need some. But before you fill yours with a flock of pink flamingos (even two seems a lot), figure out what your garden style is. If pink flamingos aren't your taste but a Lutyens bench is, maybe even that won't fit into the style of garden you've chosen.

Totems are important in any garden. These are usually small objects that are imbued with personal meaning. Something with emotional significance takes on a special patina when it is placed in the garden. One of my totems is a shell my father gave me as a child, which I have placed next to a hosta from a collector who has since died. My last chore of the season is to put my garden totems in places where they are noticeable from the windows. They become prominent in winter to provide a continuum for me as the garden rests.

Totems are a useful part of the landscape as well; they could be special rocks, a large glass ball or even a nice old finial (the ornaments they used to put on top of fenceposts). They should be used as surprises scattered around the garden—under a shrub, near a hidden garden seat, by a large leaf. All will enhance the garden immeasurably.

## SCULPTURE IN THE GARDEN

Statuary can be almost anything: busts, plaques, masks, full-length portraits of people, gods, goddesses, Pan, cupids and little boys peeing. But garden sculpture or statuary isn't as easy to place as you might think.

A piece of sculpture, figurative or abstract, used as the focal point of a whole garden can be very interesting, but there are some guidelines to follow. If it's plunked right in the middle of a lawn, of course it will dominate everything around it. By being so conspicuous, it will look oddly vulnerable. What's needed here is a context.

You can use almost anything as a focal point for small compositions within the garden. In a less formal garden you might want to think about using statuary as part of smaller garden pictures along the main axis.

When siting a statue, think about how the light on it will change throughout the day and in different seasons. A dark piece in a shadowy place will be quite lost. But maybe that's the effect you want—something enigmatic you must see up close to appreciate.

A piece of sculpture can be far more interesting if it's placed in a way that draws you into the garden—in a secret bower or at the side of a patio framed by shrubs, for example. The garden then becomes a shelter for the piece. If you're drawn to a rendition of a herd of deer, think how much more appealing they'd be surrounded by trees and shrubs.

---

RIGHT: *Murray Haigh designed this enchanting entrance to Wendy and Gordon McLean's compact back garden. Center: polyantha rose 'The Fairy' underplanted with impatiens. The viewer can see through the plants to a* COTONEASTER APICULATUS *standard, cranberry cotoneaster. Upper right:* CLEMATIS MAXIMOWICZIANA *(formerly* C. PANICULATA*), sweet autumn-flowering clematis, clambers over the arch. Ontario Z6.*

The first principle of garden furnishing: display a piece of sculpture against a background. A glorious deep green hedge is ideal, but almost any neutral planting or fence will do the job. Any light-colored piece is going to look more dramatic and interesting against a somber background.

Once you have the right location, be sure the surrounding plants complement the piece. A column set into a pool of grass-like LIRIOPE, lilyturf, seems more anchored than when it is a solitary projection from the earth.

Try to match any pieces with the mood of the landscape and the architecture. You'll find that a formal, symmetrical piece looks best in a more formal part of the garden, and informal pieces reverberate with the mood of an informal landscape.

Always think about the scale: a figurative piece should be either much smaller or much larger than life size. There is nothing quite as nerve-wracking as happening upon an exact life-size piece. It's eerily close to having a person there—enough to make you jump out of your skin—when what you want is merely to sense a presence.

An object placed at eye level usually has the most calming effect. A smaller than life-size piece is likely to establish an intimate rapport and make the viewer feel serene. It also draws the viewer's eye across the landscape or makes one want to move toward it. A small piece can be made more important by having it sit on a plinth or pillar or column. Something monumental inspires awe and allows the viewer's imagination to soar.

Make sure the shape or form of an abstract sculpture reflects what's around it. I have a black metal piece that looks like waving grass. It always looked wrong in the garden, until I put it in with some ornamental grasses. Now it resonates with the other waving grasses and replaces them when they disappear in winter.

Consider setting a mirror into a fence. It will make whatever is placed in front of it more arresting. The back of a charming cupid, for instance.

If you've bought one of the contemporary copies of antique stoneware, apply some instant age. In a blender or food processor, spritz up live moss with yogurt and buttermilk and paint this on the stone. Repeat each time it rains. Eventually the piece will develop the patina of mossy great age.

In a formal garden you might want a fountain or an important work as the central focus. Be sure it is dead center so the eye is drawn immediately to that spot.

SCULPTURE AND STATUARY TIPS

❧ Line up all garden objects or structures on an axis. A garden can be wrecked by a sculpture, a bower or an arch that is off-kilter even by a few inches or centimeters.

❧ If the garden design is asymmetrical, have vegetation or something of equal solidity to act as a counterpoise to a piece of sculpture.

❧ As in much of contemporary design, the combination of antique and modern styles can work very well indeed if pieces are chosen thoughtfully.

❧ You might want a statue to be reflected in a pool. A vertical statue over a pool creates an interesting tension between the two planes.

## LIGHTING THE GARDEN

Lighting a garden can be as important as all your other ornamentation. In a tiny garden, it may be the only addition you want other than some comfortable seating. In a garden of any size, the play of light and shadow takes on sculptural values, as well as adding tension and drama.

The most effective lighting is to have several important specimen plants lit from below or, if you're illuminating a massive tree, to have the light installed halfway up so the canopy is lit.

Always place lights above or below eye level and be especially careful with lights along a steep path. Blinding lights are just as dangerous as no lights at all.

Trees or shrubs with weird forms look especially good when backlit. CORYLUS AVELLANA 'Contorta',

ABOVE: *This garden, designed by Tom Sparling, includes climbing* LONICERA JAPONICA *'Purpurea'. Rear:* VIBURNUM x CARLCEPHALUM; *middle:* RHODODENDRON CATAWBIENSE *'Album'; foreground:* MAHONIA AQUIFOLIUM. *Ontario Z6.*

LEFT: *Lee Goossens' captivating arbor marks the entrance to a new garden room. To the left:* RUDBECK-IA ACCUMULATA, *coneflower. The arbor is draped with an unnamed vine. To the right: phlox and irises. Ontario Z7.*

corkscrew hazel, is an example of one that becomes much more fascinating at night when there's a light behind it. Tacky as it sounds, a string of fairy lights tossed over weeping shrubs looks wonderful—summer and winter.

The only kind of lighting I'm not crazy about is cross lighting—having two lights in different parts of the garden illuminating one subject. The light becomes almost too brilliant, too stagy. Unless you have a property of palatial dimensions this always seems rather pompous.

Lighting the garden in winter has almost become a necessity in our northern climate. To spend months without being able to see the garden in the evening simply isn't fair. Lighting on snow makes any effort worthwhile.

You don't need elaborate technology—a long outdoor extension cord and a simple outdoor fixture are easy to set up. Intricate installations on rheostatic controls are available but expensive.

The shape of lighting fixtures should reflect the style of your garden. Don't get ones that are huge and put them in obvious places. Lighting should be subtle—an illuminating emphasis of the garden's style.

LIGHTING TIPS

⁊ Disguise the source of light as much as possible.

⁊ Lighting is a safety feature as well—a well-lit garden may discourage intruders.

⁊ Use light to emphasize areas beyond trees and shrubs.

## GARDEN STRUCTURES

As focal points, garden buildings and structures assume great significance. They can augment the style of the garden or, indeed, establish the style of an entire garden. When you are adding structures to your garden, think first about the placement, the seasons of use, then the appropriate material and finally the plants they will support.

Whatever style you choose, design the structure in keeping with the architecture of the house. Generally speaking, the closer to the house the more a structure should mirror that architecture. Save informal or more rustic buildings for outlying sites. If the house isn't distinctive, you can have a lot of fun designing outbuildings to add some flamboyance to the garden.

On the other hand, an ostentatious arbor or pergola stuck in the middle of nowhere, without a context, looks awkward. As in all things gardenesque there has to be an underlying principle at work for gracious results. Scale and context of plants are two of the most important considerations to keep in mind.

TRELLISAGE ⁊ Trellis work is becoming increasingly popular. And a good thing too. A handsome bit of trellis can perk up the dullest garden. It can augment the verticality of the garden and provide climbing structures for plants such as roses and clematis.

I like the fashion of using trellis with false perspective. This is an ideal way of making a deck, balcony or tiny courtyard look more impressive and larger.

Depending on the placement of trellis work, keep the color neutral. Dead white sticks out, and unless you have something else white nearby—a fence or furniture—it will be too conspicuous.

I'm a big fan of square trellis. (Most of the crisscross style seems too busy.) You can buy square trellis in sheets. But it's also simple enough to construct, which means you can control the size of the openings to make them harmonious with the surroundings.

RIGHT: *Trellis work in the garden of Cecily and Norman Bell provides a private entrance to the door. Top left to right: unnamed dark red rose;* ROSA *'Coral Dawn' and* R. *'Pink Dawn';* R. *'Schoolgirl';* R. *'Mrs. Herbert Stevens'. The clematis from left to right:* CLEMATIS *'Vyvyan Pennell';* C. *'Ramona',* C. *'Pink Chiffon' and* C. X JACKMANII. *In front: a very old unnamed variety of white single tree peony;* ANEMONE JAPONICA; ASTILBE *'Hyacinth';* A. CHINENSIS *'Pumila' and a clump of pale yellow lilies. Ontario Z6.*

LEFT: *Sheila Paulson's garden room has a raised bed filled with hybrid tea roses (left). In raised bed with cranes: Siberian irises and an* ACER PALMATUM. LOBELIA CARDINALIS *in the water;* HOLCUS MOLLIS *'Variegatus'. Lower left to center:* AJUGA REPTANS *'Burgundy Glow' in front of pink* GERANIUM CINEREUM *'Ballerina'; pink-flowering* ERIGERON SIMPLEX. *Alberta Z4.*

RIGHT: *Carol Woodward's country property has a secret garden with a rose-embraced arbor. Center left to right: red spirea;* ROSA RUGOSA *'Pink Grootendorst'; white hydrangea 'Annabelle'; Spanish bluebells;* DICTAMNUS, *gasplant, with yellow sundrops. Right foreground: peonies, wood fern and* VINCA MINOR. *Quebec Z4.*

BELOW: *Collector-designer Richard H. Birkett has a wonderful gazebo that's used as a lathe house.* RHODODENDRON *'Narcissiflorum', yellow deciduous azalea;* R. CATAWBIENSE *'Album', large white-flowering rhodo. Ontario Z6B.*

**GAZEBOS** ❧ Open garden houses called gazebos have a history going back to the seventeenth century in Europe and even further back in Chinese gardens. Styles have been influenced by the fashionable chinoiserie of the eighteenth century and can be simple or fabulous confections. Temples, gothic and otherwise, tea houses—everything has been acceptable at one time or other.

These days we feel that a gazebo should be in scale with the rest of the garden and have a purpose. A gazebo can be useful as a focal point, or to house seating from which to appreciate a view.

❧ If you use a gazebo as an eating area, make sure it's close enough to the house. Too removed a getaway won't be used.

❧ A gazebo can be placed so that it's almost hidden from the rest of the garden—a place to stroll to, perfect for contemplative thought.

❧ Make it comfortable enough to sit in—to read or entertain in.

❧ To keep a gazebo cool, cover it with vines that will bloom in succession. Avoid silver lace vine, which is too dense and attracts swarms of bees.

**PERGOLAS** ❧ A pergola is a structure that usually covers a path, deck or patio and provides shade. The form originated in Italy, where it was a projection from a roof. Therefore, many pergolas in European gardens are attached to houses.

A pergola can be decorative in itself or merely the framework for climbing plants. This versatile conceit can be a link between two sections of the garden or garden rooms.

I have a pergola across the back of my house. It acts as a transition from house to garden and provides an extra room in the summer. We eat all our meals under the shelter of a wisteria and several different clematis. Not only is it a place to sit, it's also a shelter for shade-loving plants in pots. Getting it right took a fair amount of careful deliberation. The pergola had to reflect what the house looks like, and the question of whether to use any sort of design as embellishment was vexing. Since the house is plain (rather non-descript, actually), I went with simple wood squares that echo an adjacent square lattice fence.

As long as the proportions are right a simple pergola can fit in almost anywhere. It should be subtle, scaled properly and utilitarian, not demanding architectural statement. Horizontals should be in proportion to the distance between the verticals. Don't make it too narrow. Elaborate ornamentation isn't necessary. It's the plants climbing over that count.

THE TUNNEL

Another form of linking structure is the tunnel. This is where the underpinnings are so densely planted that they are obscured. In this case the silver lace vine works well: it provides autumn blooms and makes a gorgeous entry into a vegetable garden. The privacy factor here is also important.

**ARBORS AND BOWERS** ❧ These structures are similar to trellises but are usually fitted over a gate, a path or a garden bench. They can be a passageway from one garden room to another or give definition to both. Have roses, honeysuckle and clematis ramping over them for sheer delight.

Traditionally an arbor had a little seat in it for appreciating the scent of the plants climbing about it. A seat built into an arbor can be a focal point.

Almost any material can be used, from painted wood to slender posts stripped of bark. No matter how you use an arbor or bower, think about how it will look in winter when it is stripped of adornment.

LEFT: *The Lynch-Staunton garden is graced with the ideal pergola: covered with a white native grape, the proportions are perfect, leading the eye to the fields beyond. Hanging basket: white* BEGONIA PENDULA. *The flagstone is planted with* ARENARIA MONTANA *and* THYMUS SERPYLLUM, *mother-of-thyme. Quebec Z4.*

ABOVE: *Gary Roxborough designed this fence and entrance for William J. Hurren's garden. The tunnel is concealed under a thick blanket of Virginia creeper and silver-lace vine. Ontario Z6.*

LEFT: *In Janet Rosenberg's garden, an unnamed rose is allowed to run rampant. The chair was designed and constructed by her; the scale is perfect. Right:* THUJA PYRAMIDALIS; LABURNUM X WATERERI *'Vossii'; annual cosmos, blue salvia and canna lilies;* VIBURNUM X CARL-CEPHALUM. *Ontario Z6.*

ABOVE: *An elegant poolside arbor was designed by Janet Rosenberg for the DeLuce garden. Rear left clockwise:* THUJA PYRAMIDALIS; HAMAEMELIS VIRGINIANA; RHODODENDRON *'Roseum Elegans';* R. *'P.J.M.' (lavender);* EUONYMUS FORTUNEI; E. F. *'Emerald Gaiety';* WISTERIA SINENSIS *'Boskoop';* TAXUS X MEDIA *'Hicksii';* ASTILBE X ROSEA. *Ontario Z6.*

RIGHT: *Andrew Yeoman's herb garden creates this idyllic garden picture. Left of the Lutyens-style bench: a mixture of St.-John's-Wort; juniper; rosemary; hardy or French marjoram; far right:* LAVANDULA ANGUSTIFOLIA, *English lavender. Center: hyssop; French thyme; germander. British Columbia Z8.*

ABOVE: *The garden of Marilyn Sale has many corners designed for retreat—a pleasure any garden should include.* CORNUS FLORIDA *'Rubra', the pink-flowering dogwood is like a cloud over the gray-green leaf of* COTONEASTER DIELSIANUS *var.* MAJOR. *Left:* SPIRAEA NIPPONICA *'Snowmound'; coming forward: delphiniums and* IRIS SIBIRICA. *Ontario Z6B.*

**FENCES** ❦ I like square lattice fencing because it makes a good background for climbing plants and gives a feeling of airiness. Try to get the cooperation of your neighbors to keep fencing consistent. I'm stuck with several different styles of fence and the only thing that saves this mess is mature climbing plants everywhere. But my neighbors and I are experimenting with a living fence—one length of fence was removed and posts were put in with plain finials on top. Instead of filling in the spaces between with fencing, we planted a variety of shrubs. They will eventually fill out to provide a wall of color changing with each season.

My biggest hate is for chain-link fencing. It's ugly and offensively jail-like. If you can't get rid of it, cover it up as quickly as possible with ivy or some other screening plant.

Most places in Canada have a 6-foot (2-meter) limit on how high you can put up a privacy fence. But you can cheat a little by having a panel of trellis work on top, or something as elaborate as planters (filled with trailing plants, of course) to give just a bit more height.

## GARDEN FURNITURE

The very first quality you want in garden furniture is comfort. But it should be beautiful as well. Many owners willingly spend a fortune on garden design and planting, then plunk in cheap plastic furniture, undoing the whole effect. I'd rather see one good piece of furniture, perfectly placed, than a whole bunch of dreck.

Keep scale in mind. Don't use bitty pieces on a vast deck or terrace or cram something grand into a small area. Then think about the placement: the horizontal angularity of a bench can make a welcome contrast to the verticality of a tree.

Invest in great garden furniture just the way you would a work of art or fine furniture for the house. It will be not only something for the eye but useful as well. In summer a beautiful garden bench is a place of respite. In winter, covered in snow, it is sculpture.

As for the style of furniture, use your indoor furniture as a point of departure—keeping what's in the garden in the same mood, if not exactly the same style. But the style of furniture will also depend on the style of your garden. Weatherproof wicker looks quite wonderful for a relaxed, casual garden. Willow furniture is having a big, big revival. Some of it looks great, some designs tend to look awkward. Choose with great care.

Color is important. As mentioned before, white stands out glaringly unless it's connected with something logical nearby, such as white lattice work or fencing. Any natural color or wood with pale natural stain looks more comfortable. Greens usually war with the plants around, so look for more subtle muted tones of gray-green, earthy bronze or a green so dark it's almost black.

Don't put chairs and tables under a tree such as mulberry or cherry—you risk having fruit dropped into the soup. Soften any furniture with an enclosure of plants or one beautiful specimen that will provide a sheltering canopy.

# CHAPTER NINE

# WATER IN THE GARDEN

Water in the garden takes many forms: a fountain, pool, pond or waterfall. What it does for the garden is incalculable. You can be captivated by the changing beauty of its surface. Still water mirrors the sky and surrounding trees. The sound masks intrusive noise. This has become such a necessity in our crowded cities that it's hard to think of these features as a luxury anymore. Everyone feels a little bit better around running water—it adds healthy negative ions to the air, much like stepping into the shower and immediately bursting into song.

Garden size isn't important—it's the *presence* of water that's most significant. A simple container to collect rain, a miniature fountain, even a bird bath is effective. In the tiniest courtyard a wall-mounted outlet with a small basin and circulating pump will be enough to create a quiet oasis. The larger a garden, the more important a water feature it will hold, one that's important enough to be a focal point, part of a vista or a place to stroll in a special part of the garden.

Where to put water is a major decision in your garden design. Water needs to be anchored with sculptural elements or plantings, though in a very formal garden little else besides the pool itself and perhaps an urn or a statue is needed. In an informal garden the planting around a water feature should act as a frame.

If you put in a pool, make sure it gets lots of sun and is protected from the prevailing wind. A berm, the house or a distant stand of trees can keep a pool from being buffeted by winds. If you don't have a pool but want the effect of water, a small course of stones and rocks provides a similar tranquillity. Be sure to choose rocks from your area and don't overdo it. Overstoning the environment is ugly and cold and lacking in aesthetics.

If a fountain is a focal point, make sure it lines up with the axes of the garden. As usual, anything off-center is off-putting.

### WATER IN THE COUNTRY GARDEN

Having a pond or pool on a country property has become a tradition. A natural-looking pond can be placed in the landscape in such a way that it will have the appearance of always having been there. Placement should be subtle. The water shouldn't dominate the view but be subservient to it. If you sink it into the land so that it is concealed from the house, the landscape beyond—the borrowed view—becomes increasingly important.

The most natural pond site is in the lowest part of the land and is as large as possible to get a proper ecological balance. Provide plenty of plants for attendant birds and waterfowl. By making a dam to slow down a fast-flowing stream you can give the garden more serenity.

---

RIGHT: *Francis Cabot is one of the finest gardeners in North America. This inspired creation has many garden rooms, each with its own style and spirit. He has perfected the concept of making garden pictures—as is evident in this beautiful watercourse—which provides a cooling system. The subtle murmuring of the water flow masks any intrusive noise that might penetrate through to the garden. Cedar hedges define the border of the water flowing down the slight incline. In the foreground:* RHEUM PALMATUM, *ornamental rhubarb, a large architectural plant that stands up in a whimsical manner to the grandeur of the scene behind. Quebec Z4.*

LEFT: *Don Armstrong's subtle double-level pond fits perfectly into a tiered rock garden of impeccable design. Upper left:* PAEONIA LUTEA *with unnamed rhododendron. Ferns back up against the fence. Against fence:* P. DELAVAYI *with* P. MLOKOSEWITSCHII. *In the middle storey:* IRIS ENSATA *far left;* LYSIMACHIA PUNCTATA; *unnamed* PICEA *backed by* P. OBOVATA *'Alba'; left of the fern:* ABIES *fronted by* ADIANTUM PEDATUM; *to right:* DICENTRA SPECTABILIS; STEWARTIA PSEUDO-CAMELLIA; RHODODENDRON KEISKEI. *Upper far right:* ALSTROEMERIA AURANTIACA. *Around the pond:* ABIES LASIOCARPA; GENISTA PILOSA; PHLOX DOU-GLASII; *an unnamed rhododendron; unnamed* PICEA. *British Columbia Z8.*

RIGHT: *Rex Murfitt's pond mirrors the early morning sky.
Left:* SALIX HELVETICA, *alpine willow; above bridge:*
PINUS MUGO, *mugo pine, with* TSUGA MERTENSIANA
*'Glauca', mountain hemlock; farther back:* JUNIPERUS
COMMUNIS *'Compressa'. Right of bridge:* HELIANTHE-
MUM *'Buttercup'. Center behind bridge:* SAPONARIA
PUMILA *(pink);* THYMUS *(pink-lavender);* ACHILLEA X
JABORNEGGII *(white-gray foliage);* SAPONARIA OCY-
MOIDES *'Rubra Compacta'. British Columbia Z7.*

ABOVE: *The pond in Thomas Hobbs' garden doesn't even
hint that a busy street is only a few feet away. This is a prac-
tical and elegant solution to a difficult corner. The pond is
surrounded by cypress trees;* HOSTA SIEBOLDIANA *'Elegans';*
H. *'Frances Williams' (rear);* ADIANTUM PEDATUM, *maidenhair ferns, and primula. British Columbia Z7.*

ABOVE: *Francine and Peter Trent designed this pond as a focal point for their garden. Clockwise from center:* HEDERA HELIX, *English ivy;* WEIGELA *'Pink Princess';* PHYSOCARPUS; PRUNUS; LAMIUM GALEOB-DOLON; CAMPANULA CARPATICA *'Blue Clips';* C.C. *'Glacier';* COTONEASTER DAMMERI *'Skogholm'. Quebec Z6A.*

RIGHT: *Audrey Meiklejohn's wonderful pond includes granite rocks that emulate a mountainside. Upper left clockwise:* DEUTZIA *'Pride of Rochester';* ROSA *'Mme Alfred Carrière';* THUJA OCCIDENTALIS *'Emerald';* R. *'Blanc Double de Coubert'; Japanese Katsura;* THUJA OCCIDENTALIS; R. *'Clair Matin'. Lower left clockwise:* HOSTA *'Royal Standard';* EUONYMUS *'Emerald Gaiety';* DEUTZIA X LEMOINEI; ALCHEMILLA MOLLIS; LAMIUM MACULATUM *'White Nancy'. Ontario Z6.*

ABOVE: *Terry McGlade designed Annette McCoubrey's pond to perfect scale for a city garden. Lower left:* SEDUM KAMTSCHATICUM *'Variegatum';* COREOPSIS VERTICILLATA *'Golden Shower'. Right:* THUJA *'Nigra' behind* DICENTRA SPECTABILIS *'Alba';* ACHILLEA *'Summer Pastels' and white agapanthus (in pots). Ontario Z6.*

LEFT: *The Richardson garden designed by Janet Rosenberg has a cascading waterfall over different garden layers. Clockwise from center left:* TSUGA CANADENSIS *'Geneva';* IRIS SIBIRICA; VIBURNUM X CARL-CEPHALUM; T. CANADENSIS *'Prostrata';* TAXUS CUSPIDATA; JUNIPERUS HORIZON-TALIS *'Prince of Wales';* MAGNOLIA STELLA-TA; V. PLICATUM *'Summer Snowflake';* COTONEASTER APICULATUS; PENNISTETUM ALOPECUROIDES, *fountain grass;* PICEA PUNGENS *'Glauca Globosa'. Ontario Z6.*

ABOVE: *The formal pond in the DeLuce garden is the central focal point. Left clockwise:* BUXUS *'Green Mound';* PRUNUS X CISTENA; THUJA OCCIDENTALIS; MAGNOLIA STELLATA; HYDRANGEA, *peegee hydrangea;* MALUS NIPPISSING; PINUS MUGO; COTONEASTER APICULATUS; LIATRIS SPICATA; PHLOX SUBULATA; IRIS SUBULATA. *Ontario Z6.*

RIGHT: *In designing her Japanese-inspired pond and fountain, Rosemary Pauer uses a fine background of arborvitae hedge. Rear of bamboo fence: Japanese plum pruned into a small tree; variegated golden dogwood; juniper. Center:* ACER PALMATUM, *Japanese maple; right of lantern: astilbes; dwarf dogwood; emerald cedar. Lower far left:* SORBUS; SORBARIA, *false spirea, underplanted with* ALCHEMILLA MOLLIS *and* LAMIASTRUM. *Ontario Z5.*

## POOL PLANTINGS

To highlight a water form you'll need a strong planting. Any tree or shrub that droops naturally as well as grasses and vines look unaffected next to a pond or a pool. Grasses are particularly useful. Here are some to try:

❧ MISCANTHUS SINENSIS, eulalia grass; MOLINIA ARUNDINACEA, purple moor grass; CALAMAGROSTIS ACUTIFLORA STRICTA, feather reed grass; PENNISETUM ALOPECUROIDES, Chinese fountain grass.

❧ Hardy bamboos look wonderful near water: ARUNDINARIA VIRIDISTRIATA, bamboo; A. PUMILA, a dwarf bamboo, grows only to 2 feet (60 centimeters) but it spreads. A. JAPONICA and BAMBUSA METAKE grow to 13 feet (4 meters) and need protection from winter wind and sun. Though they take a fair amount of cold, bamboos cannot take wind, so never use as windbreaks. FARGESIA NITIDA, hardy clump bamboo, is not invasive and is one of the hardiest bamboos. PHYLLOSTACHYS NIGRA, black bamboo, grows to 16 feet (5 meters) and is spectacular.

❧ Weeping plants over ponds underplanted with ivy or European ginger look gorgeous.

❧ Arum lily, any rushes and aquatic grasses and ferns look natural around an informal pond.

❧ Most water plants resent a lot of disturbance, so keep them away from pumps and waterfalls.

## SWIMMING POOLS

Swimming pools can be a bonus or the bane of a garden. Far too often they are plunked into the best part of a garden without any thought as to how they fit into a design. Any swimming pool creates an artificial situation at best and seems even more crazily at odds with our northern climate.

The very first thing to do about a swimming pool is to either settle it into the landscape so that it isn't terribly obvious, or put it in a separate part of the garden with as much distinction between areas as possible. Siting it where it won't be seen in winter is an appropriate solution to the stark and not very beautiful reality of a covered winter swimming pool. By placing the pool on a terrace, it can be dropped or raised so that it isn't obvious from the house.

The configuration of a pool is important—kidney-shaped numbers are hard to make gardenesque; rectangles and ovals are much easier. The more formal the garden, the more geometric the outline should be. Always make sure the paving around the edge is at least 3 feet (1 meter) wide to accommodate most necessary bits of furniture.

If you can get your mind around the more utilitarian aspect of a swimming pool, visualize it blended with the rest of the garden. There are some constraints on this. It must be placed out of the wind and have at least six hours of sun a day on it—just for comfort's sake.

The color of the pool lining is important. Brilliant turquoise has no relationship to nature. Go for a dark color—slate, navy or ultramarine for a mirror-like surface. White reflects all the colors around it as well as the sky. Green tends to look muddy with all the variety of green inevitably in the neighborhood.

Choose interesting patio stones. If they are of poured concrete, add color to the mix so that they will be softened or at least mimic the color of the pool.

During excavation keep your eye on where the soil is going. Too often, contractors cart topsoil off to be sold at handsome prices. Instead, you may want to provide an area for this soil to be stored so you can later create a sheltering berm around the pool. If absolutely nothing will grow around the pool, you're working with subsoil and it will have to be bumped up with plenty of compost and manure to bring life back into it. Even then, you will have to find plants such as lavenders that flourish in poor soil.

ABOVE: *In Maureen and Brian Bixley's garden, the swimming pool functions as a private separate garden room.* THUJA OCCIDENTALIS, *white cedar, makes a soft line between sky and trees.* THYMUS SERPYLLUM, *mother-of-thyme, creates a mat surface pleasant to walk on—its slight fragrance floats across the pool. Ontario Z4B.*

LEFT: *Murray Haigh's garden for Gillian and David Stewart's country swimming pool borrows the view of surrounding fields. The lollypop dwarf* SYRINGA VELUTINA *punctuate the horizon line without being intrusive. In the island beds:* VERONICA AUSTRIACA *'Crater Lake Blue';* SEDUM SPECTABILE; STACHYS BYZANTINA; ARTEMISIA *'Silver Mound';* HOSTA *sp. Center urn: pansies underplanted with petunias. Ontario Z5.*

One of the tricks landscape architect Murray Haigh used around his pools was to make a garden out of the retaining wall. He liked to nestle the pool into an embankment and have a retaining wall on two sides. He used plants to cascade down the wall toward the pool for a singular effect. This eliminates the need for fencing.

Be sure to build in some attractive method of hiding the pool equipment. A nicely designed cabana with one side for a changing room and the other for pool equipment works well both as a disguise and as a way of deadening the sound of the pump. An evergreen hedge or lattice work will also screen filter and pump.

If you have to deal with a swimming pool already in place, you can do a number of things to make it more aesthetic:

❧ Paint the pool surface navy blue, slate gray or black to turn it into a reflecting pool.

❧ Use Murray Haigh's solution—plant sculpturally at each corner: ornamental grasses, Siberian irises and daylilies set in gravel and rock.

❧ Make a custom look by creating special designs with brick or patio stones. If you are pouring new concrete squares, add color to the mix. Or extend the style of indoor tiles to the exterior.

❧ Take off the diving board—they're ugly. Most small city pools don't need them, and in a large country swimming pool it's an even more revolting appendage.

❧ If an existing pool is close to the house, disguise it with a screen of planting or a good-looking fence, or cover a chain-link fence with ivy. Bare chain-link looks depressing and ugly in winter.

**POOLSIDE SUMMER GARDEN** ❧ All pools should have a garden setting, but here are some plants that work particularly well with swimming pools.

❧ Any of the silver plants soften the look of stone and water: PEROVSKIA, ARTEMISIAS and CARYOPTERIS are among my favorites.

❧ Don't plant large trees and shrubs so close they'll interfere with the pool. And don't let them interfere with the amount of sun shining on the pool.

❧ Swimming pool plants will have to be tough enough to stand the occasional splashing with chlorine.

❧ Summer-flowering shrubs: spiraeas; COTINUS, smoke bush; hydrangeas; VIBURNUM PLICATUM 'Summer Snowflake', hibiscus and perennials.

❧ Perennials: COREOPSIS VERTICILLATA 'Moonbeam'; SEDUM SPECTABILE 'Autumn Joy'; ACHILLEA FILIPENDULA, fern-leaf yarrow; HEMEROCALLIS spp, daylilies; IRIS SIBIRICA; ASTER X FRIKARTII 'Moench'.

A pool can be a beautiful thing if it's properly designed. And it is most successful when it's fitted in so that it becomes a strong feature in the landscape.

# YOUR MICROCLIMATE AND
# THE XERISCAPED GARDEN

*G*iven our profligate use of resources, we're going to be facing either water rationing or water shortages in the future. As gardeners, we have to think up new ways to be better stewards of the land. Xeriscaping is one of those methods.

The term *xeriscaping*—a combination of the Greek word *xeros*, for dry, and *landscaping*—means organizing your garden so that little water other than natural rainfall is needed for plants to thrive. Many styles of design benefit from xeriscaping: prairie gardens, meadows, ordinary borders, cottage, vegetable gardens and even formal landscapes. The principles are the same though the plants change from region to region. You can apply the principles of xeriscaping to parts of your garden or to the whole garden.

Knowing the microclimate of your garden is the first step in making a xeriscape garden. Indeed, this is an important consideration in any garden design, no matter how you choose to go.

To determine your microclimate, you'll need to find out: the height you are above sea level; the annual rainfall in your area; how many growing days you have; the dates the first frost comes into your garden and when last frost leaves in spring. From these, you will find out exactly what zone you are in. Your microclimate may be a whole zone warmer than the general climate zone for your area if you have high light-colored fences or walls. Your house and nearby trees will also modify temperatures and change the velocity of the wind. As well, there may be different climate zones in the same garden; it all depends on the proximity of surrounding fences, buildings and trees.

The climate zones identified in the listings will give you a vague idea of what plants will work in your general region. However, you can experiment with plants that would seem to be a bit tender for your zone because the microclimate in your garden may be warmer.

When working out your xeriscape design, keep the following principles in mind:

❧ Work with nature rather than against it. Don't impose more on your site than it can accommodate; if your land has contours, follow them. This works better than trying to change them for the sake of convenience or aesthetics.

❧ Use native species and place plants in their natural environments. For example, use woodland plants in a woodland setting. The advantages of using native plants are that most can adapt to just about any kind of soil and they are resistant to diseases and pests. It's built into their genetic code to survive, and survive they will in the worst possible circumstances. They have also adapted to the amount of rainfall and the type of soil in the area and therefore require little care.

❧ Know your soil type and choose appropriate plants for the conditions. In general, you won't have to amend the soil, but mulching will help retain moisture. If you have really porous, sandy soil, add compost and leaf mold or soaked peat moss to help the soil retain water. (For more information, see Chapter 7, "The Maintenance of Foliage Plants.")

❧ Organize your garden into watering zones. Group plants with similar water requirements together. Remember that plants in shade tend to require less water than plants in full sun.

Trees and shrubs are extremely important in a xeriscaped garden. They provide shade, which reduces plants' water requirements, and act as wind barriers, thereby reducing evaporation. All plants need water to become established, and this usually takes at least a year or two. After this, however, most plants require less water since they suck it up from deep in the earth.

I don't find it difficult to have and maintain a xerophytic garden. Most of the plants I adore are silvery or gray and those plants—lavenders, artemisias, and stachys—accept dry conditions. Plants with fleshy stems and leaves, like sedums, live happily with them and also need little water. In fact, too much water and many a sedum will croak.

In the xeriscaped garden, *controlled* watering is the key. One of my best investments was an underground leaky pipe system of watering. The pipe is made of recycled tires with tiny holes punched into it. The pipe is laid underground, deep enough so that it feeds the roots where water is needed. The only time I turn it on is when the indicator plants in the garden are wilting. The rest of the time I water by hand those plants that need it.

If you're using an aboveground hose, about 80 per cent of the water will evaporate at high noon. Don't water in the middle of the day. Water early in the morning or late in the afternoon. Do as much as you can by hand instead of sprinkling the whole garden. Invest in a rain butt and catch the water that comes off your roof (make sure the container is covered to keep out leaves, bugs and prevent evaporation).

There's not much room for huge swathes of nonnative grasses in a xeriscaped garden. Such landscapes may soon be a thing of the past anyway. Vast swards of needy grasses such as Kentucky bluegrass need gallons of water to stay brilliant green. Get rid of, or cut back, your grassy areas. Use ground covers or drought-resistant native varieties of grass instead. You'll be amazed by their dramatically reduced water requirements: Kentucky bluegrass needs 35 to 60 inches (90 to 150 centimeters) of water a year; smooth bromegrass needs only 20 inches (50 centimeters).

In a xeriscaped garden, the emphasis is on drought-tolerant plants. Here are some general characteristics that will help you identify such plants:

⋙ The smaller the leaf, the less water the plant requires; conversely, the larger the leaf, the more water it needs to sustain itself.

⋙ Any of the gray-leaved plants, those with hair and those with deeply divided foliage usually tolerate drought.

⋙ Plants that hug the ground and thereby keep themselves out of wind need less water. Herbs and plants that produce aromatic oil (lavender, for example) don't dry out readily.

Good plants for a xeriscaped garden in full sun with dry soil:

*Trees:* KOELREUTERIA, golden-rain tree; GLEDITSIA, honey locust; CARAGANA ARBORESCENS, pea tree; ACER GINNALA, Amur maple; A. CAMPESTRE, hedge maple.

*Shrubs:* ARTEMISIA; CERATOSTIGMA; CYTISUS, broom; ELAEAGNUS; GENISTA; JUNIPERUS; CEANOTHUS; RHAMNUS, buckthorn.

*Perennials:* ACAENA; ALYSSUM; ACANTHUS; ACHILLEA; ANTHEMIS; ARABIS; ARMERIA; AUBRIETA; BAPTISIA AUSTRALIS; CAMPANULA ALLIARIIFOLIA; CERASTIUM; DIANTHUS; GERANIUM ENDRESSII; LIMONIUM LATIFOLIUM; LIRIOPE; NEPETA; SEDUM; STACHYS; TEUCRIUM; THYMUS; POLYGONATUM ODORATUM; CENTRANTHUS RUBER; HELIOPSIS HELIANTHOIDES; OENOTHERA MISSOURENSIS; LINUM PERENNE; RUTA GRAVEOLENS; EUPHORBIA; LAVANDULA ANGUSTIFOLIA.

*Wildflowers:* ACHILLEA, yarrow; CAMPANULA, bellflower; FILIPENDULA VULGARIS, meadowsweet; MALVA MOSCHATA, musk mallow.

See also "Ornamental Grasses" on page 119. And check in the Plant Listings of both this book and *The Canadian Gardener* for each plant's water requirements.

My book *Ecological Gardening* has more information on how to be a good steward in the garden.

# LISTINGS OF TREES, SHRUBS, VINES AND GROUND COVERS

In this section are plants from the gardens we've looked at and from our own gardens in alphabetical order rather than by zone or plant type.

Apart from personal experience, the major references here are Michael A. Dirr, *Manual of Woody Landscape Plants;* Brian Davis, *The Gardener's Illustrated Encyclopedia of Trees and Shrubs;* and John J. Sabuco, *The Best of the Hardiest;* Donald Wyman, *Trees for American Gardens: The Definitive Guide to Identification and Cultivation;* Roger Phillips and Martyn Rix, *The Random House Book of Shrubs.*

Most listings will include other species, varieties or cultivars.

### ABELIA X GRANDIFLORA (ab-EE-lia) ❧ Glossy Abelia *ZONE:* 5.
*Origin:* Mexico.
*Value:* A marvelous hedge that dies back and revives quickly in spring, within 3 weeks. Also makes a pretty specimen.
*Hardiness:* Evergreen in temperatures above 5°F (-15°C); herbaceous in lower ones.
*Size:* 5' (1.5 m).
*Color:* Lightly scented white blossoms with a touch of pink from July to first frost.
*Soil:* Warm humusy soil.
*Maintenance:* Cut back to the ground in early May so that the plant will grow back quickly; flowers form on new wood.

### ABELIOPHYLLUM DISTICHUM (a-BE-lio-fill-um) ❧ Korean Abelia-leaf or White Forsythia *ZONE:* 5 to 8.
This often overlooked, undemanding flowering shrub grows quickly under ideal conditions. The arching branches will root where they touch the soil. Not for exposed places.
*Origin:* Korea.
*Value:* Early spring color before most foliage is out. Blooms even earlier than forsythia, a good companion to the yellow forsythia but not as showy.
*Hardiness:* Flowering buds may be injured in a severe winter, but more dependable than FORSYTHIA X INTERMEDIA types. Tolerates 5°F (-15°C).
*Size:* After 3 years, 4' (1.2 m) high, with a spread of 3' (1 m).
*Color:* Tiny white scented flowers with a mauve tinge are borne in late winter to early spring. Light green foliage.
*Soil:* Easily transplanted. Prefers well-drained acid or alkaline soil.

*Maintenance:* No pruning required, but does best on its own in full sun or light to medium shade, can be propagated from rooted tips of the branches.
*Problems:* Some say that this is a weak and uninteresting shrub.
A. D. **'Rosea'**, pure pink form.

### ABIES BALSAMEA (A-beez) ❧ Balsam Fir
*ZONE:* 3 to 5, maybe 6.
There are about 40 species of fir, found from Canada to Guatemala. Slow growing, requires cool, moist conditions.
*Origin:* North America.
*Value:* Specimen tree, excellent Christmas tree, though Dirr claims it does not hold its needles long in a dry house. I have seen it in zone 5 used as a screen from wind and as beautiful protection from prying eyes.
*Hardiness:* Slow to medium growth rate, intolerant of air pollution.
*Size:* Average height is 45' - 75' (14 m - 23 m) with a 20' - 25' (6 m - 8 m) spread.
*Color:* Dark rich green.
*Soil:* Shallow rooted, shade tolerant, prefers well-drained soil. Will grow in damp conditions in moist fertile soil.
*Maintenance:* Requires very little pruning or maintenance. Transplants readily in spring. Adapts to cold climates.

### A. CONCOLOR White Fir
*ZONE:* 3 to 7.
Needles resist burning. Very green; good Christmas tree. Drought tolerant. Formal habit with bluish cast.
*Origin:* North America.
*Value:* Beautiful foliage and soft look. Good replacement for spruce in the garden.
*Size:* Average 30' - 50' (9 m - 15 m), but can reach 100' (30 m) with a spread of 15' - 30' (4.5 m - 9 m).
*Color:* Bluish green leaf color.
*Soil:* Deep, rich, moist, well-drained soils; dislikes clay.
*Maintenance:* Transplants well.
*Problems:* Nothing special.

### A. FRASERI Fraser Fir
*ZONE:* 4 to 7.
Best Christmas tree.
*Origin:* Native to the mountains of West Virginia and Tennessee.
*Value:* Ornamental tree, excellent and popular as a Christmas tree.
*Hardiness:* Suffers in hot climates.

*Size:* 30' - 40' (9 m - 12 m) with a spread of 20' - 25' (6 m - 8 m). Can reach 70' (21 m).
*Color:* Shining dark green needles.
*Soil:* Prefers moist, well-drained loamy soil in the sun or partial shade.
*Maintenance:* Transplants well with some pruning. Best transplanted in the spring.

### ACANTHOPANAX SIEBOLDIANUS (ak-an-tho-PAY-nax) ❧ Fiveleaf Aralia
*ZONE:* 5 to 8.
*Origin:* China.
*Value:* A handsome, almost impenetrable hedge, use as a barrier or screen. The thorns will discourage intruders. At its best in full sun to partial shade. Near water it complements GUNNERA MANICATA.
*Hardiness:* Tolerates 25°F (-5°C). Adapts to most unfavorable conditions.
*Size:* After 10 years, 6' by 6' (2 m by 2 m) to a maximum of 8' by 8' (2.5 m by 2.5 m).
*Color:* Rich bright green leaves, brown stems and small greenish white flowers in June.
*Soil:* Prefers well-drained soil, acid or alkaline, sand to clay; sun or shade.
*Maintenance:* No pruning necessary, but may be cut back to encourage new growth; it will tolerate heavy pruning. Tends to sucker so may need some restraining.
A. S. **'Variegatus'** is a variegated variety.

### A. HENRYI Henry's Aralia
A multistemmed upright shrub with dark green leaves and flowers that give way to black, long fruits. Grows 8' - 10' (2.5 m - 3 m).

### ACER CAMPESTRE (AY-ser) ❧ Hedge Maple
*ZONE:* 4 to 8.
*Origin:* Near East.
*Value:* Good for lining urban streets. Excellent for hedging and dry areas.
*Hardiness:* Extremely adaptable, easily transplanted, tolerant of air pollution. Full sun or light shade, is adaptable to dry conditions.
*Size:* 25' - 35' (8 m - 11 m) with comparable spread. Averages 2' (.5 m) of growth a year.
*Color:* Light brown stem with dark green leaves.
*Soil:* Prefers rich well-drained soils; does well in acid conditions.
*Maintenance:* No pruning necessary. Branches hang low to the ground, but can be trimmed up.
A. **'Compactum'**, dwarf multistemmed shrub, 2' - 4' (.5 m - 1.2 m) high, is not as hardy, but develops beautiful yellow fall color.

ACER GINNALA ❧ **Amur Maple**
*ZONE:* 2 to 8 (but does best north of 7).
*Origin:* China and Japan.
*Value:* This plant is almost unkillable. Does well as a privacy hedge or container plant; useful in groups; excellent screening for the small garden. Likes full sun or light shade; requires practically no care and is excellent in dry locations.
*Hardiness:* Adaptable to a wide range of soils; withstands heavy pruning; resistant to drought and extremely hardy.
*Size:* 20' - 30' (6 m - 9 m) but has been known to reach 40' (12 m).
*Color:* Scarlet leaves in autumn, glossy deep green in spring and summer. The winged keys turn red in late summer and the flowers in spring are white and fragrant.
*Soil:* Well-drained soils from acid to alkaline.
*Maintenance:* Practically none; withstands heavy pruning and shaping.
Some cultivars: **'Compactum'**, more dense and compact, grows to 6' (2 m), flowers are fragrant; fall color a deep red. **'Durand Dwarf'**, dwarf, shrubby and dense, 5' (1.5 m) high with less showy color in fall. **'Red Fruit'**, brilliant red fruit, but otherwise a clone. **'Flame'**, used for its form and brilliant scarlet color almost a deep red-purple; effective screen.

A. JAPONICUM **Fullmoon Maple**
20' - 30' (6 m - 9 m) high; light green turning to yellow and red in fall, purple flowers in spring; zone 6.

A. PALMATUM **Japanese Maple**
*ZONE:* Depending on cultivar, 5 to 6 to 8.
*Origin:* Japan.
*Value:* Good accent plant for border or groupings. The seasonal changes of color in ACER PALMATUM **'Atropurpureum'** make it an invaluable plant: wine-colored foliage changes to green and then to a blaze of fall scarlet.
*Hardiness:* Tolerates temperatures to -5°F (-20°C). Needs protection from spring frost and summer midday sun.
*Size:* 15' - 25' (4.5 m - 8 m) high with a spread as great as or greater than the height.
*Color:* Green in summer, becoming yellow, purple-red in late summer and into fall.
*Soil:* Neutral to acid; tolerates alkalinity with moisture.
*Maintenance:* No pruning, but some shaping may be desirable; remove the lower branches.
*Problems:* Vulnerable to frost, midday sun can scorch foliage or make the colors fade; coral spot may be a problem in some areas, diseased branches should be cut off.

Some cultivars: **'Atropurpureum'**, deep purple leaves, crimson in fall; in some areas it suffers from coral spot. **'Bloodgood'**, strong form, fine purple leaves, grows upright. **'Chitoseyama'**, bronze-green foliage, turns bright red in the fall, form is tighter than others, not as hardy. **'Burgundy Lace'**, reddish purple leaves, lobes produce a lacy appearance. **'Senkaki'** often called the coral bark maple, gorgeous for winter effect; yellow leaves in fall. **'Shishio'**, spring foliage a crimson red, aging to green with a pink outline.

A. PSEUDO-SIEBOLDIANUM **Purplebloom Maple**
Small tree similar to other acers; zone 5.

A. SIEBOLDIANUM **Siebold Maple**
Yellow flowers, but otherwise similar to other acers, fall color is orange; good for any garden, almost guaranteed success.

ACTINIDIA ARGUTA (ak-tin-ID-ia) ❧ **Tara Vine** *ZONE:* 4.
*Origin:* China.
*Value:* Good for areas where no other vine will grow. It's rarely used, but according to Dirr, it is adaptable to difficult situations.
*Hardiness:* Vigorous, high climbing with support.
*Size:* Can grow 20' - 30' (6 m - 9 m) in a 2 or 3 year period.
*Color:* Dark green leaves in summer with red tinge in the fall. Holds leaves late into the fall.
*Soil:* Will grow in any soil; best in infertile soil to stunt growth.
*Maintenance:* Cut back to 1 or 2 main branches for fruit, which is borne on year or older wood.

A. CHINENSIS **Chinese Gooseberry or Kiwi Fruit**
White flowers in June, hairy reddish shoots, large leaves, produces edible brown-green berries; any soil, sun or part shade.

A. KOLOMIKTA **Kolomikta Actinidia**
Climbs to 30' (9 m); fragrant white flowers in May and June.

A. POLYGAMA **Silver Vine**
Not a strong climber; long silver-white leaves, white flowers, fragrant in June and July. Needs lots of pruning or it will rapidly take over.

AESCULUS GLABRA (EES-kew-lus) ❧ **Ohio Buckeye** *ZONE:* 3 to 7.
*Origin:* Southeastern United States (Alabama, Georgia to Florida).
*Value:* Good for parks and large areas, but not for street planting.
*Hardiness:* Tolerant to -15°F (-25°C).
*Size:* 20' - 40' (6 m - 12 m) high with a similar spread; can grow to 80' (24 m) under ideal conditions.

*Color:* Bright green leaves when unfolding, dark green in summer, brilliant red-orange to reddish brown in fall.
*Soil:* Well-drained, slightly acid, moist soil.
*Maintenance:* No pruning required, but remove dead branches.
*Problems:* Leaf scorching in drought conditions; vulnerable to leaf blotch, leaf mold, wood rot, bagworm, walnut scale, constock mealy bug, marked tussock moth.

A. DISCOLOR
Red flowers, glossy leaves; rarely grows higher than 10' (3 m); zone 5.

A. PARVIFLORA **Bottlebrush Buckeye**
Few problems, but slow to show its true beauty. Flowers in July; glorious yellow fall color. Likes sun or part shade. Suckers. Zone 5.

ALNUS CRISPA (AL-nus) ❧ **American Green Alder, Mountain Alder** *ZONE:* 1.
*Origin:* Many are native to North America.
*Value:* Excellent in wet areas where no other trees will grow. Most useful for screening; acts as a great coverup of the blights on the earth; fixes nitrogen and adds organic matter to the soil; flower catkins last through the winter.
*Size:* 100' (30 m); 30" (75 cm) trunk.
*Color:* Reddish twigs, dark green oval leaves.
*Soil:* Will grow even in barren soil.
*Maintenance:* Nothing special.
*Problems:* No diseases from zone 3 north. Insects thrive on it, especially the tent caterpillar.
Cultivars are not as hardy as the species.

A. CORDATA **Italian Alder**

A. GLUTINOSA **European Alder**
Will naturalize near water; shade tolerant; lovely glossy green leaves; almost red-black bark.

A. RUBRA **Red Alder**
Fast growing native with long, long male catkins. Leaves often remain green until they fall. Pollen can cause allergic reaction.

AMELANCHIER ARBOREA (am-el-ANK-ier) ❧ **Downy Serviceberry, Juneberry, Shadbush, Service-tree or Sarvis-tree**
*ZONE:* 4 to 9.
Sabuco says that A. ARBOREA is known in the trade as A. CANADENSIS and that few nurseries carry true A. CANADENSIS, a stolonifera 4' - 10' (1.2 m - 3 m) shrub. The serviceberry provides a food source for birds in winter. Makes a beautiful edging screen.
*Origin:* North America.
*Value:* Blends in well with woodland plants near ponds. Makes a splendid show in spring with showers of white flowers.
*Hardiness:* Hardy to -5°F (-20°C).

*Size:* 15' - 25' (4.5 m - 8 m). Can grow to 50' (15 m) depending on climate.

*Color:* Grayish leaves in spring to green in summer. White flowers in spring, orange berries turn purplish black in late fall.

*Soil:* Performs well in many soils, tolerates high alkalinity and acidity.

*Maintenance:* No pruning necessary; remove dead limbs at maturity.

*Problems:* Rust, witches broom caused by fungus, leaf blight, pear slug fly, powdery mildews.

### AMELANCHIER ALNIFOLIA **Saskatoon Serviceberry**

A great tree for prairie gardens. Sun or shade; wet or dry soil. White flowers in mid-May in Edmonton; thicker rounded leaves. Fruit grown commercially. Grows 3' - 18' (1 m - 5.5 m) high. Berries are bluish purple, juicy and edible. Tolerates harsh winter climate. Zone 2. Survives to -70°F (-55°C). Grows close to the Arctic Circle. Excellent prairie cultivars are: **'Altaglow'**, **'Northline'**, **'Pembina'** and **'Smokey'**.

### A. ASIATICA **Asian Serviceberry**

More of a tree than a shrub; grows 15' - 40' (4.5 m - 12 m). The white and fragrant flowers appear in late spring after the leaves; purplish fruit; winter buds are very deep red; native to China and Japan; zone 5.

### A. CANADENSIS **Shadblow Serviceberry**

Fruit is black and very juicy; fall color is yellow gold; grows 6' - 20' (2 m - 6 m); zone 4.

### A. LAEVIS **Allegany Serviceberry**

The best ornamental serviceberry; showy white flowers are fragrant; pink to bronze leaves in spring. Fragrant. Black berries are good eating. Zone 2.

### A. STOLONIFERA **Running Serviceberry**

Does just that—a low stoloniferous shrub that grows to 6' (2 m). Incredible scarlet fall color. Zone 3.

### AMPELOPSIS BREVIPEDUNCULATA

(am-pel-OP-sis) ❦ **Porcelain Ampelopsis** ZONE: 5.

This vine can be invasive.

*Origin:* Asia.

*Value:* The berries are long lasting and look like porcelain. Makes a light screen.

*Size:* Will grow up to 20' (6 m) a year, if not controlled.

*Color:* The leaves are variable, but it's the fruit you look for—it changes from yellow to green to lavender to bright blue.

*Soil:* Almost any soil will do.

*Maintenance:* Sabuco recommends planting it in a pot to keep it from becoming too rampant in a sunny situation, but I haven't found this to be a problem. Repot every five years. Propagate by layering: weight down one length of vine with a small stone and it will root quite readily.

*Problems:* Might become rampant.

A. B. **'Elegans'** is the variegated version that I'd recommend over all others. The new growth is pink. I love this vine especially combined with GALEGA for summer bloom, and a pink chrysanthemum for fall bloom.

### ANDROMEDA POLIFOLIA (an-DROM-ed-a) ❦ **Bog Rosemary** ZONE: 2.

*Origin:* Europe, northern Asia and North America (circumpolar in habitat range).

*Value:* Used in acid soil with heathers and ericaceous plants such as rhododendrons. Grows from creeping rootstock.

*Hardiness:* Must have cold. In zone 2 it can be found in sand and scree or heavy bottomland.

*Size:* After 5 years, 2' by 2' (.5 m by .5 m); after 20 years, at maturity, 3' by 5' (1 m by 1.5 m).

*Color:* Hanging clusters of soft pink to purple bell-shaped flowers; slender blue-green foliage.

*Soil:* Moist rich acid soil, resists alkalinity, commonly found in peat.

*Maintenance:* Nothing special.

A. P. **'Compacta'**, a dwarf, compact variety.

### A. GLAUCOPHYLLA

Slightly lighter-colored flowers; leaves have a downy underside.

### ARALIA SPINOSA (a-RAIL-a) ❦ **Devil's-walking Stick or Hercules'-club** ZONE: 4 to 9.

*Origin:* Central Pennsylvania to Florida and Texas.

*Value:* The shoots that sprout up from the base should be taken into consideration when planting. Use in shrub border or out-of-the-way places.

*Hardiness:* Does well under city conditions.

*Size:* 10' - 20' (3 m - 6 m) high; can grow to 40' (12 m).

*Color:* Dark green in the summer; white flowers at the end of branches in July, veil-like over the plant. The fall color is basic yellow. Fruit is plentiful, purple-black in late August to October; good for the birds.

*Soil:* Prefers moist well-drained fertile soils, but grows in dry, rocky or heavy soils, acid or slightly alkaline conditions, sun or partial shade.

*Maintenance:* Remove the shoots sprouting at the base to control growth. Transplants well; shoots at the base can be removed and used to start new plants.

A. ELATA **Japanese Angelica**

Grows 30' - 50' (9 m - 15 m); long-lived, slow grower. Yellow tinge on the huge bipinnately compound leaves, which can be 6' (2 m) long. Great fall color. Once the leaves drop, the spiny stems look weirdly sculptural. White flowers July to September. Origin Japan, Russian Far East. Zone 5.

### ARBUTUS MENZIESII (AR-bew-tus) ❦ **Madrone, Strawberry Tree** ZONE: 8.

*Origin:* Native to the West Coast of North America; Mediterranean region.

*Value:* Evergreen; beautiful peeling bark falls away to expose a pinkish wood; wonderful shape.

*Hardiness:* Should be considered tender in areas with winter frost, withstands temperatures to 15°F (-10°C); in some areas expect winterkill and new growth from the ground each year.

*Size:* 100' (30 m) in native habitat; 20' - 30' (6 m - 9 m) under cultivation.

*Color:* Fruit orange and red; pale flowers in May.

*Soil:* Does well in all types of soil, likes peat or compost in soil.

*Maintenance:* Likes fast drainage, nonalkaline water. Remove winterkill if necessary.

*Problems:* None other than frost.

### ARCTOSTAPHYLOS UVA-URSI (ark-to-STAFF-il-oss) ❦ **Bearberry, Hog Cranberry, Kinnikinick** ZONE: Dirr says 2 to 5; Sabuco says 1 to 4.

For good ground cover plant 6" (15 cm) apart in a sandy peaty mixture.

*Value:* Reliable ground cover for hills, coasts.

*Origin:* Northern hemisphere.

*Hardiness:* Temperatures to 5°F (-15°C); likes full sun and resents shade.

*Size:* 6" - 12" (15 cm - 30 cm) high; 2' - 4' (.5 m - 1.2 m) in width to infinity. Each plant may cover 15' (4.5 m).

*Color:* Glossy bright green leaves, white-tinged pink flowers; in late May, red fruit.

*Soil:* Must have loose, well-drained acid soil.

*Maintenance:* During the first year it needs water every week. Pinch back to control growth. Difficult to transplant from wild.

*Problems:* Davis says none; Dirr says rust, leaf galls and black mildew.

### ARISTOLOCHIA DURIOR (a-riss-to-LO-kia) ❦ **Dutchman's-pipe** ZONE: 4 to 8.

A deciduous vine often used as a screen on old porches. Gives a lovely old-fashioned look and is a nice respite from the usual plants.

*Origin:* North America.

*Value:* Grows quickly, can cover an arbor or trellis in a single season; excellent thick screen.

*Hardiness:* Very hardy; will withstand both partial shade and full sun.

*Size:* Can grow up 20'- 30' (6 m - 9 m) with the aid of trellis.
*Color:* Deep green; leaves can be a foot (30 cm) long. The pipe-shaped flowers are foul-smelling and yellowish brown.
*Soil:* Well-drained soil of any type.
*Maintenance:* Nothing special.

BETULA LENTA (BET-yew-la)
❧ **Sweet Birch or Cherry Birch** *ZONE:* 3.
*Origin:* Native to most northern climates.
*Value:* Good for parks; best birch for fall color. Sabuco does not recommend this tree.
*Size:* 40'- 60' (12 m - 18 m) in landscapes; 70' - 80' (21 m - 24 m) in the wild.
*Color:* Dark green, yellow in fall.
*Soil:* Deep, rich, moist, slightly acid, well-drained soils; often found on rocky drier sites.
*Maintenance:* These trees are short-lived.
*Problems:* Birches have several problems and this variety is no exception: leaf spot, leaf blisters, leaf rust, canker, dieback, wood-decay, mildew. Insect pests include: aphids, witch-hazel, leaf gall, birch skeletonizer, leaf miner, bronze birch borer and seed mite gall.

B. ALLEGHANIENSIS **Yellow Birch or Grey Birch**
Valuable timber tree. Grows to 75' (23 m); can reach 100' (30 m). Bark is yellowish; leaves light green, to yellow in fall. Prefers cool temperatures. Zone 3.

B. FONTINALIS **River Birch**
Grows to 30' (9 m). Native to the prairies up to 5,000 feet (1500 m) in foothills of the Rockies from Calgary south.

B. LUTEA **Yellow Birch**
Tolerates cold, wet soil and some shade in zone 5. Splendid yellow fall color. Typical growth is 45' (14 m).

B. NANA **Dwarf Arctic Birch**
A pretty little shrub that likes scree conditions, but is adaptable. Grows 3' - 4' (1 m - 1.2 m). Zone 1 to 4 (I'm growing it in zone 6, but it may be subject to diseases).

B. NIGRA **River Birch**
Likes wet soil and will defoliate in dry spots. Stunning exfoliating bark. Zone 4.

B. OCCIDENTALIS **Water Birch**
This red-twigged western native will grow along river banks in thickets 15' (4.5 m). Sabuco likes this plant better than red-stemmed dogwoods.

B. PAPYRIFERA **Paper Birch, Canoe Birch or White Birch** *ZONE:* 2 to 6 possibly 7 (Dirr); adaptable to zone 1 (Sabuco); bronze birch borer in areas warmer than zone 4. Likes the north and does poorly south of zone 4.
*Origin:* North America; native to Alberta.
*Value:* Good in parks or large planting areas. Excellent white bark for the winter garden.

*Hardiness:* Best in colder climates. Does well in the wild; not in polluted areas. Likes full sun.
*Size:* 50' - 70' (15 m - 21 m) though can reach 120' (37 m).
*Color:* Dark green, to yellow in fall.
*Soil:* Adapts to wide variety of soils; likes well-drained, acid, moist, sandy or silty loams best.
*Maintenance:* Cut out dead limbs. Doesn't take well to pruning or to fall planting on the prairies. Needs lots of water in a drought.
*Problems:* Not as susceptible to bronze birch borer like the European species of birch. There are many species but according to Dirr they are difficult to separate. B. P. 'Gracilis' has lacy drooping branches.

B. PENDULA **European White Birch** *ZONE:* 2 (Wyman); or 2 to 7 (Dirr).
If young trees don't look as though they'll weep, be patient.
*Origin:* Europe and Asia Minor.
*Value:* Popular in many gardens, extensively used in parks and cemeteries.
*Size:* 60' (18 m).
*Color:* Green, to yellow in fall.
*Soil:* Will tolerate wet or dry soils.
*Maintenance:* Should be pruned to shape in the summer.
*Problems:* Short-lived tree. Subject to attack by bronze birch borer.
Some cultivars: B. P. 'Dalecarlica', cutleaf weeping birch is the most common in cultivation; pendulous coarsely toothed leaves. B. P. 'Fastigiata', branches erect, resembles Lombardy. B. P. 'Gracilis', a popular small tree that holds foliage later than others and has drooping branches with clusters like witches broom; B. P. 'Purpurea', deep reddish leaves. B. P. 'Tristis', a clone similar to 'Elegans'. B. P. 'Youngii', slender and pendulous.

BUDDLEIA DAVIDII (BUD-lia) ❧ **Butterfly Bush, Summer Lilac** *ZONE:* 5 to 9.
*Origin:* Central and western China.
*Value:* Has a beautiful fountain shape and blooms that last well into fall.
*Hardiness:* Withstands temperatures to 5°F (-15°C).
*Size:* This large shrub grows 10' - 15' (3 m - 4.5 m).
*Color:* Pale to blue fragrant flowers borne mid to late summer, fragrant.
*Soil:* Prefers well-drained fertile soils.
*Maintenance:* Previous year's wood must be cut before spring growth begins. Cut back to 4" (10 cm) from origin close to the ground with secateurs; prune hard in midspring to produce larger flowers in fall. I have one of these shrubs and it blooms gloriously until mid-October if it's deadheaded.

*Problems:* None serious; important to prune or it will be short-lived. Subject to winterkill but returns very nicely.
Some cultivars: **'Black Knight'**, dark purple flowers, slightly hardier than the following: **'Charming'**, pink flowers. **'Dubonnet'**, dark purple flowers. **'Empire Blue'**, rich violet upright flowers. **'Fascinating'**, vivid lilac-pink. **'Royal Red'**, rich purple-red flowers. **'White Bouquet'**, white flowers. **'White Profusion'**, white flowers.

BUXUS MICROPHYLLA (BUK-sus) ❧ **Littleleaf Box or Boxwood** *ZONE:* 6; some cultivars will grow in 4 to 9.
This formal hedging requires proper placing to show up well. Will thrive in containers that are more than 14" (35 cm) in all directions. Slow growing and hates root disturbance.
*Origin:* Japan, western Asia; grows wild in the British Isles.
*Value:* Excellent evergreen hedge for foundations and borders in formal gardens. Attractive in container gardens and tubs.
*Hardiness:* Hardy if all its requirements are met. Withstands winter temperatures of -15°F (-25°C); protect from severe winds.
*Size:* After 5 years, 3' by 3' (1 m by 1 m); after 20 years, in maturity, 13' by 13' (4 m by 4 m).
*Color:* Glossy green.
*Soil:* The better the soil, the better the growth. Likes mulching, peat or leaf mold, and cool temperatures.
*Maintenance:* Can be trimmed to any shape. Do not cultivate around because it is a surface rooter. The roots will take richness from soil and prevent growth of nearby plants. Plenty of compost and mulching will help reduce pest and disease problems.
*Problems:* Canker, blight, leaf spot, root rot, winter injury and sun scald, mealybugs, scales, boxwood psyllid, boxwood leaf miner, giant hornet, boxwood webworm.
Some cultivars: **'Compacta'**, small dense slow growing form. **'Green Beauty'**, thick dense foliage year-round. **'Green Pillow'**, similar to **'Compacta'** but larger leaves. **'Green Mountain'** and **'Wintergreen'**, recommended by Sabuco for zone 5, green all winter. **'Sunnyside'**, hardy with large leaves. **'Tide Till'**, green foliage all winter. **'Winter Beauty'** and **'Winter Gem'**.

B. M. JAPONICA
Flowers more freely than other cultivars and grows 3' - 6' (1 m - 2 m), but Dirr wonders if these plants have been labelled correctly.

B. M. KOREANA
Extremely hardy zone 4; good choice for northern areas. Foliage turns yellow. Grows loose and open, twice as wide as high. **'Medad'**, **'Morris Dwarf'**, **'National'**, **'Nomar'**, **'Tall Boy'**.

CALLICARPA JAPONICA (kal-i-CARP-a)
❧ **Japanese Beautyberry** *ZONE:* 5 to 8.
*Origin:* Japan.
*Value:* This fountain-shaped plant is good in either the shrub border or in groups.
*Hardiness:* Dieback of new growth in extreme cold temperatures.
*Size:* 4' - 6' (1.2 m - 2 m) high, similar width.
*Color:* Pink flowers, leaves medium green, to yellowish in fall, fruit is violet to purple.
*Soil:* Well-drained soil in full sun or light shade.
*Maintenance:* Prune to within 4" (10 cm) of the ground every spring—flowers are produced on new growth. Grow in protected, moist, sunny spot in slightly acidic soil. Will do okay in clay. Mulch. This plant takes time to flourish. Don't fertilize.
*Problems:* Leaf spot, black mold; nothing serious. Subject to dieback.
C. J. 'Leucocarpa' has white fruit.

C. AMERICANA **American Beautyberry**
Light lavender-pink flowers. Grows 3' - 8' (1 m - 2.5 m). Zone 7 to 10.

C. BODINIERI **Bodinier Beautyberry**
Late-flowering shrub, small lilac blooms; leaves turn purple in fall. Reaches 6' - 10' (2 m - 3 m).

C. DICHOTOMA **Purple Beautyberry**
The most spectacular variety of all. Shorter height of 3' - 4' (1 m - 1.2 m) and larger spread. Oval leaves; lilac flowers from June to August. Likes clay soil.

CALLUNA VULGARIS (kal-LOON-a)
❧ **Heather** *ZONE:* 3 to 6.
Wind is the enemy of heather. Likes shade in winter and sun in summer.
*Value:* Flowers from the middle of summer well into fall. Wonderful evergreen ground cover of uniform height.
*Hardiness:* Choose your cultivars carefully, can be tender.
*Size:* 4" - 30" (10 cm - 75 cm).
*Soil:* Moist, infertile, acid.
*Maintenance:* Only cut back in spring to renew old plants. You'll kill it any other time. Take either softwood and hardwood cuttings in summer to propagate.
There are an enormous number of cultivars. Here are the ones recommended by Sabuco: 'Blazeaway', orange-red foliage and lilac flowers; 18" (45 cm). 'County Wicklow', spectacular pink flowers, July to October; grows to 9" (23 cm). 'H. E. Beale', pink flowers; grows to 24" (60 cm); August to November. 'J. H. Hamilton', rose flowers August to October; 10" (25 cm). 'Martha Herman', vivid green foliage and white flowers June to September; 12" (30 cm). 'Mullion', deep pink flowers; July to September; 12" (30 cm).

'Tib', rose-colored flowers from July to October, dark rosy-green foliage; 24" (60 cm).

CAMPSIS RADICANS (KAMP-sis) ❧ **Trumpet Creeper, Trumpet Vine** *ZONE:* 4 to 9.
*Origin:* North America.
*Value:* Grows quickly everywhere and on anything providing excellent screening.
*Hardiness:* Very hardy though some tip dieback at -25°F (-32°C). Possible to grow in almost any garden.
*Size:* 30' - 40' (9 m - 12 m) high.
*Color:* Dark green leaves, changing to yellow in fall. Flowers are a rich orange and scarlet, trumpet shaped.
*Soil:* Will grow in any soil but needs to be planted 24" - 36" (60 cm - 90 cm) from the wall or trellis.
*Maintenance:* Pruning is necessary to maintain control and encourage flowering. Has a propensity to sucker from roots and strangle everything in its path.
*Problems:* Blight, leaf spot, powdery mildew, plant hoppers, scale and whitefly—Dirr says nothing serious enough to warrant controls. Some cultivars: 'Flava', handsome with yellow flowers. 'Praecox', red flowers in June.

C. GRANDIFLORA **Chinese Trumpet Creeper**
Grows 20' - 30' (6 m - 9 m); deep orange and red flowers. Native to Japan; zone 7 to 9.

CARAGANA ARBORESCENS (kar-rag-AY-na) ❧ **Pea Tree, Pea Shrub** *ZONE:* 2 to 7.
*Origin:* Siberia and Manchuria.
*Value:* Good as a hedge or screen. This oval shrub can be grown in containers or on dry banks. Can also be grown as a tree; erect branches may create a fastigiate appearance. Recommended for prairie windbreaks. It's a great plant that takes incredible abuse and manages to come back refreshed.
*Hardiness:* Tolerates 5°F (-15°C), poor soils and drought, severe winds and salt; extremely hardy.
*Size:* 15' - 20' (4.5 m - 6 m) high with a spread of 12' - 18' (3.5 m - 5.5 m).
*Color:* Bright yellow flowers early to mid-May; flowers on last year's wood; light green leaves.
*Soil:* Tolerates poor soil, drought, alkalinity, winds, salt. Fixes nitrogen in the soil.
*Maintenance:* Needs to be trained.
*Problems:* Slow starter.
Some cultivars: 'Lorbergii', fern appearance with narrow flowers and wide leaves. 'Nana', dwarf, 6' (2 m) high by 3' (1 m) wide. 'Pendula', weeping ornamental. 'Sutherland', upright form effective for screening; grows up to 10' (3 m).

C. AURANTIACA **Dwarf Pea Shrub**
Lovely fountain shape and grows to 4' (1.2 m). Zone 5.

C. MICROPHYLLA **Littleleaf Caragana**
Small, grayish, delicate-looking leaves; zone 2. 'Walker', usually top-grafted and the prettiest of all.

CARPINUS BETULUS (kar-PY-nus) ❧ **European Hornbeam** *ZONE:* 4 to 7.
*Origin:* Europe and Asia Minor.
*Value:* Good as screens or hedges. Excellent for use around large buildings and malls or in planters. Should be used more here.
*Hardiness:* Tolerates -15°F (-25°C), partially tolerant of difficult conditions.
*Size:* 40'- 60' (12 m - 18 m) high with a 30'-40' (9 m - 12 m) spread.
*Color:* Hanging catkins in spring and light green leaves turning yellow in fall.
*Soil:* Wide range of soil conditions, acid to alkaline. Likes full sun and good drainage.
*Maintenance:* Seldom needs pruning unless for shaping.
*Problems:* None serious.
Some cultivars: 'Columnaris', densely branched with spirelike foliage. 'Fastigiata', zone 6; common cultivar with vase shape and fan-ribbed branches; grows 50' (15 m) high; close-knit branches are an effective screen in winter. 'Frans Fontaine', fastigiate form. 'Globosa', rounded, no central trunk, serves as screen, slow growing. 'Pendula', zone 7; shrubby dwarf tree with droopy branches.

C. CAROLINIANA **American Hornbeam, Blue Beech** is hard to transplant, so best moved balled and burlapped or from a container in spring. Beautiful ashy gray trunk; grows to 40' (12 m). Zone 3b.

CARYA ILLINOINENSIS (KAY-rya) ❧ **Pecan** *ZONE:* 5.
*Origin:* North America.
*Value:* Liberal quantities of fruit in the South, ornamental in the midwest.
*Hardiness:* Tolerates 15°F (-10°C), but damage to previous years' shoots can occur in winter.
*Size:* 70' - 100' (21 m - 30 m) high with a spread of 40' - 75' (12 m - 23 m).
*Color:* Light green leaf.
*Soil:* Grows in most soil conditions, but does best in well-drained, deep and moist soil.
*Maintenance:* Can be pruned to shape; remove dead limbs; has a long tap root.
*Problems:* Resents root disturbance, requires full sun or semi-partial shade.

C. OVATA **Shagbark Hickory**
A spectacular huge specimen. Zone 4b.

CARYOPTERIS X CLANDONENSIS
(ka-ri-OP-ter-is) ❧ **Bluebeard, Blue-spirea**
*ZONE:* From protected parts of 6 up.
*Origin:* East Asia.
*Value:* Good alone or in groups; makes a colorful interesting hedge.
*Hardiness:* Won't survive below 25°F (-5°C).
*Size:* 2' (60 cm) mounded.
*Color:* Bright blue flowers, felted gray foliage.
*Soil:* Any soil, but especially likes alkaline; loose and loamy is ideal, needs good drainage.
*Maintenance:* Cut back shoots to almost ground level in mid to late spring to encourage flowers which are borne on new growth of the season. This plant seeds like crazy and, so far, I've done not too badly with seedlings.
*Problems:* Winterkill, but nothing to worry about, they will come back.

CATALPA SPECIOSA (kat-ALP-a) ❧ **Northern Catalpa, Western Catalpa or Catawba**
*ZONE:* 4 to 8.
*Origin:* South-eastern United States.
*Value:* This is a glorious-looking tree for a substantial garden. Sabuco says this is not the weak-wooded tree it is reputed to be. Magnificent scented blooms in spring.
*Hardiness:* Takes hot summers and dry soil.
*Size:* 40' - 60' (12 m - 18 m) high, with a spread of 20' - 40' (6 m - 12 m). I have seen them 90' (27 m) high, which is not uncommon according to Wyman.
*Color:* Grayish brown trunks, medium green foliage turning yellow in fall. Leaves often fall before they turn; white flowers in June.
*Soil:* Prefers deep moist fertile soil; sun or part shade; withstands wet and dry soils.
*Maintenance:* Nothing special.
*Problems:* Catalpa midge (CECIDOMYIA CATAL-PAE) chews circular areas in leaves. First manifested as an infestation of tiny yellow maggots; adult is a fly appearing in late May or early June. Cultivate the soil beneath the tree to destroy the pupae. Catalpa Sphinx (CER-ATOMIA CATALPAE), a yellow and black caterpillar, completely strips leaves. Winters in pupal stage in the ground. Best control is to hand pick caterpillars. Rake up and burn or get rid of infected leaves. Keep the garden clean.

C. BIGNONIOIDES **Southern Catalpa**
Grows 30' - 40' (9 m - 12 m) high with equal spread; flowers are white with yellow spots in mid to late June; 'Nana' is a dwarf bushy form that rarely flowers. Zone 5 to 9.

CEANOTHUS AMERICANUS (see-an-O-thus)
❧ **New Jersey Tea, Redroot, Wild Snowball, Mountain Sweet** *ZONE:* 4 to 8.
*Origin:* Canada to South Carolina and Texas.
*Value:* Excellent for difficult areas.

*Hardiness:* The most hardy of the CEANOTHUS.
*Size:* 3' - 4' (1 m - 1.2 m) high and 3' - 5' (1 m - 1.5 m) wide.
*Color:* Dull green foliage with white odorless flowers in June and July; red fruits in fall.
*Soil:* Will thrive where the soil is too poor for other shrubs.
*Maintenance:* Prune back to point of origin of previous year's growth. Will often die back in a fierce winter, but flowers on current season's growth so blooms aren't lost. Cut after flowering. Does well against a wall.
*Problems:* Tip blight, root rot, black scale and Deodar weevil, which can be fended off with lots of compost and mulching.

C. X DELILIANUS *ZONE:* 7.
West Coast hybrid group that flowers in April and has evergreen leaves. 'Gloire de Versailles', pale blue flowers; 'Gloire de Platieres', deep blue flowers; 'Autumnal Blue', deep blue flowers.

C. OVATUS **Inland Ceanothus** *ZONE:* 5.
Native to New England; grows to a dense rounded 2' - 3' (.5 m - 1 m). Best for naturalizing though flowers are not showy; dry capsules turn bright red in July and August. This genus fixes nitrogen from atmosphere. Don't fertilize; likes dry soil.

C. VELUTINUS **Snowbrush** *ZONE:* 3.
Can grow in high Rockies. Likes dry infertile soil: Sabuco says this is the best CEANOTHUS for a wide variety of gardens. Leaves are shiny and leathery; flowers white and fragrant. Blooms in spring, often re-blooms in fall. Spreads by seed and stolon reproduction.

CELTIS OCCIDENTALIS (SELL-tis)
❧ **Common Hackberry** *ZONE:* 2 to 9.
*Origin:* Eastern North America.
*Value:* Similar in shape to elm.
*Hardiness:* Tolerates wind and dry conditions, full sun plus city grime.
*Size:* 40' - 60' (12 m - 18 m) high with a nearly equal spread; have been known to grow up to 120' (37 m).
*Color:* Light green foliage in summer, yellow-green in fall; bark is light grey-brown; fruit is fleshy orange-red to dark purple and ripens in September.
*Soil:* Prefers rich, deep, fertile, moist soils, but grows in dry, heavy or sandy soils.
*Maintenance:* Nothing special; transplants well in the spring.
*Problems:* Leaf spot, witches-broom, powdery mildew, scale, gall, fungus.

CERATOSTIGMA PLUMBAGINOIDES
(ser-at-OS-tig-ma) ❧ **Blue Ceratostigma**
*ZONE:* 5 to 6.
*Origin:* China.

*Value:* One of the splendors of autumn in the right place, this shrubby ground cover has brilliant color. Works well with lavenders and artemisias for textural contrast.
*Hardiness:* This is one of my favorite ground covers. It has 3 seasons of value.
*Size:* 6" - 12" (15 cm - 30 cm) high, 3' - 4' (1 m - 1.2 m) wide.
*Color:* The flowers are a marvelous cobalt blue in late summer; foliage turns brilliant red in fall, and is long lasting.
*Soil:* Tolerant of any soil.
*Maintenance:* Mulch in zone 5 and in the colder parts of zone 6. Expand your supply by taking vegetative cuttings in spring; plant them about 8" (20 cm) apart, if you want to make this a proper ground cover.
*Problems:* Winter dieback.

CERCIDIPHYLLUM JAPONICUM
(ser-sid-i-FILL-um) ❧ **Katsura Tree**
*ZONE:* 4 to 8.
*Origin:* Japan.
*Value:* A gorgeous tree—if you have room for only one more this is it. It's a shade tree and the loose foliage allows for good air circulation. Excellent as a street tree and for parks, golfways, residential properties, commercial areas, and around pools for shade.
*Hardiness:* Hardy, medium to fast grower.
*Size:* 40' - 60' (12 m - 18 m) high, but can reach 100' (30 m) in the wild.
*Color:* New leaves are reddish purple, changing to bluish green, then apricot in fall; they are heart-shaped and very beautiful.
*Soil:* Should be rich, moist well-drained soil. Acid soils enhance fall color. Needs full sun and water in dry hot season.
*Maintenance:* Nothing special.
*Problems:* None too serious, though some sun scalding and bark splitting.
C. J. 'Pendula', zone 5; a weeping variety with mounds of blue-green foliage creating the look of cascading water; fast growing, 15' - 25' (4.5 m - 8 m) high.

CERCIS CANADENSIS (SER-sis) ❧ **Redbud**
*ZONE:* 4 to 9; perhaps in 3.
*Origin:* North America.
*Value:* Good in shrub borders, woodlands.
*Size:* 20' - 30' (6 m - 9 m) high with a spread of 12' - 35' (3.5 m - 7.5 m).
*Color:* Purplish red flowers opening to rosy pink. In early April foliage is a lustrous green.
*Soil:* Does well in any soil.
*Maintenance:* Some pruning of dead branches may be necessary to allow more light into the tree canopy. Difficult to transplant so make sure it's properly sited.
*Problems:* Subject to canker and verticillium wilt.

Some cultivars: 'Forest Pansy', purple-leaved type, not hardy much below 10°F (-12.5°C); established plants can be wiped out over winter; loses its color in late May and becomes a dark green. 'Flame', double pink that is difficult to find. 'Pinkbud', true bright pink flower. 'Royal', white flowers. 'Silver Cloud', variegated leaves with creamy white splotches, best in shade.

### CERCIS CHINENSIS  Chinese Redbud

Grows 10' (3 m) high; erect, small rosy purple flowers, very showy in early spring; native to central China. 'Alba', white flower form, zone 5; grows 15' - 20' (4.5 m - 6 m); tolerates heat and humidity; sometimes attacked by stem canker or verticillium wilt, but not serious.

### CHAENOMELES JAPONICA (kee-NOM-ee-lees)

֎ Japanese Quince, Japanese Flowering Quince ZONE: 5 and sometimes 4, though not flower-bud hardy.
*Origin:* China.
*Value:* Good as a border shrub or an informal open hedge. Freestanding shrub, or against a wall it likes cool exposed areas.
*Hardiness:* Tolerates -15°F (-25°C).
*Size:* Approximately 3' (1 m).
*Color:* Flowers are orange-red or scarlet-red on year-old wood in April; fruit bright yellow; elliptic leaves light to dark green.
*Soil:* Any soil, but liable to chlorosis in very alkaline areas; full sun to heavy shade.
*Maintenance:* Remove previous year's growth after flowering unless training for espalier.
*Problems:* Very sharp thorns; prone to fungus disease, but simply remove the affected wood and get it right out of the garden.

### C. SPECIOSA

Zone 4 to 8; grows 6' - 10' (2 m - 3 m) high, with similar spread; flower color varies according to type, from scarlet to white or pink; yellowish green fruit used for jellies; good in poor soil and sun or shade; excellent for massive plantings, hedges; freestanding.

### CHAMAECYPARIS LAWSONIANA

(kam-ee-SIP-a-ris) ֎ Lawson Cypress, Port Orford Cedar ZONE: 5 to 7, possibly 8, but no excessive heat.
*Origin:* Coast of Oregon and California.
*Value:* Handsome pyramidal shape and graceful habit. There are numerous variations of form and color.
*Hardiness:* Does best in the moist atmosphere of the West Coast.
*Size:* 40' - 60' (12 m - 18 m) but can grow 140' - 180' (43 m - 55 m) in the wild.
*Color:* Deep green foliage, reddish brown bark, flowers steely blue, bluish green fruit.
*Soil:* Moist rich well-drained soil is best, but will survive high, dry climate and sandy soil. Thrives in full sun.

*Maintenance:* Nothing special.
*Problems:* A fungus, PHYTOPHTHORA LATERALIS, rots the root system and kills the tree. No satisfactory controls have been found. Some cultivars: (More than 200 in the trade.) 'Allumii', steel blue foliage, columnar form, zone 5. 'Argentea', silvery white leaves, zone 5. 'Erecta', columnar, dense foliage, bright green leaves, zone 5. 'Fletcheri', ornamental, excellent variety, close feathery blue foliage, pyramidal form, 12' - 20' (3.5 m - 6 m), zone 5.

### C. OBTUSA  Hinoki False Cypress ZONE: 4 to 8.

*Origin:* Japan.
*Value:* Good in rock gardens; dark green foliage is dense. It is considered one of the most attractive of its genus.
*Size:* 25' (8 m) in 20 years.
*Color:* Glossy green leaves, some whitish markers beneath, cones are orange-brown.
*Soil:* Needs sharp drainage.
*Maintenance:* Needs lots of water. Some cultivars: 'Aurea', yellow foliage tips. 'Crippsii', fernlike, golden yellow foliage. 'Erecta', ascending branches. 'Filicoides', straggly branches, frondlike. 'Gracilis', golden foliage, bronze in the winter, slow grower. 'Lycopodioides', cordlike, blue-green foliage. 'Magnifica', vigorous, wide, pyramidal, lustrous green fan-shaped foliage. 'Nana', slow growing compact.

### C. PISIFERA  Sawara Cypress, Japanese False Cypress ZONE: 3 to 8.

*Origin:* Japan.
*Value:* Good in rock gardens when small, but not so great when mature. Good accent plant and excellent for winter gardens. Too often used as foundation plantings.
*Size:* 50' - 70' (15 m - 21 m) high with 10' - 20' (3 m - 6 m) spread.
*Color:* Dark green foliage with a hint of silver-white.
*Soil:* Any conditions.
*Maintenance:* Constant pruning controls the growth; remove dead branches in the winter. Some cultivars: 'Filifera', 6' to 8' (2 m to 2.5 m), drooping foliage, forms a dense mound. 'Filifera Aurea', threadlike, golden yellow foliage. 'Plumosa', slightly feathery foliage, frondlike. 'Plumosa Aurea', soft, feathery, golden yellow foliage, retains color in summer. 'Squarrosa', very feathery, frondlike, soft gray-green in color. 'Boulevard' ('Squarrosa Cyanoviridis'), silver-gray, feathery, grayish blue in the winter.

### CHIMONANTHUS PRAECOX

(ky-mo-NAN-thus) ֎ Wintersweet
ZONE: 6 or 7, to 9.
*Origin:* China.

*Value:* In warmer, protected gardens, a wonderful winter shrub. Excellent for a shrub border and, because of its fragrance, along walkways and near entrances. Combine with other winter flowering shrubs.
*Hardiness:* Tolerates 15°F (-10°C); autumn growth; may die back in winter.
*Size:* After 5 years, 4' (1.2 m) by 3' (1 m), and after 20 years 8' (2.5 m) by 8' (2.5 m).
*Color:* Dark green foliage turns yellow in fall; flowers, borne in midwinter in mild climates, are fragrant, transparent, yellow.
*Soil:* Most soils, especially alkaline, full sun to light shade.
*Maintenance:* Nothing special.
*Problems:* Slow to flower; not bothered by diseases or pests.

### CHIONANTHUS VIRGINICUS (ky-o-NAN-thus)

֎ Fringetree, Old-man's-beard
ZONE: 3 to 9.
*Origin:* North America.
*Value:* Wonderful summer flowering shrub, an asset to any garden. Fragrant, best used around entrances. Its size allows for use in front of large buildings,
*Hardiness:* Extreme cold can cause dieback. Tolerant of air pollution.
*Size:* 12' - 20' (3.5 m - 6 m) in landscape situations; can grow taller in the wild.
*Color:* White fragrant flowers, dark green foliage, dark blue fruit.
*Soil:* Good in any soil; likes sun.
*Maintenance:* Can be shaped to control growth. Male and female need to fruit.
*Problems:* None serious; the occasional canker, leaf spot, and powdery mildew.

### CLEMATIS (KLEM-at-is)

Organize vines so that you've got them blooming through three seasons. They can scramble through shrubs, cover walls and trellises, trail along fences, around a door, up a tree, droop over a stone wall; and combine well with other climbers such as wisteria, flowering quince, akebia, and climbing roses. Interplant with tall plants that need no staking. There are over 230 species; those hardy in North America are divided into three groups:
*Group One:* Species and cultivars that flower early, usually on the previous season's stems—C. ALPINA; C. MACROPETALA and C. MONTANA.
*Group Two:* Cultivars that produce flowers on stems ripened the previous year. Early flowering, large-flowered cultivars include 'Nelly Moser', 'The President', 'Vyvyan Pennell', 'Marie Boisselot'.
*Group Three:* Jackmanii types that flower on new growth—C. HERACLEIFOLIA; C. INTEGRIFOLIA; C. ORIENTALIS; C. TEXENSIS and C. VITICELLA.

*Pruning instructions:*
The best guide is the plant itself—observe it carefully and you'll probably end up doing the right thing. However, there are general guidelines for each group.
*Group One:* Simple pruning is best, after flowering is over. Remove dead wood; attach to tree, shrub or lattice immediately. New growth will produce next year's flowers. First spring, cut back to 12" (30 cm); second year, cut back to 3' (1 m); third year and after, remove dead wood or any weak stems after flowering.
*Group Two:* Remove all dead wood and cut back by 6" - 10" (15 cm - 25 cm) to strongest pair of leaf axil buds. Tie into position immediately. First spring, cut back to 12" (30 cm); second year, cut back to 3' (1 m); third year and after, cut back to one pair of buds.
*Group Three:* Remove all the old top growth down to new leaf axil buds to about 30" (75 cm) by late winter. First year, cut back to 12" (30 cm); second spring and after, cut back to just above previous year's growth that is within 30" (75 cm) of the soil.
*Problems:* Leaf spot, stem rot, mites, clematis blister beetle and earwigs.
*Clematis Blister Beetle:* Larvae are C-shaped, white grayish grubs, adults are yellowish gray and exude a liquid causing blisters when it touches bare skin; holes in the leaves and flowers are evident. Control by handpicking; wear gloves; crush the beetle or drop into soapy water; one hortbuddy sprays the whole plant with hot soapy water and this seems to work.
*Wilt:* Considered the major blight: it's a fungus and once you spot it, remove the affected areas. If it recurs, you might have to pull up the whole plant, ditch it or cut out any affected part of the root system and give it a soak in soapy water and reposition the plant. Make sure you don't confuse wilt with starvation. If you plant vines too close to other plants, you have them in a rain shadow. Replant.

CLEMATIS X JACKMANII ❧ **Jackman Clematis, Group 3** *ZONE:* 3 to 8, possibly 9.
*Origin:* Continental Europe.
*Value:* This is the most popular of the hybrids in North American gardens.
*Hardiness:* Flowers until frost kills it off.
*Size:* 5' - 6' (1.5 m - 2 - m) unsupported and 18' (5.5 m) on a proper structure.
*Color:* Bright green leaves in summer, no fall color. Flowers are violet-purple borne in June.
*Soil:* Loamy, moist, well-drained mulched soil. Root system should be kept cool for ideal growing environment.

C. ALPINA
Native to the alps; zone 3 to 9; flowers in July and August, bluish with a rare white; well-drained soil, partial shade, shade the root; no

pruning required. 'Pamela Jackman', 'Ruby' are popular cultivars.

C. ARMANDII
Evergreen, fast growing vine that clings by tendrils; large glossy green leaves; fragrant white flowers that appear in March to May; low tolerance of cold. Origin China; zone 7. 'Hendersoni Rubra' is pink. 'Apple Blossom' is pale pink.

C. MACROPETALA
Lantern-shaped flowers; blooms in May; zone 5. 'Maidwell Hall', 'Markham's Pink'.

C. MAXIMOWICZIANA **Sweet Autumn Clematis**
White flowers; likes full sun; zone 4.

C. MONTANA
'Elizabeth', 'Picton's Variety', 'Pink Perfection', 'Rubens', 'Tetrarose'; zone 5.

C. ORIENTALIS, 'Bill Mackenzie'.

C. STANS
This clematis is almost shrubby, with glorious blue flowers and particularly lovely seedheads; zone 5.

C. TANGUTICA **Golden Clematis**
Bright yellow flowers in June to July; prune after flowering; origin China; zone 5.

C. TEXENSIS **Scarlet Clematis**
Red flowers July to October; full sun to light shade; zone 4. 'Duchess of Albany', 'Etoile Rose', 'Gravetye Beauty'.

C. VITALBA **Prairie Traveller's Joy**
White blooms June to September; ornamental seed head; grows 50' (15 m) a year; zone 5.

C. VITICELLA **Virgin's Bower**
Parent of C. X JACKMANII; blooms range through the blues to purple; good color range from June to September; doesn't succumb to clematis wilt; looks good in trees and shrubs. 'Blue Belle', 'Polish Spirit' (purple-blue). Adaptable to zone 2.

*Large Flowered Hybrid Cultivars:* Except where indicated, these require pruning after bloom is over to keep within bounds. zone 3, unless indicated otherwise.
'Barbara Jackman', hardy to -5°F (-20°C), deep violet, striped deep carmine, flowers from May to June and again September. Plant away from the sun to prevent fading of flowers; light pruning only. 'Comtesse de Bouchard', medium-sized satiny pink flowers June to August, vigorous grower, hardy to -5°F (-20°C), requires hard pruning. 'Gillian Blades', white ruffled flowers May to June and again in September. Zone 4. 'Jackmanii Rubra', vigorous form of double flowers in midsummer, deep red, doubles on old wood, single blooms until frost, pruning required. 'Nelly Moser', the most common of all. Zone 4. 'Ramona', large lavender-blue flowers with dark anthers, June flowers on old wood, light

pruning. 'Ville de Lyon', July to October flowers carmine to crimson; zone 4.

*Clematis as Ground Cover:* Many species clematis can flop over the ground looking wonderful, but don't tread on them. You can use C. ALPINA; C. MACROPETALA; C. MONTANA and C. TEXENSIS as ground covers. If you run clematis through a hybrid tea rose border it will cover up unsightly legs and the soil. Combine clematis with other low-growing plants, such as the heathers, as suggested by clematis guru Raymond Evison. The other standard text is by Christopher Lloyd. See **bibliography** page 203.

CLETHRA ALNIFOLIA (KLETH-ra)
❧ **Summer-sweet, White Alder**
*ZONE:* 3 to 9.
*Origin:* Eastern North America and East Asia.
*Value:* Summer flower, July into August, shrub border. Bees love it and the fragrance is wonderful around sitting areas. Clean looking in the winter garden. Good in woodland settings.
*Hardiness:* 5°F (-15°C); protect young plants from the frost.
*Size:* 3" - 8" (7.5 cm - 20 cm) high, and 4" - 6" (10 cm - 15 cm) wide.
*Color:* Fluffy white to pink flowers in early fall; fruit remains in winter. Leaves light green with toothed edge, stems light gray to green.
*Soil:* Acid, dislikes alkaline; prefers light shade, but tolerates sun.
*Maintenance:* Nothing special required.
Some cultivars: 'Paniculata', large flowers, zone 5, superior variety. 'Pink Spires', pink to rose, European form, zone 5. 'Rosea', buds pink, fade to pinkish white, glossy green foliage, particularly beautiful, zone 5.

C. ACUMINATA **Cinnamon Clethra**
A suckering shrub, 8' - 12' (2.5 m - 3.5 m), dark green leaves and white fragrant flowers in July, zone 5; grows on dry, rocky, gravelly mountainsides in the wild.

C. TOMENTOSA **Woolly Summersweet**
Similar to C. ALNIFOLIA, downy stems, larger leaves, white fragrant flowers in August to September, grows 6' - 8' (2 m - 2.5 m); zone 5.

CORNUS ALBA (KOR-nus) ❧ **Tartarian Dogwood, Tatarian Dogwood**
*ZONE:* 2 to 8, but best not too far south.
*Origin:* Siberia to Manchuria and through North Korea.
*Value:* Best in shrub border. Can be clipped into a formal hedge. Large masses effective around ponds and large areas. Spreads rapidly under ideal conditions.
*Hardiness:* Tolerates temperatures as low as -15°F (-25°C); full sun to mid-shade.
*Size:* 8' - 10' (2.5 m - 3 m) high, spreads 5' - 10' (1.5 m - 3 m).

*Color:* Stems turn blood red in the winter, leaves a yellow-green in spring, dark green in summer, and purple-red in fall. May to June flowers are bright yellow, some flowering in the summer.

*Soil:* Does well in any soil, including wet. Moisture produces stronger roots.

*Maintenance:* Cut back every second year in late spring for the strong red new shoots, which provide winter interest.

*Problems:* Leaf blight, leaf spot, powdery mildew, twig blight, leaf miner, scales, crown canker, root rot, borer. Dogwood club-gall: club-shaped swellings, 1" (2.5 cm) long, on twig or flower; reddish brown midge attacks in late May, orange larvae drop to ground in early fall.

Some varieties: **'Elegantissima'**, silverleaf dogwood is a favorite. I plant it in the shade to keep the grayish leaves with creamy white edges protected from the sun. **'Sibirica'**, a clone, is the hardiest; **'Westonbirt'**, bright coral red stems and rounded leaves; is best on current season's growth, so watch when pruning; fruit is bluish. Zone 2. **'Spaethii'**, yellow-margined leaves form a bushy clump, very hardy; bright color all season; will take more sun than other cultivars. Zone 2.

CORNUS ALTERNIFOLIA **'Argentea'**, a very pretty form with variegated leaves, shrubby habit. Zone 3b.

C. CONTROVERSA **'Variegata'**, an ornamental small tree with yellowish white edged leaves. Grows to 60' (18 m). Zone 5.

C. FLORIDA ❦ **Flowering Dogwood Tree**
*ZONE:* 5 to 9. Dirr feels 5 is pushing it unless the parent tree is also zone 5, but no other author mentions this. Wyman says 4 to 9 and Cole says 6. Take your chances.

*Origin:* Eastern United States.

*Value:* Has character for 4 seasons. Excellent near patios, large buildings, in parks and in groupings.

*Hardiness:* Full sun, tolerates 15°F (-10°C).

*Size:* 40' (12 m) maximum, 20' (6 m) seems average.

*Color:* Young stems are purple, gradually turning gray; dark green leaf in summer, fall color red to purplish; flowers are unimportant—greenish yellow according to Dirr, but everyone else says white bracts.

*Soil:* Neutral to acid, dislikes alkaline.

*Maintenance:* Nothing special.

*Problems:* Numerous diseases and pests affect the dogwood; it seems the more stressed the tree, the more susceptible to canker, borer and various petal and leaf spot; plant in ideal conditions and hope for the best. In the east this plant is affected terribly by anthracnose.

Some varieties: **'Apple blossom'**, light pink flowers, shading to white, zone 6. **'Cherokee Chief'**, ruby red flowers, zone 7. **'Cloud 9'**,

slow growing, showy white flowers, zone 7. **'Hohman's Gold'**, variegated golden yellow and green foliage, turns deep red in fall, zone 7. **'Pendula'**, weeping, white flowers, zone 6. **'Rainbow'**, variegated yellow and green, turns red with white bracts in spring, zone 7. **'Spring Song'**, deep rose-red flowers, zone 7. **'White Cloud'**, creamy white flowers, zone 7.

CORNUS KOUSA ❦ **Japanese Dogwood, Kousa** *ZONE:* 5 to 8.

*Origin:* Japan and Korea.

*Value:* Handsome small shrub, works well in the shrub border or as foundation planting. Gorgeous strawberry-like flowers appear in June when most shrubs have finished flowering. Attracts birds in winter. After 20 years this becomes a small tree with a top that nods to one side rather puckishly. Blooms 3 weeks after C. FLORIDA.

*Hardiness:* Prefers light shade, but tolerates full sun. Must have sun to fruit well.

*Size:* 20' - 30' (6 m - 9 m) high, equal spread.

*Color:* Large creamy white flowers, turn pinkish white in fall; foliage is dense, dark green in summer turning reddish purple to scarlet in fall; stems of older wood are multicolored gray-tan rich brown.

*Soil:* Neutral to acid, moist conditions, tolerates slightly alkaline.

*Maintenance:* Avoid pruning.

C. KOUSA var. CHINENSIS **Chinese Dogwood**
Grows 30' - 40' (9 m - 12 m) high and just as wide; produces large flower, zone 6. **'Milky Way'**, broad bushy form of CHINENSIS, suitable for small landscapes; an American variety, large white flowers, zone 6.

CORNUS MAS ❦ **Cornelian Cherry, Sorbet**
*ZONE:* 4 to 8, but not as robust in 8.

*Origin:* Central and southern Europe.

*Value:* A hedge screen and winter-flowering shrub that can be grown to a small tree. Highly recommended.

*Hardiness:* Tolerates 5°F (-15°C); full sun and light shade.

*Size:* 20' - 25' (6 m - 8 m) high, 15' - 20' (4.5 m - 6 m) wide.

*Color:* Dark green leaves, yellow flowers on bare stems in late winter or early spring, stem is light green to gray.

*Soil:* Any soil.

*Maintenance:* Nothing special.

Some varieties: **'Alba'**, white fruit. **'Flava'**, yellow fruit, big and sweet. **'Nana'**, low growing, small-leaved. **'Variegata'**, creamy white leaves.

CORYLOPSIS PAUCIFLORA (ko-ry-LOP-sis) ❦ **Buttercup Winter Hazel** *ZONE:* 6.

*Origin:* Japan.

*Value:* Flowers mid to late April. Ideal for woodlands and as a freestanding shrub or in the shrub border.

*Hardiness:* Protect from wind, full sun and alkaline soils.

*Size:* 4' - 6' (1.2 m - 2 m).

*Color:* Primrose-yellow flowers, leaves give good fall color with orange-red shading, stem is medium brown.

*Soil:* Best on neutral soil, dislikes alkalinity.

*Maintenance:* Nothing special.

C. SPICATA **Spike Winter Hazel**
Wide spreading, 4' - 6' (1.2 m - 2 m) high, yellow fragrant flowers in mid-April; leaves are blue-green; prefers light to medium shade, neutral soil; slow to establish; zone 5.

CORYLUS AMERICANA (KO-ry-lus) ❦ **American Filbert, American Hazelnut**
*ZONE:* Sabuco says zone 2.

*Origin:* North America.

*Value:* Shade tolerant, thicket-forming shrub, very early blooming. Though too big for most city properties, it's excellent for naturalizing on a large country property.

*Hardiness:* Tolerates winter temperatures down to -15°F (-25°C).

*Size:* 15' - 18' (4.5 - 5.5 m) high; spread is ⅔ of the height.

*Color:* Dark green leaf in summer, yellowish green with red tint in the fall, male catkins brownish and long; very showy in the spring.

*Soil:* Any soil, wet or dry.

*Maintenance:* Nothing special.

*Problems:* Blight that injures leaves and branches.

C. AVELLANA **European Filbert, European Hazelnut**
Grows 12' - 20' (3.5 to 6 m); dense thicket of stems, native to Europe and North Africa; prized for the nut, zone 4 to 7. **'Aurea'**, yellow leaf, weak growing, zone 5. **'Contorta'**, (Harry Lauder's Walking Stick)—8' - 10' (2.5 m - 3 m), the stems' twisted and curled form makes an impressive winter statement. Dramatic effect when back lit. **'Fusco-rubra'**, a purple form, zone 5. **'Pendula'**, weeping branches, 8' (2.5 m) high, zone 5.

C. COLURNA ❦ **Turkish Filbert or Turkish Hazelnut** *ZONE:* 4 to 7.

*Origin:* Southeast Europe and Western Asia.

*Value:* Good for lawns and street lining. Similar to maple but isn't subject to scorching.

*Hardiness:* Thrives in hot summers and cold winters; tolerant of adverse conditions.

*Size:* 40' - 50' (12 m - 15 m) high.

*Color:* Dark green leaves, yellow to purple in fall; catkins in early spring can be attractive; fruit is grouped together in threes.

*Soil:* Loamy well-drained soil is preferred; full sun; drought tolerant.

*Maintenance:* Nothing special.

**CORYLUS CORNUTA Beaked Filbert, Beaked Hazelnut**

Native to North America, this refined shrub grows 4' - 6' (1.2 m - 2 m) high and just as wide. Known for its beaked fruits, will survive under willow. Leaves often persist through winter; zone 2.

**C. MAXIMA 'Purpurea' Purple Giant Filbert**

Similar to C. AVELLANA, except dark purple leaves in early spring, catkins retain purplish cast, leaves fade to green in summer; reaches 15' - 20' (4.5 m - 6 m); native to Europe. Zone 4 to 8.

**COTINUS COGGYGRIA (ko-TY-nus) ⚘ Smoke Tree, Smokebush** *ZONE:* 5 to 8.

*Origin:* Central and southern Europe.
*Value:* Good for the shrub border, masses or groupings, fall color, specimen plant; the color links the deeper greens and the lighter foliage.
*Hardiness:* To -30°F (-35°C); tips of new growth can experience winter dieback.
*Size:* 10' - 15' (3 m - 4.5 m) high.
*Color:* Blue-green leaves in summer and yellow-red-purple in fall; hairs pass through several colors, but are best when they are a smoky pink, June to September.
*Soil:* Prefers rich deep soil, but tolerates any.
*Maintenance:* Plant only in spring or fall. Prune to the ground for the first few years, but leave mature plants unpruned to give full flowering potential. Prune out dead wood and mature shoots every 3 or 4 years.
Some varieties: **'Purpureus'**, leaves are green, inflorescences a shade of pink; zone 5. **'Royal Purple'**, foliage is a rich maroon, darkens to purple, inflorescences are purplish red, color does not fade, zone 5. **'Velvet Cloak'**, dark purple leaf, fall color is red, zone 5.

**COTONEASTER APICULATUS (kah-toe-nee-AS-ter) ⚘ Cranberry Cotoneaster** *ZONE:* 4 to 7, best in colder climates.

*Origin:* China.
*Value:* This low shrub works well on banks, walls where it can hang down, or as edging in shrub border. Also used as ground cover.
*Hardiness:* -15°F (-25°C); full sun to medium shade.
*Size:* 3' - 6' (1 m - 2 m) spread.
*Color:* Glossy green foliage; pink flowers in May; fruit is cranberry red, August to frost.
*Soil:* Any.
*Maintenance:* Dense foliage prevents thorough cleaning, fall leaves are difficult to remove, prune only to within bounds. In colder areas, spring pruning of winter-damaged wood is essential and helps keep plants shapely.
*Problems:* Mites in dry conditions, fire blight.

**C. ADPRESSUS Creeping Cotoneaster**

Dwarf, compact, rigidly branched, 1' - 2' (30 cm - 60 cm) high, spreading up to 6' (2 m). Glossy green leaves; flowers are in pairs and white-tipped rose color; fruit is red, hardy in zone 4.

**C. DAMMERI Bearberry Cotoneaster**

*ZONE:* 5 to 8.
*Origin:* Central China.
*Value:* Good as ground cover on banks or slopes, also in shrub border. Covers large area quickly.
*Hardiness:* Fast growing.
*Size:* 1' - 1.5' (30 cm - 45 cm) high, 6' (2 m) spread.
*Color:* Dark green leaf, in winter purplish leaf, flowers white in late May, fruit in late summer is bright red.
*Soil:* Adaptable, but prefers well-drained areas.
*Maintenance:* Resistant to fire blight and scab. In colder areas, spring pruning of winter-damaged wood is essential and helps keep plants shapely.
Some cultivars: **'Coral Beauty'**, pink, zone 4. **'Lowfast'**, extremely hardy, glossy foliage, zone 4. **'Major'**, vigorous, zone 4. **'Moon Creeper'**, low growing mat form, dark foliage, zone 4. **'Skogholm'**, covers fast.

**C. DIELSIANUS ⚘ Diel's Cotoneaster**

*ZONE:* 5.
*Origin:* China.
*Value:* Great way to break up a foliage bed.
*Hardiness:* Very hardy and easy to grow.
*Size:* 6' (2 m) high.
*Color:* Red leaves in autumn with small red fruits.
*Soil:* Almost any.

**C. DIVARICATUS Spreading Cotoneaster**

*ZONE:* 4 to 7.
*Origin:* Central and western China.
*Value:* Multifaceted shrub that blends well in hedges, borders, foundation plantings, masses or groupings.
*Hardiness:* Deciduous in all zones.
*Size:* 5' - 6' (1.5 m - 2 m) high, spreads to 8' (2.5 m).
*Color:* Leaf is dark glossy green, flowers rose in late May to early June, masked by the foliage; fruit is dark red.
*Soil:* Any.
*Maintenance:* In colder areas, spring pruning of winter-damaged wood is essential and helps keep plants shapely.

**C. HORIZONTALIS Rockspray or Rock Cotoneaster** *ZONE:* 4.

*Origin:* Western China.
*Value:* Good on banks, slopes or in mass plantings. Also used as ground cover and can be espaliered very successfully.
*Hardiness:* Possible winterkill in extreme cold.
*Size:* 2' - 3' (.5 m -1 m) high, and 5' - 8' (1.5 m - 2.5 m) in spread.

*Color:* Glossy dark green leaves, turning purplish and holding to November; flowers are perfect pink mid-May to early June; small fruit in August is red.
*Soil:* Any conditions.

**C. LUCIDUS Hedge Cotoneaster** *ZONE:* 3 to 7.

*Origin:* Siberia and northern Asia.
*Value:* Primarily used as a hedge.
*Hardiness:* Withstands dry climate and poor conditions.
*Size:* 5' - 10' (1.5 m - 3 m) high, just as wide.
*Color:* Dark green leaf, turning yellow to red in fall; flower pinkish white in May, insignificant; berrylike fruit is black and holds through winter.
*Soil:* Any conditions.
*Maintenance:* Prune anytime.
*Problems:* Leaf spot, canker, fire blight, scale, spider mites and cotoneaster webworm. Cotoneaster webworm is manifested by pale yellow or green caterpillars, 1" (2.5 cm) long. They attack in August—find web nests by locating leaves skeletonized from webworm feeding, cut out and remove nests, spray with Bacillus Thuringiensis every 3 days.

**CRATAEGUS (krat-EE-gus) ⚘ Hawthorn**

*ZONE:* 3 to 7.
*Origin:* North America.
*Value:* Great for avenues, streets and large areas. Gorgeous orange, red or pinky fall color. Takes enormous stress.
*Hardiness:* Tolerates -15°F (-25°C); will take some shade.
*Size:* 20' - 30' (6 m - 9 m) high, with spread of 20' - 35' (6 m - 11 m).
*Color:* Small white florets produced in clusters; mid-green leaves, yellow or orange fall color; fruit clusters in fall are orange or crimson.
*Soil:* Any, but not dry soil. Can tolerate poor soil.
*Maintenance:* Can cut back for shaping.
*Problems:* Fire blight, lace bug, leaf miners, Japanese beetle.

**CRYPTOMERIA JAPONICA (krip-to-MEER-ia) ⚘ Japanese Cedar, Japanese Cryptomeria**

*ZONE:* Warmer parts of 5 and 6, south to zones 8 and 9.
*Origin:* Japan.
*Value:* Useful as a street tree.
*Hardiness:* Will take -22°F (-30°C); cannot cope with wind.
*Size:* Maximum 100' (30 m), average range is 20' - 30' (6 m - 9 m).
*Color:* Leaves are blue-green in summer, needles take on a bronzy tone during winter, becoming green again in spring; cones are globular and brownish.
*Soil:* Any conditions.
*Maintenance:* Nothing special.

*Problems:* Leaf blight, leaf spot.

Some varieties: There are over 50. The following are all zone 6: '**Compacta**', compact and conical, 45' (14 m) high, short needles, stiff and bluish. '**Elegans**', tall, bushy, 9' - 15' (3 m - 4.5 m) high, soft feathery green foliage, turns brown-red in winter. '**Elegans Nana**', similar to above, but flattened, 3' (1 m) high, slow growing, bluish green to purple-tinged in winter. '**Globosa**', dense, neat, dome-shaped, grows 2' - 3' (.5 m - 1 m) high, bluish green, foliage turns rusty red in winter. '**Lobbii**', pyramidal, dense, compact, grows to 60' (18 m), glossy green needles do not change color. '**Sekkan-sugi**', broad column, grows 3' - 4' (1 m - 1.5 m), branching upright, loose pendulous inner foliage, yellow in winter, creamy white in summer.

## X CUPRESSOCYPARIS LEYLANDII (kew-press-o-SIP-aris) ❦ Leyland Cypress

*ZONE:* 6, possibly 5, to 10.
*Value:* Makes an excellent evergreen screen, hedging or grouping. Good accent; makes a light airy backdrop for any garden.
*Hardiness:* Withstands salt spray, any soil condition and grows fast.
*Size:* 60' - 70' (18 m - 21 m), can grow to 100' (30 m) in natural habitat.
*Color:* Leaf a bluish green, bark a reddish brown, cone-shaped fruit.
*Soil:* Adaptable to any soil.
*Maintenance:* Withstands heavy pruning for shaping or hedging purposes. Easy to transplant but not easy to propagate—cuttings taken in late March may be successful.
C. L. '**Castlewellan Gold**', yellow foliage, a hybrid, grows over 100' (30 m) in zone 7.

## CYTISUS X PRAECOX (SIT-is-us) ❦ Warminster Broom *ZONE:* 5.

*Origin:* Europe.
*Value:* Fragrant when in flower.
*Hardiness:* Has been known to tolerate -30°F (-35°C).
*Size:* 6' (2 m).
*Color:* Dark green with pealike yellow blossoms in May and June.
*Soil:* Sandy, not too rich.
*Maintenance:* According to Sabuco, do not use nitrogen fertilizer, phosphorus, or potassium more than once in 5 years. Don't prune or the shape will be wrecked.
Some cultivars: '**Albus**', white. '**Allgold**', flowers earlier, 5' (1.5 m). '**Goldspear**', golden flowers, 3' (1 m).

## CYTISUS SCOPARIUS Common Broom, Scotch Broom *ZONE:* 5b to 8.

*Origin:* Europe.
*Value:* Can take harsh sites.
*Hardiness:* Prefers sandy soil; water for sun and wind scorch in winter.
*Size:* 6' (2 m).

*Color:* Stems of olive green; flowers are vivid yellow.
*Soil:* Sandy soil; rich medium will cause winter dieback.
*Maintenance:* Protect the stems from winter sun and wind with mulch.
*Problems:* Nothing special.

## DAPHNE CNEORUM (DAFF-ne) ❦ Rose Daphne *ZONE:* 4 to 7, Sabuco says zone 3.

*Origin:* Central and southern Europe.
*Value:* Evergreen ground cover especially good for rock gardens and slightly shady spots.
*Hardiness:* Protect over the winter with pine boughs and mulch to maintain moist soil. Plant in partial shade; in coastal areas full sun.
*Size:* 6" - 12" (15 cm - 30 cm) high and spreading up to 10' (3 m), usually at least 4' (1.2 m).
*Color:* Leaf color is deep green throughout the year, rosy pink flowers in April and May, and again in late summer; fruit berry is a yellowish brown.
*Soil:* Well-drained, moist, neutral, slightly gritty soil. Needs a cool root run and hates wet soil. Water only when they've been dry for 10 or more days.
*Maintenance:* Doesn't need fertilizing. Does not move readily; transplant as a container plant in the early spring or early fall.
*Problems:* Genetic virus causes mature plants to die suddenly.

### D. X BURKWOODII  Burkwood Daphne

Creamy white flowers with a pink tinge, fragrant, borne in May; grows 3' - 4' (1 m - 1.2 m) high; semi-green foliage; easily cultivated in summer with cuttings; zone 4.

### D. GENKWA  Lilac Daphne

Grows 3' - 4' (1 m - 1.2 m); deciduous; slender branches, lilac flowers produced during May; native to China or Korea; zone 5.

### D. GIRALDII  Giraldi Daphne

Deciduous bushy shrub grows 2' - 3' (.5 m - 1 m); flowers are fragrant, golden yellow, borne in May; red berries mature in July, quite hardy, zone 3, native to northwest China.

### D. MEZEREUM  February Daphne

Semi-evergreen deciduous shrub, fragrant flowers are lilac to rosy purple, red berries in June. Grows up to 5' (1.5 m) high and just as wide,  All sources indicate that this plant lasts about 5 to 10 years and then croaks. China, zone 5.

### D. ODORA  Winter Daphne

Fragrant winter shrub; origin is Japan and China; rose, pink or white flowers; may need winter protection; at maturity up to 5' (1.5 m) high and similar spread; zone 5.

## DAVIDIA INVOLUCRATA (dav-ID-ia)  ❦ Dove Tree, Handkerchief Tree *ZONE:* 6.

*Origin:* China.
*Value:* Spectacular specimen, similar to linden in shape. Slow to establish.
*Hardiness:* Not hardy as a young tree, but does well once established.
*Size:* Up to 60' (18 m).
*Color:* Bright green leaf in summer, no fall color, flowers borne in mid-May, white with red tips; bract is creamy white.
*Soil:* Well-drained and moist, water in summer if drought, likes light shade, tolerates sun with moist soil.
*Maintenance:* Prune only if necessary; difficult to propagate; cuttings in January work about 20% of the time.

## DEUTZIA GRACILIS (DOIT-zia) ❦ Slender Deutzia *ZONE:* 5 to 8.

*Origin:* China and Japan.
*Value:* Good for hedges, borders, group plantings or as a stand-alone shrub; beautiful when in flower but bedraggled the rest of the season. If you have limited space and want a showy shrub, plant something else—this one is too much trouble for little gain.
*Hardiness:* Tolerates -15°F (-25°C); full sun or light shade, needs snow or mulch to keep from stem tip damage.
*Size:* Grows to 6' (2 m), average of 2' - 4' (.5 m - l.2 m) high and 3' - 4' (1 m - 1.2 m) wide.
*Color:* Flat green foliage in summer, white flowers borne in May smother the shrub for about 2 weeks.
*Soil:* Any good garden soil; prefers moist soil but will grow in dry soil if watered.
*Maintenance:* Prune dead wood and at least one-third of the oldest flowering wood after flowering; easily rooted from softwood any time during the growing season.
*Problems:* May not survive drought, requires pruning each year, flowering period is short.

### D. G. '**Nikko**' is a dwarf shrub 2' - 3' (.5 m - 1 m) high by 8' - 12' (2.5 m - 3.5 m) wide; white flowers in May; leafs out early; zone 5.

### D. X ELEGANTISSIMA, fragrant with good fall color; needs tip-pruning occasionally; remove non-flowering stems every 3 years. '**Rosalind**', very handsome plant with dark pink flowers, zone 5.

## D. X LEMOINEI  Lemoine Deutzia *ZONE:* 4.

*Origin:* China.
*Value:* Few problems and never requires corrective pruning.
*Hardiness:* Very hardy.
*Size:* Rounded from 4' - 7' (1.2 m - 2 m).
*Color:* White flowers, dark green foliage.
*Soil:* Any garden soil, very adaptable.
*Maintenance:* Prune after flowering.

*Problems:* Unruly without creative pruning. D. × L. **'Compacta'**, dwarf dense 3' (1 m) shrub; hardiest of all; zone 4.

### DEUTZIA × MAGNIFICA **Showy Deutzia**
ZONE: 5.
*Value:* Excellent flower display.
*Size:* Grows up to 6' (2 m), but 8' (2.5-m) plants have been seen.
*Color:* Double white flowers in mid-May.
*Soil:* Prefers moist soil but any garden soil will do.
*Maintenance:* Prune after flowering.
Clones: **'Eburnea'**, single white flowers are bell-shaped. **'Erecta'**, single white flowers, erect panicles. **'Latifolia'**, single white flowers, wide spreading. **'Longipetala'**, single long white flowers, narrow petals. **'Staphyleoides'**, white reflexed single flowers.

D. × ROSEA has pink petals outside, paler inside; spreading plant with arching branches, grows 3' (1 m) high, zone 6.

### ELAEAGNUS ANGUSTIFOLIA (el-ee-AG-nus)
❧ **Russian Olive** ZONE: 2 to 7.
*Origin:* Southern Europe to western and central Asia.
*Value:* Good for roadside plantings, withstands wind, salt, and poor growing conditions; excellent privacy screen. I love this plant both for the silvery foliage and the general feeling of age its twisted boughs lend to a garden.
*Hardiness:* Very hardy, fast grower.
*Size:* Up to 20' (6 m) high, similar width; some grow 30' - 40' (9 m - 12 m).
*Color:* Gray foliage is outstanding, silver-gray flowers in June.
*Soil:* Grows in any soil, but does best in sandy loams; full sun.
*Maintenance:* Can stand creative pruning to keep its interesting shape. Transplants easily.
*Problems:* Leaf spot, canker, rusts, crown gall.

### E. COMMUTATA **Silverberry**
This wide shrub grows 6' - 12' (2 m - 3.5 m) high, suckers easily; fragrant yellow flowers in May, silvery white foliage, very untidy in growth habit. Propagate from suckers at the base. Great Plains native, zone 2 to 6.

### E. MULTIFLORA **Cherry Elaeagnus**
Wide-spreading shrub, 6' - 10' (2 m - 3.5 m) high and just as wide; silvery green foliage; red fruit in June and July; good for the birds; flowers are fragrant and silvery green, similar to the underside of the foliage; origin is China and Japan; zone 5 to 7.

### E. UMBELLATA **Autumn Elaeagnus**
Grows 12' - 18' (3.5 m - 5.5 m) high, wide spreading; foliage is bright green above and silver green beneath; fragrant silvery white flowers in May and June; fruits are silvery brown and turn red when ripe in September; prefers loamy and sandy soil; excellent drought tolerance; China, Korea, Japan; zone 3 to 8.

### ELSHOLTZIA STAUNTONII (el-SHOLT-zia)
❧ **Mint Shrub** ZONE: 5.
*Origin:* Northern China.
*Value:* Can be planted on balconies. Profuse bloomer in fall. Minty scent.
*Size:* 2' - 3' (.5 m - 1 m) high. In warm zones grows up to 5' (1.5 m).
*Color:* Dark green foliage on top and light green with dots beneath; flowers of lavender to lilac to pink bloom in September.
*Soil:* Well-drained soil in a sunny location.
*Maintenance:* Though not strictly necessary, prune before new growth begins, as flowers bloom on the new wood. Propagates easily from cuttings during growing season.

### ENKIANTHUS CAMPANULATUS (en-ki-ANTH-us)
❧ **Redvein Enkianthus** ZONE: 5 to 7.
*Origin:* Japan.
*Value:* Excellent for color, good for patio gardens. It should be placed so that the gorgeous campanula-like bells can be appreciated up close. Needs consistent moisture to do well.
*Hardiness:* Does not grow tall in cold areas.
*Size:* 6' - 8' (2 m - 2.5 m) in cold climates; can grow to 30' (9 m) where it's warmer.
*Color:* Foliage is almost blue-green, brilliant red-orange in the fall, creamy yellow flowers borne in May to June, dainty and delicate.
*Soil:* Acid soil in full sun or partial shade; prefers rich soil.
*Maintenance:* Remove one shoot each year to rejuvenate old plants.

### ERICA **Heath**
A marvelously undemanding small shrub or ground cover that gives year-round pleasure in a variety of foliage hues and blossom colors.

### E. HERBACEA (Syn. E. CARNEA) ZONE: 4.
Leaves are similar to CALLUNA.
*Origin:* Central and southern Europe.
*Value:* Makes a good ground cover around shrubs since it won't compete with root systems. Combines well with rhododendrons. Ericas make a wonderful contrast with hellebores and EUPHORBIA MYRSINITES. Plant spring bulbs under them. Attract bees.
*Hardiness:* Needs protection from wind and winter sun. This heath tolerates lime.
*Size:* 8" (20 cm).
*Color:* Foliage is bronzy green in summer and red-bronze in winter; blooms pink to red. Will bloom January to May in zone 7; February to June in zone 6; March to June in zone 5; April to July in zone 4.
*Soil:* Coarse, does better in neutral to slightly acid soil.
*Maintenance:* Trim lightly after flowering; if it dries out from winter wind and sun, cut back to green; mulch lightly.
*Problems:* Nothing serious.

Some varieties: **'Mediterranean Pink'**, zone 5. The following are all zone 6: **'Mediterranean White'**. **'Vivellii'**, dense needlelike foliage. **'Springwood Pink'**. **'Springwood White'**. **'Ruby Glow'**. **'Pink Beauty'**.

### E. CINEREA **Bell Heather, Scotch Heather**
ZONE: 6.
*Origin:* Western Europe.
*Value:* A gorgeous low spreading ground cover for large rock gardens or banks of mass plantings.
*Hardiness:* Tolerates 5°F (-15°C).
*Size:* 1' (30 cm) high, 1' (30 cm) spread.
*Color:* Hanging bell-shaped white flower, borne in midsummer to early autumn, dark green leaves in summer, purplish in fall.
*Soil:* Neutral to acid; full sun to light shade.
*Maintenance:* Trim lightly after flowering.
*Problems:* Susceptible to drought, protect with mulch; protect from wind chill and prolonged freezing.
The following cultivars are all zone 6: **'Alba Minor'**, white flowers, dwarf. **'Atropurpurea'**, deep pink. **'C.D. Eason'**, dark red-pink. **'Cindy'**, purple. **'Contrast'**, deep purple, bronze leaves. **'Eden Valley'**, lilac and white. **'Foxhollow'**, mahogany-maroon. **'Golden Drop'**, pink flowers, orange leaves. **'Knaphill Pink'**, deep pink flowers, olive foliage. **'Lavender Lady'**, pink and red. **'Pentreath'**, rich red-purple. **'Pink Ice'**, deep purple. **'Patrick'**, deep purple. **'Rosabelle'**, salmon, dwarf. **'Rozanne Waterer'**, maroon flowers, purple leaves. **'Stephen Davis'**, scarlet flowers. **'Vivienne Patricia'**, soft purple.

### E. × DARLEYENSIS **Darley Heath**
Origin England; good ground cover for large rock gardens; colors of flowers range from white to pink to dark pink; dark green foliage; tolerates 5°F (-15°C); neutral to acid soil; full sun to light shade; protect with mulch in winter; zone 5. **'Arthur Johnson'**; **'Darley Dale'**; **'Silberschmelze'**; **'George Rendell'**.

### E. ERIGENA **Mediterranean Heath**
Originally from southern France, Spain and Northern Ireland; use for mass plantings and rock gardens; flower is small, hanging, narrow, fragrant and bell-shaped, in shades of white and pink, borne in early to late spring; full sun to light shade; trim after flowering; same problems as other species; at maturity 3' by 3' (1 m by 1 m); zone 7.

### E. TERMINALIS **Corsican Heather**
Origin western Mediterranean and Northern Ireland; upright shrub for groupings or single plantings; flower is small, pink and bell-shaped, borne in late summer; foliage dark green; does well in both acid and alkaline soils; full sun to light shade; 3' (1 m) high, 2½' (.7 m) spread; zone 7.

ERICA TETRALIX **Cross-leaved Heather, Bog Heather**

Sabuco says this shrub is adaptable to the warmest parts of zone 3 and has a long period of bloom. Must be kept out of wind; origin western Europe; bell-shaped flowers pure white and shades of pink, early summer to early fall; leaves gray-green; acid soil; full sun to light shade; trim after flowering; same problems as other varieties; grows 1¼' (37.5 cm) high, spread of 2' (.5 m). '**Con Underwood**', bright red. '**George Fraser**', zone 4, deep pink. '**Mollis**', white from July to October.

EUONYMUS ALATA (yew-ON-im-us)
⚘ **Winged Euonymus** ZONE: 3 to 8.
*Origin:* China and Japan.
*Value:* Superb fall color, turns brilliant scarlet. Used in moderation, this is a marvelous plant. Excellent for hedging, group planting, screening, massing, near water. Good foundation plant with clean foliage.
*Hardiness:* Hardy to -30°F (-35°C), one of the hardiest of them all.
*Size:* 15' - 20' (4.5 m - 6 m) high, similar spread.
*Color:* Dark green foliage in summer, bright red in fall, red fruit in the fall.
*Soil:* Does well in all soil types; the richer the soil, the more winged bark appears on stem.
*Maintenance:* Occasional pruning. Easily transplanted, withstands heavy pruning.
E. A. '**Compacta**', slender branches, 10' (3 m) high; excellent hedge or screen without pruning; tolerates -15°F (-25°C); zone 3.

E. BUNGEANA **Winterberry Euonymus** ZONE: 4.
*Origin:* Japan, Korea.
*Value:* Semi-evergreen leaves. Capsules split open in fall to reveal scarlet seeds.
*Size:* Small tree, 10' - 15' (3 m - 4.5 m) high.
*Color:* Leaves light green, flowers in May, yellow but not showy, fruit is pinkish purple.
*Soil:* Any soil type.
*Maintenance:* Nothing special.
*Problems:* Scale.

E. EUROPAEA **European Euonymus** ZONE: 3 to 7.
*Origin:* Europe.
*Value:* Although the fruit is the great attraction, this plant is also good for screenings and hedging.
*Size:* 12' - 30' (3.5 m - 9 m) high, 10' - 25' (3 m - 8 m) wide.
*Color:* Leaves dark green in summer, turning yellow-green to yellow or to a good reddish purple in fall; flowers in early spring are not showy; fruit is pink to red.
*Soil:* Tolerates all soil.
*Maintenance:* Nothing special.
*Problems:* Scale, but not a big deal.

E. FORTUNEI **Wintercreeper**
ZONE: 5 to 9, needs snow cover or a good mulch in zone 4.
*Origin:* China.
*Value:* Depending on cultivar, a ground cover, vine, wall cover, low hedge, grouping or massing. Great in winter garden.
*Hardiness:* Below -20°F (-30°C), most cultivars will be injured.
*Size:* 4" - 6" (10 cm - 15 cm) as a ground cover, scrambles 40' - 70' (12 m - 21 m) on a structure.
*Color:* Dark bluish leaves; on adult plants flowers are white, fruit is orange-red, opens to expose seed in October.
*Soil:* Will tolerate any soil.
*Maintenance:* Trim for control. To propagate, collect cuttings in June, July and August.
*Problems:* Crown gall, aphids, thrips, powdery mildew, leaf spot, but the major problem is scale.
Some varieties: '**Colorata**', ground cover form that will also climb with help; deep glossy green, turns plum-purple in winter then back to green in spring, Japan origin, zone 5. '**Dart's Blanket**', origin Holland; dark green waxy leaves, bronze in fall, ground cover, 16" (40 cm) high, wide spreading, hardy, resists salt conditions, zone 5. '**Emerald Beauty**' will grow vinelike to 6' (2 m). '**Emerald Charm**', shrub, 3' (1 m) high, glossy green elliptic leaves, fruit yellow, orange seed coats, origin North America, zone 6. '**Emerald Gaiety**', small erect shrub, 4' to 5' (1.2 m - 1.5 m) high, leaves deep green with a white margin that turns pink in fall; this is the only hardy variegated plant that's excellent for winter gardens in zone 5. '**Emerald Leader**', grows to 5' (1.5 m), 30" (75 cm) spread, pink capsules with orange seed, similar to '**Emerald Beauty**', zone 6. '**Green Lane**', green foliage, upright. '**Kewensis**', forms a low mat with dainty leaves, will climb a tree or trellis, may flower, zone 5. '**Minima**', low growing, vigorous, heat tolerant, zone 6.

E. F. var. RADICANS Climbing form, fruiting, thick foliage, woody stems, dark shiny leaves, wavy in appearance. '**Sarcoxie**', upright form, 4' (1.2 m), glossy, non-fruiter, dark green leaves with white veins, zone 5. '**Sun Spot**', rounded, compact, winter hardy, thick green variegated leaves, zone 5. '**Woodland**', lustrous, and slightly smaller than varieties or '**Vegeta**', zone 5.

E. F. '**Vegeta**', similar to RADICANS, heavy fruit form, leaves are medium green, grows 4' - 5' (1.2 m - 1.5 m), clinging vine, trainable.

E. JAPONICA **Spindle Tree, Japanese Spindle Tree** ZONE: 7 to 9.
*Origin:* Japan.

*Value:* Evergreen shrub used on its own. Also climbs walls and can be trained to hedge. Dirr says it has lost favor in its native south where it was at home; it is now a houseplant.
*Hardiness:* Likes full sun, tolerates winter temperatures of -5°F (-20°C).
*Size:* 10' - 15' (3 m - 4.5 m) high, about 5' - 8' (1.5 m - 2.5 m) wide.
*Color:* Leaves a waxy dark green; flowers a greenish white borne in June; fruit is pinkish capsule, orange aril, in late summer or early fall.
*Soil:* Any soil, sandy or coastal included.
*Maintenance:* Propagate in early summer, softwood cuttings root easily.
*Problems:* Crown gall, anthracnose, mildew, leaf spot, aphids, scale.

EXOCHORDA X MACRANTHA (ex-o-KORD-a)
⚘ **Pearlbush** ZONE: 4 to 8.
*Origin:* China.
*Value:* Late-flowering shrub glorious in a shrub border.
*Hardiness:* Shake ice off its arching branches.
*Size:* 9' - 15' (2.7 m - 4.5 m) high, 10' - 15' (3 m - 4.5 m) spread.
*Color:* Flowers in early spring, white and yellow, arching outwards and downwards; gray-green foliage, faint yellow fall color.
*Soil:* Most soils.
*Maintenance:* Flowers on last year's growth, cut immediately after blossoms fade. Prune out any branches winter killed or diseased. Softwood cuttings root well in early summer.
*Problems:* None.
E. X M. '**The Bride**' is the major cultivar and it is a beauty, even when not in bloom.

FAGUS GRANDIFOLIA (FAY-gus) ⚘ **American Beech** ZONE: 3 to 9.
*Origin:* Northeastern North America (New Brunswick to Ontario).
*Value:* A sturdy imposing tree that makes a handsome row or group; needs lots of space, not good for city streets, nothing grows beneath it, but good in open areas where it has room to grow. Striking in combination with ACER RUBRUM. Beautiful colored trunks for the winter garden.
*Size:* 50' - 70' (15 m - 21 m).
*Color:* Silvery green leaves, dark green in summer, in fall a golden bronze, bark a bluish gray, smooth finish.
*Soil:* Prefers moist well-drained soils, full sun, root system is shallow, nothing will grow under the tree.
*Maintenance:* Prune in summer or early fall; don't disturb the wide-reaching roots.
*Problems:* Nothing serious but watch for: leaf spot, powdery mildew, bleeding canker, aphids, beech scale, caterpillars.

*Beech scale:* Beech scale is a mealybug. Apply dormant superior oil spray in the early spring; use insecticide when you have consulted a professional to determine the type of scale.

FAGUS SYLVATICA **European Beech Tree**
*ZONE:* 4 to 7.
*Origin:* Central and southern Europe.
*Value:* Beautiful but not a street tree. Good for hedges, will blend into any landscape.
*Hardiness:* Can't tolerate extreme heat.
*Size:* Up to 90' (27 m), average 50'- 60' (15 m - 18 m), spread of 35' - 45' (11 m - 14 m).
*Color:* Bark is smooth gray, darker than the American Beech, leaves resemble elephant hide and are lime green in spring, dark green in summer, golden bronze in fall.
*Soil:* More tolerant than the American Beech, prefers well-drained and moist soils.
*Maintenance:* Can be trimmed for shape in summer or early fall. Transplants well.
*Problems:* Same as American Beech.
Some varieties: '**Asplenifolia**', fernlike, dark green leaves, turn golden brown in fall, sometimes confused with '**Laciniata**' cultivar, zone 5. '**Atropunicea**' ('**Purpurea**'), original purple-leaved beech, found in the wild, leaves are a black-red at bud, turning purple-green by fall, zone 6. '**Aurea Pendula**', weeping beech, yellow leaves that change in late summer to almost a green, zone 6. '**Cockleshell**', slow growing, columnar form, handsome dark green leaves, zone 6. '**Dawyck Gold**', narrow columnar, golden yellow leaves, zone 6. '**Dawyckii**' ('**Fastigiata**'), columnar and a great substitute for Lombardy poplars. '**Pendula**', weeping form, each one is different, fantastic shapes and forms, zone 6. '**Purpurea Pendula**', broad mushroom shape with a gorgeous purple color, never becomes too large, slow grower, branches in a broad arch, no central leader, zone 6. '**Riversii**', deep purple, holds color to early fall, zone 6. '**Rohanii**', vigorous grower, brownish purple leaves, color fades with time, zone 6. '**Roseo-marginata**', purple-leaved form, some white in the leaves, some white looks pink, zone 6. '**Spathiana**', deep purple leaves, holds color, veins lighter than body, buds later than other beeches, zone 6. '**Tricolor**', this is a real show-stopper; warm part of zone 6. '**Zlatia**', slow growing, yellow leaves, green in summer, zone 6.

FORSYTHIA X INTERMEDIA
(for-SY-thi-a or for-SITH-ia) ✃ **Border Forsythia** *ZONE:* 5, with limited hardiness to flower buds.
*Origin:* China.
*Value:* Freestanding flowering shrub, in large shrub borders and massing. Beautiful in the spring, this shrub is one of the first signs of spring—but it's widely over-used, often in the wrong place. It can be trained up a wall.

*Hardiness:* Dirr says zone 4. In zone 5 the shrub is slow to recover from winter temperatures, and often only flowers below the snow line. Takes city conditions, but not wind.
*Size:* 13' (4 m) high, 12' (3.5 m) wide.
*Color:* Leaf color is a medium green; flowers are a pale yellow, scentless, tiny, borne in early April for 2 or 3 weeks.
*Soil:* Does well in any soil, but prefers loose good soil and needs full sun to flower.
*Maintenance:* Prune back to control growth, remove one-third after flowering, oldest branches will rejuvenate with pruning but won't flower for 2 or 3 years. Softwood cuttings are easy to root anytime during the growing season.
Some cultivars: '**Beatrix Farrand**', bright yellow flowers, vigorous bush, grows 8' - 10' (2.5 m - 3 m) high and wide, zone 6. '**Karl Sax**', deep yellow flowers borne in great numbers along branches, hardier and bushier than the above, zone 6. '**Lynwood**', Northern Ireland origin, brilliant yellow flowers, zone 6. '**Spectabilis**', commonly called the Showy Border Forsythia, 10' (3 m) high and just as wide, very unruly, rich bright yellow flowers, flower buds are more hardy than other varieties, zone 6. '**Spring Glory**', dense sulfur yellow flowers, 6' (2 m) in height, zone 5.
F. '**Arnold Dwarf**', greenish yellow flowers, slow to produce flowers, could be 5 to 6 years, 3' (1 m) high, 7' (2 m) wide; excellent for planting on banks or in large areas where you want cover; roots develop wherever branches touch the soil; zone 5.
F. '**Bronxensis**', a miniature hardy plant that is less than 3' (1 m) at maturity, zone 4.

F. OVATA, 4' - 6' (1.2 m - 2 m) high, 8' - 10' (2.5 m - 3 m) wide, stiff shrub, grows erect, early blooming, yellow-green flowers, large and bright, origin is Korea, zone 5.

F. VIRIDISSIMA (Greenstem Forsythia), 6' - 10' (2 m - 3 m) high, equal spread, flat-topped, stiff and upright growth, bright yellow flowers in April, origin China, zone 5.

FOTHERGILLA MAJOR (foth-er-GILL-a) ✃ **Large Fothergilla** Syn. with FOTHERGILLA MONTICOLA. *ZONE:* 5 to 8.
*Origin:* Southeastern United States.
*Value:* Excellent shrub for borders, foundation plantings, mass groupings or freestanding; flowers from spring to fall.
*Hardiness:* Needs winter protection.
*Size:* 6' - 10' (2 m - 3 m) high.
*Color:* Dark green leaf in summer, turns yellow, orange, scarlet in fall with all colors in the same leaf; flowers are bottle-shaped and white with a strong fragrance like honey.

*Soil:* Sabuco goes on a rant about how much disinformation there is about this shrub. The conventional wisdom is that it won't grow anywhere but in moist rich woodland-type soil, that it likes acid, dislikes alkalinity, prefers light shade, and that full sun discolors fall showing. He says nonsense. Hortguru Marion Jarvie has two plants that color well in part shade—in acid soil.
*Maintenance:* Softwood cuttings can be readily rooted when cut in June, July or August.

F. GARDENII Doesn't need a highly acid soil. Needs lots of mulch. First to break out in spring, it's the perfect small shrub 3' (1 m). '**Blue Mist**' is particularly lovely; zone 5.

GAULTHERIA PROCUMBENS (gawl-THEE-ria) ✃ **Checkerberry, Wintergreen** *ZONE:* 3.
*Origin:* North America.
*Value:* Ground cover for acid soil areas, in full sun or light to medium shade.
*Size:* 2' (.5 m) high with a spread of 10' (3 m).
*Color:* Evergreen ground cover, dark green, often variegated, leaves turn reddish with the cold weather; when crushed leaves emit wintergreen odor; flowers are pinkish white, borne May through September; fruit is bright red, which persists all winter.
*Soil:* Acid soil, dislikes alkalinity.
*Maintenance:* Needs lots of water and acid soil; transplant in early spring or fall, or from suckers during the growing season. This plant should always be used in "drifts"—not planted singly.

G. SHALLON **Salal, Shallon**
Grows to 2' (.5 m) and in warmer spots up to 6' (2 m). It grows well on the West Coast; likes lots of water; has shiny thick leaves, reddish in winter; small white flowers. Normally considered hardy in zone 6, but Sabuco puts it at zone 3, says it's been seen near Grande Prairie, Alberta, zone 2.

GENISTA TINCTORIA (jen-ISS-ta) ✃ **Dyer's Greenweed, Woadwaxen** *ZONE:* 4 to 7.
*Origin:* Europe and Western Asia.
*Value:* Low-growing plant for poor soil conditions; handsome, good informal hedge.
*Hardiness:* Prefers hot sunny location.
*Size:* 2' - 3' (.5 m - 1 m) high, equally wide.
*Color:* Bright green leaves; yellow or golden flowers borne on new growth in June to September.
*Soil:* Any soil type, best in well-drained soil.
*Maintenance:* If necessary, prune after flowering; difficult to transplant; should not be moved once established.
*Problems:* Resents pruning, no serious disease.
Some cultivars: '**Plena**', a dwarf shrub, superb almost prostrate mound, 3' (1 m) high, very floriferous double, brilliant yellow flowers; a real gem; zone 3. '**Royal Gold**', 2' (.5 m) high; flowers golden; zone 3.

GENISTA PILOSA **Silky-leaf Woadwaxen**
Low growing, 1½' (.5 m) high; forms tangled mass of twiggy shoots; leaves are grayish green; flowers bright yellow; prefers sandy, dry soils; native to Europe. **'Vancouver Gold'** is gorgeous as a ground cover or hanging over a wall; zone 5.

GINKGO BILOBA (ging-ko) ⚘ **Ginkgo Tree, Maidenhair Tree** *ZONE:* 3 to 8.
*Origin:* China, Japan, Korea.
*Value:* Apart from the fact that this is one of my favorite trees, it is ideal for the city—withstands pollution, is slow growing and strong and has heart-meltingly beautiful fan-shaped leaves and unique growth silhouette. It's possible to grow almost anything under and around this tree. Use only male tree.
*Hardiness:* Very hardy.
*Size:* 50' - 80' (15 m - 24 m) high, spread of 30' - 40' (9 m - 12); at maturity this tree can grow to 100' (30 m).
*Color:* Leaf bright green, excellent yellow in the fall; fruit, a seed really, is an orange color, eaten by the Chinese, smells when ripe.
*Soil:* Grows in almost any soil, prefers sandy, deep, moist soils.
*Maintenance:* Transplants easily.
G. B. **'Autumn Gold'**, broad forming, handsome, wide spreading, male.

GLEDITSIA TRIACANTHOS (gled-IT-sia)
⚘ **Common Honey Locust** *ZONE:* 3 to 9.
*Origin:* Central North America.
*Value:* Although overused, still an excellent tree for dappled shade. Fast growing even in zone 4 for people who have not the time to wait years.
*Size:* 30' - 70' (9 m - 21 m) high on average, 135' (41 m) maximum.
*Color:* Green in summer to a yellow-green in fall, leaves drop early in autumn; fragrant clusters of green-yellow flowers in May-June.
*Soil:* Adaptable to most soils but does best in limy types.
*Maintenance:* Nothing special; transplants easily. Drought tolerant.
*Problems:* Leaf spot, canker, witches broom, powdery mildew, rust, midge pod gall, webworm, spider mites.
Some varieties: **'Imperial'**, 30' - 35' (9 m - 11 m) high, branches spread at right angles from trunk; some dieback in severe winters, zone 4. **'Moraine'**, first of the thornless honey locusts, 40' - 50' (12 m - 15 m), fruitless, zone 4. **'Ruby Lace'**, purplish foliage, ungainly, poor specimen according to Dirr, webworms love it, zone 4. **'Shademaster'**, dark green foliage, podless, zone 4. **'Skyline'**, 45' (14 m), pyramidal shape, compact, dark green leaves, good specimen according to Dirr, zone 4.

**'Sunburst'**, 30' - 35' (9 m - 11 m) broad pyramidal head, golden leaves on new growth that turn bright green and golden yellow in the fall, popular as a street tree, zone 4.

GYMNOCLADUS DIOICA (jim-NO-klay-dus)
⚘ **Kentucky Coffee Tree** *ZONE:* 3 to 8.
*Origin:* Central United States.
*Value:* Use the seeds as baseballs; it is a tough tree and underused in the modern landscape. It may be too messy for the average garden, but if you have the space it is spectacular. Lovely in winter with an attractive silhouette and craggy bark even in young trees.
*Hardiness:* Adaptable to a wide range of conditions, likes chalk-limestone soils.
*Size:* 60' - 80' (18 m - 24 m) high with a 40' - 50' (12 m - 15 m) spread.
*Color:* Dark bluish green foliage in summer; greenish white flowers borne in May to early June; female flower is fragrant; fruit ripens in October, reddish brown.
*Soil:* Deep rich moist soil.
*Maintenance:* Prune in winter or early spring, the wood is somewhat brittle. Not necessary to prune older trees, it's enough to remove the dead wood. Propagation by seed is difficult; transplant in a sunny location.

HALESIA MONTICOLA (hal-EE-sia)
⚘ **Mountain Silverbell** *ZONE:* 5.
*Origin:* West Virginia to Florida.
*Value:* Flowers beautifully; best used where it can be closely observed; attractive when planted with an evergreen background; excellent for large open area groupings. Understorey plant for open woodland.
*Hardiness:* Some dieback in zone 4; to -30°F (-35°C) without problems.
*Size:* 90' (27 m).
*Color:* Autumn color is yellow; large flowers are pale pink, fragrant and bloom early spring; fruits are large, green-yellow.
*Soil:* Prefers moist soils, grows well in clay or even poorly drained soils.
*Maintenance:* Said to be difficult to transplant; root pruning will assist in the transplanting, a specimen from the nursery is no problem.

HAMAMELIS X INTERMEDIA (ham-am-EE-lis)
⚘ **Witch-hazel** *ZONE:* 5 to 8.
*Origin:* Central China.
*Value:* Fragrant shrubs are welcome in any garden and this early spring-flowering shrub is superior to the forsythia.
*Size:* 15' - 20' (4.5 m - 6 m) high.
*Color:* Colors of flowers range from yellow, orange, red to a dark red.
*Soil:* Prefers moist, acid, well-drained, organic soils; full sun.

*Maintenance:* Prune only when necessary to keep shapely; easily transplanted, cuttings in June may root themselves.
Some varieties: **'Arnold Promise'**, clear yellow flowers with reddish cup, fragrant, grows 20' (6 m) high, flowers as early as February, zone 6. **'Carmine Red'**, red-orange flower, wide spreading, zone 6. **'Diana'**, red-flowering, rich orange fall color, zone 6. **'Jelena'** (**'Copper Beauty'**), actually glows a copper color, orange-red in fall, zone 6. **'Orange Beauty'**, deep yellow flowers, abundant and fragrant, zone 6. **'Ruby Glow'**, coppery red flowers mature to a reddish brown; original plant over 20' (6 m) high and 20' (6 m) wide, fall color orange and red, zone 6. **'Sunburst'**, the brightest yellow flowers of all, makes **'Arnold Promise'** appear dull by comparison, zone 6.

H. MOLLIS ⚘ **Chinese Witch-hazel** *ZONE:* 5 to 8.
*Origin:* China.
*Value:* One of the most fragrant shrubs—use in borders, foundation plantings near doors and near sitting areas. Bewitching scent.
*Size:* 20' (6 m) high, 10' - 15' (3 m - 4.5 m) wide.
*Color:* Dull green in summer and a brilliant yellow in fall, flowers are yellow with rich red calyx cups, fragrant, long lasting blooms in early spring.
*Soil:* Prefers moist, acid, well-drained, organic soils.
*Maintenance:* Nothing special; easily transplanted.
Some varieties: **'Brevipetala'**, deep yellow flowers, red blush base, kinked and twisted shape, fragrant, heavy flowering, holds leaves into winter, upright growing, zone 6. **'Goldcrest'**, large flowers, golden yellow, sweet scent, strong fragrance, zone 6. **'Pallida'**, soft sulfur-yellow, sweet, fragrant, lustrous leaves; not like H. MOLLIS; this cultivar was raised in the Royal Horticultural Society garden, zone 6. **'Primavera'**, broad pale yellow petals, newer introduction from Belgium, believed to be superior to **'Pallida'**.

H. VIRGINIANA ⚘ **Common Witch-hazel** *ZONE:* 3 to 8.
*Origin:* Canada to Georgia.
*Value:* Naturalized landscaping, too large for domestic gardens but excellent in shrub border; the fall fragrance of flowers adds value to any garden.
*Hardiness:* Very hardy, tolerates -15°F (-25°C).
*Size:* 20' - 30' (6 m - 9 m) high, 20' - 25' (6 m - 8 m) spread.

*Color:* Medium green foliage in summer, fall color bright yellow; flowers brilliant yellow, fragrant and sweet, blooms in November while in fall color, which takes away from the flowers.

*Soil:* Prefers moist soils, does not do well in dry conditions, tolerant of city environment, prefers full sun.

*Maintenance:* Nothing special; cuttings are difficult to root, but transplants easily.

HEDERA HELIX (HED-er-a) ❦ **English Ivy**
*ZONE:* 4 to 9.

*Origin:* Northern and Southern Hemisphere, Europe to Caucasus mountains.

*Value:* Ground cover in shaded areas, grows well on trees and buildings. Excellent on small buildings like sheds, gazebos; ties buildings to the garden and blanks out horrible views.

*Hardiness:* Fast growing, tolerates 5°F (-15°C).

*Size:* 6" - 8" (15 cm - 20 cm) high when used as ground cover, as a vine it can reach up to 90' (27 m).

*Color:* Dark green and often lustrous, greenish white flowers are found only on the mature plant in October.

*Soil:* Rich, fairly moist, well-drained soil; in full sun for maximum growth, tolerates heavy shade.

*Maintenance:* Prune back for control of growth in spring to get a gorgeous crop of sparkling fresh leaves; transplants readily from cuttings during the growing season.

*Problems:* Leaf spot, canker, mites, aphids and powdery mildew.

Some varieties: '**Baltica**', hardy, isn't a climber and must be kept out of the wind or it will get windburn; dark green leaves with white veins; zone 3. '**Bulgaria**', one of the hardiest ivies, similar to '**Baltica**' and slightly hardier; Sabuco says zone 4-8 and resistant to both heat and drought; the dark leaves are lightly veined. '**Conglomerata**', a dense slow-growing form eventually forming hummocks. Useful for growing by or over rocks or against low tree stumps. '**Thorndale**', good ground cover, not as good a climber.

H. CANARIENSIS **Algerian Ivy**
Simple evergreen, glossy dark green foliage, heart-shaped leaves 2" - 6" (5 cm - 15 cm) long, stems are a burgundy red; solid ground cover; origin Canary Islands, Azores, Portugal, and northwestern Africa; zone 7.

H. COLCHICA **Colchis Ivy**
Dark green, larger leaved than other varieties, coarser texture, fast growing, zone 6 to 9; Sabuco has it in zone 5 as a ground cover.

HIBISCUS SYRIACUS (hy-BISK-us) ❦ **Rose-of-Sharon** *ZONE:* 5 to 8.

*Origin:* Eastern Asia.

*Value:* Works best in a border surrounded by other plants that will carry it when not in bloom; can also be used as hedging; handsome as a standard.

*Hardiness:* Tolerates 5°F (-15°C), damage at -5°F (-20°C).

*Size:* 8' - 12' (2.5 m - 3.5 m) high, 6' - 10' (2 m - 3 m) wide.

*Color:* Flowers in July, August, September, range of colors, white to red, purple or violet; foliage medium green to a pale yellow in fall; fruit upright brown capsule, remains through winter.

*Soil:* Adaptable to well-drained slightly alkaline through acid conditions.

*Maintenance:* Once mature, branches can be pruned to control size; propagate from semiripe cuttings in midsummer; best to purchase an older plant as younger ones are less likely to survive, 3 to 4 years is recommended.

*Problems:* Leaf spot, canker, aphids, rust, late leaf formation; often thought to be dead in spring because it's prone to leaf out quite late. Some cultivars adaptable to zone 5—depends on variety and the microclimate. '**Ardens**', very large double, pale rose-purple petals; zone 6. '**Blue Bird**', clear violet-blue single flowers with darker central shading; zone 6. '**Hamabo**', large, single, pale rose flowers, with reddish stripes; zone 6. '**Jeanne d'Arc**', semi-double, clear white flowers; zone 6. '**Pink Giant**', large, single pink flowers; zone 6. '**Red Heart**', single, pure white with red blotch in center, zone 6. '**Rubus**', single, red flowers, compact, zone 6. '**Russian Violet**', single, deep violet, good for cold areas; zone 5. '**Speciosus**', double, white flowers with red centers; zone 6. '**William R. Smith**', large single, pure white flowers; zone 6. '**Woodbridge**', large single, bright pink to bright red flowers; zone 6.

HIPPOPHAE RHAMNOIDES (hip-OFF-ay-ee) ❦ **Common Sea-buckthorn** *ZONE:* 2b to 7.
Fast-growing shrub, deciduous, excellent screening plant, withstands seashore conditions, good as a windbreak.

*Origin:* Europe, northern China.

*Value:* Winter fruit provides color for the winter garden; birds are not crazy about the fruit; good in shrub borders, mass plantings; effective on highway landscapes in coastal areas. For sites exposed to harsh conditions.

*Hardiness:* Withstands salt spray, tolerates temperatures of 5°F (-15°C).

*Size:* Maximum height 30' (9 m); average is 8' - 12' (2.5 m - 3.5 m) after 10 years, with a spread 10' to 40' (3 m - 12 m).

*Color:* Silver-green foliage in summer, grayish green in fall; fruit is bright orange, egg-shaped, September through April.

*Soil:* Does best in non-fertile sandy soil, moist sub-soil, sunny areas are best.

*Maintenance:* Difficult to get established.

HYDRANGEA ANOMALA subspecies PETIOLARIS (hy-DRAN-jia) ❦ **Climbing Hydrangea**
*ZONE:* 5.

*Origin:* North America and Asia.

*Value:* For massive coverage on walls, arbors, trees and free structures; woody stems require support. Will take shade, is scented and gorgeous.

*Hardiness:* Slow to establish but vigorous once roots are established.

*Size:* Seems unlimited in size, climbing to 60' or 80' (18 m or 24 m); will cover large areas in spread and height.

*Color:* Leaf is glossy green and stays green into fall; flowers are white, late June to early July, sweet fragrance for 2 weeks, flower is massive.

*Soil:* Rich well-drained soil, moist, full sun and shade, best on east or north exposure.

*Maintenance:* Difficult to transplant; consider using as a container plant.

*See also* SCHIZOPHRAGMA HYDRANGEOIDES

H. ARBORESCENS ❦ **Smooth Hydrangea**
*ZONE:* 3b to 9.

*Origin:* North America.

*Value:* Excellent woodland shrub, but can be trained or shaped for any area.

*Size:* 8' by 8' (2.5 m by 2.5 m) after 5 to 10 years, can grow to 12' (3.5 m) with an equal spread.

*Color:* Creamy white flower clusters, blooms late June to September.

*Soil:* Neutral to acid soil, tolerates alkalinity.

*Maintenance:* Blooms on new wood so it can be cut back in spring; propagate from semiripe cuttings in summer, however, best to purchase container plant.

*Problems:* None.

Some cultivars: '**Annabelle**', huge white flowers held upright on stiff stems; zone 2b. '**Grandiflora**', flowers well, known as Hills of Snow Hydrangea; zone 3b.

H. MACROPHYLLA ❦ **Bigleaf Hydrangea**
*ZONE:* 5.

The species is divided into 2 groups: hortensias and lacecaps. The latter are more graceful and subtle than the huge hortensias.

*Origin:* Japan.

*Value:* For an old-fashioned garden.

*Size:* 4' - 5' (1.2 m - 1.5 m) with the same width.

*Color:* Creamy white flowers; simple green leaves.

*Soil:* Any soil.

*Maintenance:* Prune after frost in fall; flowers on year-old wood and on current year's growth, so prune out old wood. Likes lots of humus-rich mulch.

Some cultivars: '**Blue Wave**', a vigorous lacecap that grows best in light shade; zone 6. '**Forever Pink**', compact form; hortensia; pink flower heads; dark green leaves; zone 5.

HYDRANGEA PANICULATA ❧ **Panicle Hydrangea** *ZONE:* 3b.
*Origin:* Japan, China.
*Value:* Overused, but if you have enough room, it can be massed spectacularly.
*Hardiness:* Tolerates 5°F (-15°C).
*Size:* Varies in size, 15' - 25' (4.5 m - 8 m) high with a spread of 10' - 20' (3 m - 6 m).
*Color:* Flowers are yellowish white changing to purplish pink, mid to late July, borne in pyramidal panicles 6" - 8" (15 cm - 20 cm) long; leaves are dark green with a touch of yellow, sometimes a hint of reddish purple in the fall.
*Soil:* Rich deep soil, tolerates a wide range of soil conditions.
*Maintenance:* Prune in the early spring to ensure flowering, cut back to within 6" - 8" (15 cm - 20 cm) of the ground. Propagate from softwood cuttings in midsummer; best to purchase nursery plants.
*Problems:* Very brittle and easily damaged. Some cultivars: 'Floribunda', predominantly sterile flowers, yellow-white; some fertile flowers of white, flowers July to September; zone 3. 'Grandiflora', flowers are grotesquely large, white, purplish pink, then brown; this is the most common grown; for best show of flowers thin the plant to 5 or 6 stems, zone 3b. 'Pia', a recent introduction; a dwarf plant that grows 24" (60 cm) in all directions; great for containers; lovely pink flowers, zone 5. 'Variegata', zone 6.

H. QUERCIFOLIA ❧ **Oakleaf Hydrangea** *ZONE:* 5 to 9.
*Origin:* Southeastern United States.
*Value:* Good massed or in shady sites.
*Size:* 4' - 6' (1.2 m - 2 m) high, spreads 3' - 5' (1 m - 1.5 m).
*Color:* Leaf is coarse dull green, glossy in summer, shaped sort of like an oak and turning purply bronze in fall; flowers are white, changing to purplish pink and finally brown, borne in July and August.
*Soil:* Does well in most soils.
*Maintenance:* Pruning not necessary, but will recover quickly from trimming. Cut out any winter-damaged stems.

HYPERICUM CALYCINUM (hy-PER-ik-um) ❧ **Aaronsbeard, St.-John's-wort** *ZONE:* 5.
*Origin:* Southeastern Europe, Asia Minor.
*Value:* Handsome ground cover that does well in shady areas; covers an area in a short time.
*Hardiness:* Suffers from winterkill but no real damage is done.
*Size:* 12" - 18" (30 cm - 45 cm) high with 18" - 24" (45 cm - 60 cm) spread.
*Color:* Dark green leaves, flowers are yellow, very bright, 3" (7.5 cm) across, borne on new wood in July through September.
*Soil:* Does well in poor sandy soil.

*Maintenance:* Mow to the ground in spring; transplant in spring, easily rooted in spring from cuttings placed in sandy moist soil.
*Problems:* Winterkill damages plant, but since it flowers on new growth, this is not serious.

H. KALMIANUM **Kalm St.-John's-wort**
Grows 2' - 3' (.5 m - 1 m) high, bluish green leaves, yellow flowers; a hardy species, confined to riverbanks and cliffs throughout Quebec and Ontario; zone 3.

H. X MOSERANUM **Moser's St.-John's-wort**
A compact hybrid from France, tufted habit, reddish shoots, golden yellow flowers July to October, should be cut back to the ground in spring; zone 7.

ILEX CORNUTA (EYE-lex) ❧ **Chinese Holly** *ZONE:* 7, 6 if protected, to 9.
*Origin:* Eastern China, Korea.
*Value:* The cultivars are overused in many modern landscapes; useful for the shrub border, foundation planting and massing.
*Hardiness:* Tolerates temperatures to -15°F (-25°C); withstands drought.
*Size:* 8' - 10' (2.5 m - 3 m) high and often wider at maturity.
*Color:* Small dull white flowers borne in March; sweet almost sickly fragrance from the male plants; foliage dark green, fruit is bright red and persists through winter.
*Soil:* Any soil.
*Maintenance:* Transplants well.
Some cultivars: 'Burfordii', dense rounded shrub, 10' (3 m) average height, can reach 20' (6 m) at maturity; dark lustrous green leaves, heavy fruit; flowers are white, small and dull; can trim shrub to look like a tree, zone 7. 'Dazzler', upright, grows to 10' (3 m); the most fruitful cultivar; zone 7.

I. CRENATA ❧ **Japanese Holly** *ZONE:* 5 to 6.
*Origin:* Japan.
*Value:* Foundation plantings for textural differences, hedges; excellent for rock gardens.
*Hardiness:* Can take temperatures down to -20°F (-30°C).
*Size:* Depending on the cultivar, from 3' to 20' (1 m to 6 m).
*Color:* Flowers are a dull green-white, borne in May-June, dark green leaves in summer and winter; black berry-like fruit is hidden by the foliage.
*Soil:* Prefers light, moist, well-drained soils; slightly acid soil is good; sun or shade.
*Maintenance:* Prune after new growth hardens off; transplants well. Needs winter shade.
*Problems:* Spider mites, nothing serious.
Some cultivars: 'Convexa', one of the hardiest forms, can reach 9' (3 m) when mature; needs pruning for hedging; female clone that is often heavy with black fruit; zone 5. 'Golden Gem', leaves are golden, low-spreading plant, sunny location for best color, zone 6. 'Hetzii',

compact clone of 'Convexa', but less cold hardy; ornamental, zone 5. 'Mariesii', stiffly erect female clone, rounded leaves, small; zone 6.

I. GLABRA ❧ **Inkberry** *ZONE:* 3 to 9.
If seeds originated in Nova Scotia, it will be extremely hardy.
*Origin:* Nova Scotia to Florida.
*Value:* Hedges or accent plant in any garden. Creeps by stolons, can reach vast distances. Splendid for the winter garden.
*Hardiness:* Hardy but leaves will burn in the winter; plants from Nova Scotia will tolerate -30°F (-35°C).
*Size:* 6' - 8' (2 m - 2.5 m) high and a similar, if not larger, spread.
*Color:* Dark green leaf that becomes light yellow-green in summer; fruit from September to May of the following year, hidden by foliage.
*Soil:* Prefers moist acid soil, needs mulching; in the wild commonly found in swamp.
*Maintenance:* Prune for hedging and control of growth. When grown in ordinary soil, it will lose leaves but should come back by mid-May; propagate by seed only.
*Problems:* The heat of summer may scorch the leaves.
Some cultivars: 'Compacta', compact, lustrous green leaves, bears fruit heavily; 6' (2 m); zone 6. 'Nigra' is the hardiest cultivar, and changes to a maroon-purple in winter; zone 5. 'Nordic', very shiny leaves; likes drier soil; the only true dwarf, grows to 4' (1.2 m); zone 5.

I. VERTICILLATA ❧ **Common Winterberry, Black Alder, Coralberry** *ZONE:* 3 to 9.
*Origin:* Eastern North America.
*Value:* Full sun or partial shade, mass plantings, shrub borders, waterside, adaptable to very wet conditions, excellent for shoreline.
*Hardiness:* Tolerates -30°F (-35°C); a slow grower.
*Size:* 6' - 10' (2 m - 3 m) high, equal spread.
*Color:* Leaf is deep rich green; flowers have small white petals on the female only. Bright red berries.
*Soil:* Acid soil.
*Maintenance:* Can be trimmed if necessary; propagate from softwood cuttings in June, root in peat moss; transplants easily balled and burlapped, or use a container plant.
*Problems:* Powdery mildew, leaf spot.
Some cultivars: 'After Glow', compact shrub; orange-red fruit; 3' - 6' (1 m - 2 m) high; zone 5. 'Sparkleberry', large, multistemmed; abundant red fruits remain through the winter until February or March; zone 5. 'Winter Red', dark green foliage, bronzed in fall; bright red berries; zone 5.

The following hybrids are all hardy to zone 5, aren't cranky in either dry spots or the sun and can cope with sandy clay loam. Should be protected from winter sun and wind. Best with reliable snow cover. Male and female plants are essential for pollination.

I. 'Blue Angel', 'Blue Boy', 'Blue Girl'. 'Blue Princess' has very blue leaves. 'Blue Prince' has pink-white blooms for up to 3 months. 'China Boy' and 'China Girl' are a bit hardier than 'Blue Prince' and 'Blue Princess'; leaves are dark green, berries last until January. 'China Boy' has good scent.

JUNIPERUS CHINENSIS (joo-NIP-er-us) 🌿 Chinese Juniper *ZONE:* 2 to 9 depending on the cultivar.

Junipers are the toughest of the evergreen landscape plants; they will grow anywhere. There are low-growing shrubs, pyramidal trees and ground covers.

*Origin:* China, Mongolia and Japan.

*Value:* Depending on the cultivar there are many uses: foundation planting, ground cover, hedge, screen, mass planting.

*Hardiness:* Very hardy.

*Size:* Grows 50' - 60' (15 m - 18 m) high, 15' - 20' (4.5 m - 6 m) spread.

*Color:* Blue-green, grayish foliage; bluish white flowers; fruit brown when ripe.

*Soil:* Grows best in full sun; moist well-drained soils.

*Maintenance:* Pruning is not necessary; in fact, it will ultimately wreck the plant and leave it bare in the center.

*Problems:* None, except for some cultivars that tend to overgrow if not pruned.

Some varieties and cultivars: 'Armstrongii', dwarf form to 3' - 4' (1 m - 1.2 m) high with greater spread, scale-like bright yellowish green leaves; zone 5. 'Fairview', narrow pyramidal, bright green leaves, scale-like, silver berry-like cones during summer and late fall; zone 5. 'Fruitlandii', spreading form, compact, dense, bright green foliage; zone 5. 'Gold Coast', graceful, compact, spreading form with golden yellow new growth, deeper color in cold weather; zone 5. 'Iowa', loose pyramidal form of blue-green foliage, some fruiting, scale-like leaves, spreading; zone 5. 'Kaizuka', Hollywood Juniper, belongs in California, vivid green, branches slightly twisted, grown as shrub or tree, 20' - 30' (6 m -9 m); zone 5. 'Keteleeri', broad pyramidal tree, loose light green foliage, leaves scale-like, cones a gray-green; most common of the cultivars; zone 5. 'Mint Julep', compact grower, arching branches, fountain-like form; bright mint green foliage; zone 5. 'Pfitzeriana', the most widely planted juniper, wide-spreading, grows 5' (1.5 m) high and 10' (3 m) wide, bright green foliage; zone 2b.

'Plumosa Aurea', leaves mainly scale-like, yellow-green to deep green growth, golden bronze color in fall, 3' - 4' (1 m - 1.2 m) high, broad spreading, dense drooping branches, zone 4. 'Pyramidalis', male, dense, columnar form, ascending branches, bluish green, very pungent, several clones, zone 4. 'Robusta Green', upright form, tufted brilliant green foliage, 15' (4.5 m); zone 4. 'San Jose', creeping form, 12" - 18" (30 cm - 45 cm) high and 6' - 8' (2 m - 2.5 m) wide, spreads irregularly, foliage sage green, thrives in dry areas; zone 4. Var. SARGENTII, one of the best species, low growing, forming carpets 6' (2 m) across, scale-like greenish blue foliage, fruit blue; origin Japan; zone 4. 'Sea Green', compact spreader, fountain-like arching branches, dark green foliage, 4' - 6' (1.2 m - 2 m) high; zone 4. 'Variegata', conical form, slow growing, blue-green leaves splashed with creamy white; zone 4. 'Wintergreen', dense, pyramidal form, rich green foliage; zone 4.

JUNIPERUS COMMUNIS 🌿 Common Juniper *ZONE:* 2b to 7.

*Origin:* Junipers are found all over the world.

*Value:* Ground cover, naturalized areas, riverbanks, shorelines, waste areas, large open areas, foundations, useful undergrowth.

*Hardiness:* Does not do well in warmer areas.

*Size:* 5' - 10' (1.5 m - 3 m) high with an 8' - 12' (2.5 m - 3.5 m) spread.

*Color:* Gray-green foliage, often yellow in the fall, bark is reddish brown, flowers are pale yellow, cones are bluish black.

*Soil:* Grows on the worst possible soils, tolerates almost anything.

*Maintenance:* Tends to hold old needles, so give it a good hosing down to get rid of them. Transplants easily in the fall or early spring. Some varieties and cultivars: 'Compressa', dwarf, cone-shaped, dense, very slow growing, 2' - 3' (.5 m - 1 m) high, miniature cone with thin leaves, silvery look to foliage; cannot tolerate winter sun or wind; zone 6. 'Hibernica', dense upright growth to 15' (4.5 m) high, foliage bluish white, narrow, good for a formal garden; zone 4. 'Pencil Point', grows 6' (2 m) high by 12" (30 cm) wide in 10 years; excellent accent plant for small garden; blue-green needles. 'Suecica major', similar to 'Hibernica', tips of the branches droop, Swedish Juniper, bluish green foliage; zone 4. 'Suecica nana' attains 5' (1.5 m) and has a beautiful billowy shape; zone 4.

J. SQUAMATA 'Blue Star'

One of the best "blue" conifers with brightly colored foliage; grows 3' (1 m) high, 18" (45 cm) wide in 10 years.

KALMIA LATIFOLIA (KAL-mia) 🌿 Mountain-laurel *ZONE:* Warm parts of 5 to 9.

*Origin:* Northeastern and northern United States, Quebec to New Brunswick.

*Value:* Combines beautifully with broadleaf evergreens for shady borders, mass plantings or naturalized areas. Becomes wonderfully gnarled, adding depth to the garden.

*Hardiness:* Under ideal circumstances (protected site) will tolerate -40°F (-40°C).

*Size:* 7' - 15' (2.2 m - 4.5 m); with a similar spread. Slow growing.

*Color:* Glossy dark green foliage that yellows in sun; flower is white to pink-rose to deep rose with purple markings, May to June; fruit is brown and persists through winter.

*Soil:* Deep, rich, moist acid soil in cool, well-drained conditions; needs winter shade and at least half-day summer sun; mulch regularly, must have winter protection from wind. Plant almost on top of soil and then add more soil on top of the root-ball to make a slope.

*Maintenance:* Remove dead blooms and prune only if necessary for shape; to propagate, it is best to sow seed directly on peat under lights to stimulate growth.

*Problems:* Leaf spot, blight, scale, lacebug, flower blight.

Some cultivars: 'Bulls Eye', pink-white with almost a maroon band; zone 5b. 'Goodrich', continuous banded type, deep red corolla, hard to root; zone 5b. 'Nipmuck', red in bud, opens to light pink; zone 5b. 'Ostbo Red', deep red-budded clone, best of all according to Dirr, very difficult to root; zone 5b. 'Shooting Star', selection from the wild in North Carolina; zone 5.

KALOPANAX PICTUS (kay-lo-PAN-ax) 🌿 Castor-aralia *ZONE:* 4 to 7.

*Origin:* Japan, Russian Far East, Korea, China.

*Value:* Coarse-looking tree until mature; use in settings that suit its tropical appearance and when a large shade tree is required. Looks exotic with its palmate leaves.

*Hardiness:* Will tolerate -37°F (-38°C).

*Size:* Under cultivation the average height is 40' - 60' (12 m - 18 m), but in the wild 80' (24 m) with equal spread is not uncommon.

*Color:* Dark glossy green leaves in summer turn red, then rust in autumn; flowers are a perfect white, borne in July or early August, lots of blooms; black fruit ripens in late September.

*Soil:* Deep rich moist soil, full sun.

*Maintenance:* Prune in the spring, if necessary; transplants well, if in the ideal location.

KERRIA JAPONICA (KERR-ria) ❧ **Japanese Kerria** *ZONE:* 4 to 9.
*Origin:* China and Japan.
*Value:* Good in shady areas or in the winter garden for the brilliant green twigs; suitable for mass planting, highways; tough plant for use in areas where nothing else will grow.
*Hardiness:* Tolerates -5°F (-20°C).
*Size:* 3' - 6' (1 m - 2 m) high, 6' (2 m) spread.
*Color:* Bright green stems in winter; flowers bright yellow, 5 petals, borne late April and early May for 2 weeks, and now and then throughout the growing season; leaves are bright green with some yellow in the fall; holds leaves late.
*Soil:* Any soil, any area.
*Maintenance:* Propagates from rooted underground suckers; transplants well during fall or spring.

Some cultivars: **'Albaflora'**, dark green foliage, soft pale yellow flowers. **'Picta'**, leaves are edged in white, needs shade in hot climates, single yellow flowers; zone 5. I prefer this one to any other. **'Pleniflora'**, double flowers, ball-shaped, lanky gaunt plant, 8" (20 cm) high; zone 5b.

KOELREUTERIA PANICULATA (kol-roo-TEE-ria) ❧ **Varnish Tree, Golden-rain Tree** *ZONE:* 5 to 9.
*Origin:* China, Korea, Japan.
*Value:* Weak-wooded so not a good street tree; good for shade close to a house; beautiful yellow flowers accent any garden in spring; excellent for patio gardening.
*Hardiness:* Withstands air pollution, heat, drought and wind.
*Size:* 30' to 40' (9 m - 12 m) high with an equal or greater spread.
*Color:* Bright green in summer, changing in fall to yellow; perfect yellow flowers, very showy in July; fruit is black.
*Soil:* Adaptable to a wide range of soil conditions; prefers full sun.
*Maintenance:* Prune only in the winter; easy to grow from seed; transplants best in ball or burlap in early spring.

KOLKWITZIA AMABILIS (kolk-WITZ-ia) ❧ **Beautybush** *ZONE:* 5 to 9.
*Origin:* Western China.
*Value:* Informal hedging, shrub border or a stand-alone shrub; performs well as a background plant. Bark is very beautiful.
*Hardiness:* Easy to grow.
*Size:* 6' - 10' (2 m - 3 m) high, slightly smaller spread.
*Color:* Leaf a dull green, yellow to reddish in fall; flowers are a perfect pink with a yellow throat, flaring bell-shaped, two-together, May to early June; bristly seed capsules last until the following spring.
*Soil:* Well-drained, full sun, will tolerate clay soil and drought.

*Maintenance:* Nothing special.
Some cultivars: **'Pink Cloud'**, clear pink flowers, good size; zone 5. **'Rosea'**, similar to 'Pink Cloud'.

LABURNUM X WATERERI (lab-URN-um) ❧ **Waterer Laburnum, Golden-chain Tree** *ZONE:* 5 to 7.
All parts of the tree are poisonous.
*Origin:* Europe.
*Value:* Shrub border, massive plantings, beautiful long chains of yellow flowers make it an exciting plant in bloom.
*Size:* 12' - 15' (3.5 m - 4.5 m) high with a spread of 9' - 12' (3 m - 3.5 m).
*Color:* Leaf color is bright green with bluish tinge; in May yellow flowers.
*Soil:* Moist well-drained soil, light shade.
*Maintenance:* Prune after flowering.
*Problems:* None.

L. ALPINUM **'Pendula'**, weeping laburnum is tougher than the hybrid L. X WATERERI; open to much abuse; zone 5.

L. ANAGYROIDES, **Common Golden-chain**, bushy, wide-spreading tree, 20' - 30' (6 m - 9 m) high; golden yellow flowers; zone 5.

LARIX DECIDUA (LAY-rix) ❧ **Common Larch** *ZONE:* 2 to 6.
*Origin:* Northern and central Europe.
*Value:* Parks and large public areas; its dense branching (even without needles) makes it a good winter companion for rhodos.
*Hardiness:* Low tolerance of pollution.
*Size:* 100' (30 m) maximum, average height is 70' - 75' (21 m - 23 m); 25' - 30' (8 m - 9 m) wide. Pyramidal shape.
*Color:* Bright green in early spring, dark green in summer, turns yellow in fall.
*Soil:* Moist well-drained soil, wetlands, clay soils; drought resistant.
*Maintenance:* Prune in midsummer; easily transplanted.
*Problems:* Larch case-bearer eats its way into the needles and causes them to turn brown.

L. KAEMPFERI ❧ **Japanese Larch** *ZONE:* 2b to 7.
*Origin:* Japan.
*Value:* Ornamental; best in large country gardens, golf courses or public parks.
*Hardiness:* Resistant to many of the pests that bother other species.
*Size:* 70' - 90' (21 m - 27 m).
*Color:* Leaf is green in summer turning golden yellow in fall; has white band on underside; rosette cone-like fruit, long and wide.
*Soil:* Any type of soil with sufficient moisture.
*Maintenance:* Easily transplanted.
*Problems:* Similar to other larches but more resistant to infestation.
L. K. **'Pendula'**, one of the most beautiful weeping conifers.

LAVANDULA ANGUSTIFOLIA (lav-AN-dew-la) ❧ **Common or English Lavender** *ZONE:* 6 to 9.
*Origin:* Southern Europe, North Africa.
*Value:* Herb garden border, low-growing hedge or edging, use en masse and to fill in a knot garden. Grow it for color, shape and smell. It combines beautifully with other gray foliage plants.
*Size:* 1' - 2' (30 cm - 60 cm) high at maturity.
*Color:* Silver-gray foliage; flowers borne June, July or August, lavender-purple, some varieties are white-pink or blue-violet, spikes are 2" - 6" (5 cm - 15 cm) high and can be dried for sachets.
*Soil:* Prefers well-drained soil on the dry side, too much moisture will kill the plant, neutral to alkaline soil is ideal.
*Maintenance:* Stalks should be removed after flower fades; cut back to where you see the stem growth; prune back by a third every few years in spring to keep it fresh; transplants well from containers; sow seeds directly or take cuttings in August or September.
Some cultivars: **'Hidcote'**, rich purple, borne on stalks 10" - 15" (4 cm - 6 cm) high, compact habit; foliage more silver than gray; zone 6. **'Munstead'**, grows a 12" (30 cm) high, is very compact and makes a good hedge; flowers are a deep violet-blue; zone 6.

LEUCOTHOE FONTANESIANA (lew-KO-tho-ee) ❧ **Drooping Leucothoe or Fetterbush** *ZONE:* 6.
*Origin:* North America.
*Value:* Medium-sized shrub for underplanting in shady, acid areas; excellent for hiding unwanted sites, mass planting, on banks, in shrub border; good contrast with other shrubs.
*Size:* 3' - 6' (1 m - 2 m) high, same width.
*Color:* Dark green foliage, turning a bronze to purplish in fall; white fragrant pitcher-shaped flowers.
*Soil:* Rich, deep, acid to neutral soil; dislikes alkalinity.
*Maintenance:* Remove one-third of old growth to the ground each spring to encourage new and clean growth; propagate from softwood cuttings is early summer; best transplanted in the spring.
*Problems:* Leaf spot.

L. AXILLARIS **Coast Leucothoe**
Replacing L. FONTANESIANA in the nursery; not susceptible to leaf spot; grows 4' (1.2 m) high, similar width; leaves are leathery, glossy dark green; flowers white and long, borne in April and May; sandy soil; purple-red fall leaf color; zone 5.

LIGUSTRUM AMURENSE (ly-GUS-trum)
❦ **Amur Privet** *ZONE:* 5 to 7.
*Origin:* Northern China.
*Value:* This is a marvelous plant for hedges; also lends itself to forming standards.
*Size:* 12' - 15' (3.5 m - 4.5 m) high, 8' (2.5 m) spread.
*Color:* Dark green foliage; flowers are creamy white with a mildly unpleasant odor, May and June, lasting 2 to 3 weeks.
*Soil:* Adaptable to any except wet soil.
*Maintenance:* Prune if necessary, but not required. Will withstand heavy pruning. To propagate sow fruit as seed.
*Problems:* No serious problems if the hardiest and most reliable species are purchased. Can be bothered by leaf spot, spider mite, powdery mildew, root rot, twig blight, whitefly, but I've never had any of these problems.

L. OBTUSIFOLIUM **Border Privet**
Medium to dark green foliage, stem has purplish tinge when young; grows 10' - 12' (3 m - 3.5 m) high with a spread of 12' - 15' (3.5 m - 4.5 m), multistemmed, foliage turns purplish in the fall; flowers are white, and stink, borne early to mid June; fruit is black, berry-like, ripens in September; good screen or hedge; origin Japan; zone 5b to 7.

L. JAPONICUM ❦ **Japanese Privet** *ZONE:* 9a to 10.
*Origin:* Japan.
*Value:* Foundations, screens, hedges, single shrub, borders.
*Hardiness:* Grows fast, thrives with neglect, tolerates sun or shade and heavy pruning.
*Size:* 6' - 12' (2 m - 3.5 m) high, 6' - 8' (2 m - 2.5 m) wide.
*Color:* Leaf color is a lustrous dark green; flowers a perfect creamy white, fragrant, borne mid-May, odor is typically privet and offensive to many people.
*Soil:* Adaptable to any soil.
*Maintenance:* Make sure they have lots of water. For hedges cut back to about 6" (15 cm) from ground after planting; prune in spring to keep shape; cuttings root readily in spring or fall.

L. X VICARYI **Golden Privet**
Semi-evergreen with yellow-green leaves, best in sun to get the color; needs regular pruning to keep bushy; zone 6.

L. VULGARE ❦ **European Privet** *ZONE:* 5b to 7.
*Origin:* Europe, North Africa.
*Value:* Formerly the favored species, but it has lost its appeal because there are better species available.
*Size:* 12' - 15' (3.5 m - 4.5 m) high with same spread.
*Color:* Dark green foliage; flowers are white, heavy and stink, borne very densely in mid June; fruit is black, ripens in September.

*Soil:* Any soil, but avoid planting in areas where it is wet.
*Maintenance:* Easily rooted during growing season.
*Problems:* Twig blight, canker.
Some cultivars: **'Cheyenne'**, holds leaves into winter months; zone 5. **'Lodense'**, low, dense compact form; zone 5.

LONICERA (lon-ISS-er-a) ❦ **Honeysuckle**
The numerous (about 180) species and cultivars of honeysuckle generally have the same characteristics. All readily propagate from seed and cuttings, are free from serious problems and are worthy of various uses in the garden: hedging, foundations, mass plantings, standalone, fragrance gardens, shrub borders.

L. ALPIGENA **Alps Honeysuckle**
Native to mountain areas of central Europe, slow growing. 4' - 8' (1.2 m - 2.5 m) high, erect habit. Dark green leaves; flower is yellow or greenish yellow, tinged with dull red, borne in May; fruits are red, and cherry-like. Any soil will do; zone 5.

L. X BELLA **Belle Honeysuckle**
Origin is Russia. 8' - 10' (2.5 m - 3 m) high, 8' - 12' (2.5 m - 3.5 m) wide. Foliage is bluish green; flowers vary from white to pink and fade to yellow; zone 2.

L. X BROWNII **Brown's Honeysuckle**
Similar to above, hardiest honeysuckle vine in the north; **'Dropmore Scarlet'** was raised in Dropmore, Manitoba, by F.L. Skinner.

L. CAERULEA **Bearberry Honeysuckle**
A dense sturdy shrub, grows 4' - 5' (1.2 m - 1.5 m) high; yellowish flowers give way to bluish fruit; found in high altitudes; zone 2.

L. FRAGRANTISSIMA **Winter Honeysuckle**
Good hedge or screen, for the scented garden, shrub border. Origin is eastern China. Fast growing, withstands heavy pruning. 6' - 10' (1.8 m - 3 m) high and similar spread. Leaf is a dark bluish or grayish green, foliage holds late into fall; flowers creamy white, lemon-scented, extremely fragrant, early April, not that showy. Adapts to many soils, prefers good loamy soil, moist and well-drained, full sun to partial shade. Prune after flowering; cut back old shrubs to ground, they will grow new shoots readily; collect softwood shoots in June. Force branches inside in late winter. Susceptible to leaf blight, leaf spot, powdery mildew, mealybug. Zone 5 to 8.

L. X HECKROTTII **Goldflame Honeysuckle**
Loves sandy soil and semishade; prune out weak wood; flowers profusely for months; an evening scented plant; zone 5.

L. HENRYI **Henry Honeysuckle**
Semi-evergreen; will take full sun to partial shade; likes lots of mulch; white flowers and almost black berries; zone 5.

L. JAPONICA **'Aureoreticulata'**
Semi-dwarf vine, almost evergreen, oval green leaves overlaid with bright yellow veins. Fragrant white-yellow flowers, red berries, zone 4 to 10.

L. NITIDA **'Baggesen's Gold'**
Lovely yellow dwarf form; dislikes dry or water-logged soils; best in full sun; zone 6.

MAGNOLIA GRANDIFLORA (mag-NO-lia)
❦ **Southern Magnolia** *ZONE:* 5b to 9.
*Origin:* Southeastern United States.
*Value:* As a specimen needs the proper location with lots of space, should be in a protected spot.
*Hardiness:* Protect from winter winds and summer sun, will survive with as little as 3 hours of sun a day.
*Size:* 60' - 80' (18 m - 24 m) high with a spread of 30' - 50' (9 m - 15 m).
*Color:* Lustrous dark green leaves; very fragrant creamy white flowers, 8" - 12" (20 cm - 30 cm) in diameter, borne in May to early June; fruit ripens in October, rose-red, aggregate of follicles, opens to expose red seeds.
*Soil:* Rich porous, slightly acid, well-drained soil; full sun or partial shade.
*Maintenance:* Prune after flowering only to control the size and shape; any heavy pruning should wait until summer; transplant in the early spring; can be rooted but with difficulty. Do not mechanically cultivate soil around magnolias; they are shallow and fleshy rooted plants. Handpull weeds or use an acid mulch.

M. LILIFLORA X M. STELLATA **'Rosea'**
Hybrids known as the Kosar and Devos (The Girls). All slightly different but all display their gorgeous parent M. LILIFLORA with large erect buds, shrubby growth habit. **'Ann'**, **'Betty'**, large violet flowers on a compact form; zone 3. **'Jane'**, reddish medium size flowers, blooms late and highly scented; zone 3. **'Susan'**, violet flower, very bushy and compact; zone 3.

M. X LOEBNERI **'Leonard Messel'**
This hybrid blooms early to mid-season, has stellata-type flowers of soft pink-lilac, deeper in bud, small tree or shrub. Parents M. KOBUS X M. STELLATA **'Rosea'**.

M. X SOULANGIANA **Saucer Magnolia** *ZONE:* 5b to 9.
Often overused but with good reason: this specimen tree can be very beautiful when in flower; requires the right space to properly develop, and it can take your breath away.
*Origin:* France.
*Value:* In groupings, where the scent can be appreciated, as a freestanding shrub and eventually a tree, or in large shrub border.
*Hardiness:* Roots need ample room to develop, late spring frosts or freezes often kill the flower buds.

*Size:* 20' - 30' (6 m - 9 m) high with a variable spread, often equal to height.
*Color:* Leaf medium to deep flat green; flowers are white to pink to purplish with an average of 9 petals, borne before the foliage in March-April; fruiting is slight.
*Soil:* Moist deep acid soil, supplemented with leaf mold or peat moss; full sun for maximum growth, will withstand some shade.
*Maintenance:* Remove cross branches in the winter to prevent rubbing.
*Problems:* Early spring frost or freezing could cause bud damage.
Some cultivars: **'Alba Superba'**, flowers are white, fragrant, outside petals purplish, dense and erect; zone 5. **'Alexandrina'**, flowers a flushed rose-purple outside, inside white, flowers early and large, easy to root in June; zone 5. **'Lennei'**, dark purplish magenta flowers, white inside, long and wide, flowers later than other cultivars, dark green leaves, stiff and broad shrub; origin is Italy; zone 5b. **'Lombardy Rose'**, petals are dark rose in the lower areas, white in upper, flowers for several weeks; zone 5b. **'Rustica Rubra'**, rose-red large flowers, loose growing shrub, beautiful in flower; zone 5b.

MAGNOLIA STELLATA ❧ **Star Magnolia**
*ZONE:* 3 to 8.
*Origin:* Japan.
*Value:* Single specimen, accent plant, integrated into a shrub or perennial border.
*Size:* 15' - 20' (4.5 m - 6 m) high with a spread of 10' - 15' (3 m - 4.5 m).
*Color:* Dark green in summer, yellow to bronze in fall.
*Soil:* Prefers a peaty soil full of organic matter.
*Maintenance:* Propagate from softwood cuttings in June and early July; roots well in sand.
Some cultivars: **'Pink Star'**, flower buds and open flowers are pink, fading to white; zone 5b. **'Rosea'**, buds pink, fading to white; numerous clones, zone 5b. **'Royal Star'**, pure white flowers; zone 5b. **'Waterlily'**, buds pink, eventually white, highly fragrant, bushy grower; zone 5b.

MAHONIA AQUIFOLIUM (ma-HO-nia)
❧ **Oregon Holly-grape** *ZONE:* 5 to 8.
*Origin:* Western United States and British Columbia.
*Value:* Foundation plantings, retaining walls, ground cover, shrub border, shady areas. It's one of the best for the winter garden and as a background on the lower storey for smaller shrubs and perennials.
*Hardiness:* Tolerates winter temperatures down to -25°F (-32°C).
*Size:* 3' - 6' (1 m - 2 m) high, spread of 3' - 5' (1 m - 1.5 m).

*Color:* Leaf reddish bronze in spring, glossy yellow-green to dark green in summer, purplish in fall; flowers are yellow, borne in April, slightly fragrant; fruit is blue-black, ripens in October, holds until December.
*Soil:* Any soil, does not tolerate dryness.
*Maintenance:* Every 3 or 4 years cut plant to ground to rejuvenate, recovers quickly. Propagate by rooting shoots in midsummer or from softwood cuttings.
*Problems:* Leaf rust, leaf spot, leaf scorch, scale, whitefly.
M. A. **'Compactum'**, dwarf form, glossy leaves, bronze winter color, 24" - 36" (60 cm - 100 cm) high, hardy; zone 5.

M. BEALEI **Leatherleaf Mahonia**
Upright, coarse, evergreen shrub, grows 10' - 12' (2 m - 3.5 m) high; foliage is dark blue-green, flowers are lemon yellow, fragrant, March-April; native to China; zone 7 to 8.

M. REPENS **Creeping Mahonia**
Low ground cover plant, 10" (25 cm) high, dull blue-green leaves in summer, rich purple in the winter, fruit is black, grape-like; origin is British Columbia to California; zone 3.

MALUS (MAY-lus) ❧ **Flowering Crabapple**
There are 400 to 600 types of crabapple. Many species are ineffectual because they succumb to apple scab, rust, fireblight, leaf spot and powdery mildew. Most are between 15' and 25' (4.5 m and 8 m) high. They are deciduous trees or shrubs. Flowers are white to pink or carmine to red to rose. Fruit is 2" (5 cm) in diameter and ranges in color from red to yellow to green. They are adaptable to varying soil conditions, but they prefer well-drained, moist and acid soils. They are hardy and should be planted in the sun. Pruning is not required, but can be done before June.

MALUS SARGENTII ❧ **Sargent Crabapple**
*ZONE:* 5 (Sabuco rates it for zone 3).
The smallest of all the crabapples and one of the showiest.
*Origin:* Japan.
*Value:* Best grown singly in medium-sized gardens; this plant has 3 to 4 seasons of great beauty.
*Color:* Flowers are single, red in bud, opening to white, fragrant; birds like the bright red fruit.
*Soil:* Most crabs will take any soil but they like full sun.
*Maintenance:* Aside from problems listed below, nothing special.
*Problems:*
*Apple Scab:* Fruits are dark with leathery spots, leaves have dark spots—make sure you pick up all dead leaves and fruit and get them out of the garden; use dormant oil spray late in

March before budding, repeat application a week later and continue until fruits have ripened and dropped.
*Fireblight:* Caused by bacteria spread by aphids, bees and leaf hoppers; plants look scorched, tips of young shoots dry up; control of the disease is difficult, handle diseased plants carefully, prune out diseased areas.
Some cultivars: **'Adams'**, best red-flowering crab, almost disease and pest resistant; good fall color, yellow to deep red; 24' (8 m) high, 20' (6 m) wide; zone 4. **'Autumn Glory'**, brilliant red bud opening to pink, fading to white; 10' - 15' (3 m - 4.5 m); zone 4. **'Baskatong'**, introduced in Ottawa; purple buds open to pinky red flowers; bronze foliage all seasons 30' (9 m); zone 2b. **'Rosea'**, flower buds dark pink and susceptible to fireblight, zone 5. **'Selkirk'**, rose-red flowers, single to semi-double, fruit is glossy purple-red, susceptible to scab, fireblight and powdery mildew, zone 2b. **'Tina'**, red buds open to white scented flowers, 4' - 5' (1.2 m - 1.5 m) high, zone 3.

MICROBIOTA DECUSSATA ❧ **Siberian Carpet Grass** *ZONE:* 4.
*Origin:* Siberian mountains.
*Value:* Good coverup for steep slopes. This is a neat, underused shrub that is very hardy and looks a bit like a trailing arborvitae with scale-like foliage.
*Hardiness:* Not reliable below -40°F (-40°C).
*Size:* 12" to 24" (30 cm - 60 cm) high, 15' - 30' (4.5 m - 9 m) spread.
*Color:* Green foliage in summer and reddish color in winter.
*Soil:* Almost any, except heavy clay, will do.
*Maintenance:* Best in the sun.

OSMANTHUS HETEROPHYLLUS (os-MAN-thus) ❧ **Holly Osmanthus, False Holly** *ZONE:* 7b to 9.
*Origin:* Western China and Japan.
*Value:* Borders, screens, hedges—can be used formally or informally in any garden.
*Hardiness:* Slow to medium growth rate, tolerates temperatures of 25°F (-5°C).
*Size:* 8' - 10' (2.5 m - 3 m) high, spread is slightly less.
*Color:* Leaf is green on top and yellow underneath; flower is white, 4 petals, fragrant, borne in September to October and into November; fruit is seldom seen in cultivated plants.
*Soil:* Most soils, but does not like to be waterlogged, prefers well-drained moist, acid conditions.
*Maintenance:* Prune after flowering to maintain control, survives a heavy pruning; easily transplanted from containers, cuttings root easily.

OSMANTHUS HETEROPHYLLUS 'Ogon'
Bright golden yellow foliage in summer, winter color is green splashed with yellow.

PARTHENOCISSUS QUINQUEFOLIA (par-thee-no-SISS-us) ❧ **Virginia Creeper** ZONE: 2b to 9.
*Origin:* North America.
*Value:* Low-maintenance ground cover, wall covering, trellis, walls; it cements itself to any structure. Might be harmful to trees.
*Hardiness:* Fast grower, hard to kill once established, grows in windy conditions. Tolerates pollution.
*Size:* Limited only by the structure it is growing on, can reach up to 50' (15 m) or more.
*Color:* Deep green in summer, purple to crimson red in the fall; green-white flowers are borne in June; fruit is a bluish black berry, in September-October; they attract birds.
*Soil:* Any kind of soil, full sun, partial shade or full shade, hard to kill.
*Maintenance:* Keep in container until root is well established and then move to permanent area, difficult to get started, easy to root from softwood cuttings in June, July or August.
*Problems:* Lifts roof tiles; susceptible to canker, downy mildew, leaf spot.

PAXISTIMA CANBYI (syn. PACHISTIMA) (pax-ISS-tima) ❧ **Canby Paxistima, Rat-stripper** ZONE: 2b to 8.
*Origin:* Mountains of Virginia and West Virginia.
*Value:* Very beautiful shrubby ground cover, requires no attention once mature; low hedge, foundation or edging plant, in containers.
*Hardiness:* Almost unkillable.
*Size:* 12" (30 cm) high, 3' - 5' (1 m - 1.5 m) spread.
*Color:* Leaf color is dark green in summer and bronze in cold temperatures; flowers in early May are greenish or reddish; fruit is a leathery white capsule.
*Soil:* Prefers well-drained moist soils with organic materials added; in the wild it is found on rocky soils; full sun to partial shade.
*Maintenance:* Roots easily when in contact with soil; cuttings taken in summer will root.
*Problems:* Possibly leaf spot and scale.

PERNETTYA MUCRONATA (per-NET-ia) ❧ **Chilean Pernettya** ZONE: 8.
*Origin:* Chile, Argentina.
*Value:* Plantings of small or large masses.
*Hardiness:* Tolerates temperatures of 5°F (-15°C), but can suffer in cold winds.
*Size:* 2' (.5 m) high, a spread of 4' (1.2 m).
*Color:* Long glossy green foliage with red veins; cup-shaped flowers hang in small white clusters, borne in early summer; fruits range in color from white to pink to purple; must be planted in groups of 3 or more.

*Soil:* Neutral to acid soil.
*Maintenance:* Cut back rambling shoots that are more than one year old; propagate by semiripe cuttings taken in summer.
P. M. 'Alba', white medium-sized fruits, pink shaded and tipped, zone 8.

PEROVSKIA ATRIPLICIFOLIA(per-OV-ski-a) ❧ **Russian Sage**
*Origin:* East Iran to northwest India.
*Value:* Combine with other early shrubs and perennials, for a spectacular effect.
*Zone:* Warm parts of 5 up.
*Size:* 3' - 4' (1 m - 1.2 m) high.
*Color:* Soft downy gray foliage with gorgeous blue flowers in August and September.
*Soil:* Almost any, as long as it's well-drained; likes lots of sun.
*Maintenance:* Cut back to about 12" (30 cm) from ground in spring to promote new flowering growth, easily grown from seed.
*Problems:* May die back.
P. A. 'Blue spire', the most readily available cultivar; has a wonderful scent; zone 5.

PHILADELPHUS CORONARIUS (fill-a-DEL-fus) ❧ **Sweet Mock-orange** ZONE: 3 to 8.
There are 3 categories: low growing, medium high, and tall growing.
*Origin:* Southeastern Europe and Asia Minor.
*Value:* Its best asset is the sweet scent; the plant itself is not much to look at, so use it where the scent can be appreciated.
*Hardiness:* Fast growing, full sun or light shade.
*Size:* 10' - 12' (3 m - 3.5 m) high, with an equal spread.
*Color:* Medium green foliage; white fragrant flowers, May to early June.
*Soil:* Not particular about soil conditions, prefers well-drained moist soils supplemented with organic material.
*Maintenance:* Prune after flowering, remove old wood or cut to ground; propagate from softwood cuttings in June and July; transplants well, root system is large.
*Problems:* Leaf spot, canker, powdery mildew, rust, aphids, leaf miner, but none of these are serious. Cut out diseased branches, mulch.
Some cultivars: 'Aureus', yellow foliage; zone 4. 'Nanus', compact, 4' (1.2 m), dark green foliage, sparse flowering; zone 3.
P. X VIRGINALIS 'Glacier', double flowers, 5' (1.5 m) high, zone 4. 'Minnesota Snowflake', fragrant, double white flowers, 8' (2.5 m), zone 3b. 'Silver Showers' (syn. 'Silberregen'), fairly compact with large white flowers.

PHORMIUM (FORM-ium) ❧ **Green Fiber-lily** ZONE: 7 to 8.
*Origin:* New Zealand.

*Value:* As an accent plant alongside pool or patio, in shrub borders, container gardens, it adds a splendid architectural element.
*Hardiness:* Tolerates temperatures to 15°F (-10°C), accepts high degrees of pollution.
*Size:* 5' - 7' (1.5 m - 2.2 m) high at maturity, slightly larger spread.
*Color:* Flowers bloom on 3- to 4-year-old plants, red-bronze upright panicles; leaves are upright and long, leathery looking; flowers age to seed heads of brown-red color.
*Soil:* Well-drained, open soil, dislikes being water-logged (particularly in containers).
*Maintenance:* Remove dead or damaged foliage to the ground. Propagate through splitting of self-generated side plants.
*Problems:* Slow to establish and to flower.

P. TENAX **New Zealand Flax**
Rigid clumps of upright foliage, almost spike-like, leathery texture, gray to gray-green with a central creamy band; flowers grow to 3' (1 m), a bronze-red color, zone 8.
Some cultivars: 'Bronze Baby', narrow bronzy-purple leaves; 2' - 3' (.5 m - 1 m); zone 7 to 8. 'Yellow Wave', bright yellow leaves edged in green; 3' - 4' (1 m - 1.2 m); zone 7 to 8.

PHOTINIA X FRASERI (fo-TIN-ia) ❧ **Fraser Photinia** ZONE: 7 to 10.
*Origin:* New Zealand and Australia.
*Value:* Large hedge or privacy screen, softens corners of buildings, use as a small tree. Good as a focal point.
*Size:* 10' - 15' (3 m - 4.5 m) and sometimes 20' (6 m), spread is 5' - 7' (1.5 m - 2.2 m).
*Color:* New foliage is a glossy red turning to green; white flowers have offensive odor; foliage fades to green in summer.
*Soil:* Thrives in most soils, prefers well-drained, responds well to fertilizing, full sun.
*Maintenance:* Can be pruned back quite hard. For compact growth, prune out leaders by 12" (30 cm) when new growth appears in spring. Propagate cuttings taken in early summer; transplants well.
*Problems:* Shows nitrogen deficiency in some situations, leaf spot, mildew, fireblight, scale.

PHYSOCARPUS OPULIFOLIUS (fy-so-KARP-us) ❧ **Common Ninebark or Eastern Ninebark** ZONE: 2 to 7.
*Origin:* North America.
*Value:* Screening, mass plantings; looks coarse so use it at the back of the border; good with purple-leaved shrubs; ragged in winter.
*Hardiness:* Adaptable to most situations, including tough winds and dry conditions.
*Size:* 5' - 9' (1.5 m - 2.7 m) high, 6' - 10' (2 m - 3 m) spread.

*Color:* Flat green leaf, yellowish in fall; white or pink flowers, May to June, purplish stems; reddish fruit appears in September-October and is maintained into winter.
*Soil:* Most soils; tolerates dry conditions; withstands acid soils, prefers full sun or partial shade.
*Maintenance:* Remove one-third of old wood after flowering to rejuvenate for the coming year; transplants easily; root cuttings taken in summer root well in peat.
*Problems:* Leaf scorch in bright sunlight.

PHYSOCARPUS OPULIFOLIUS **'Dart's Gold'**, bright golden yellow; cut right down to ground when young; let gold spill over the ground by combining with CALLUNA VULGARIS **'H.E. Beale'** and ERICA CARNEA **'Vivellii'**, which has bronzy foliage in winter; zone 5.

PICEA (PY-see-a) **Spruce**
*ZONE:* 1 to 4, depending on species.
*Origin:* Northern Hemisphere.
*Value:* Needs a large landscape; good focal point with their muscular unchanging form. Good screen plant, windbreak and hedge. Never place this tree at the entrance to a garden.
*Hardiness:* Does not grow well in dry, hot, polluted conditions; shallow root system.
*Size:* Up to 125' (39 m), grows relatively swiftly for the first 20 years.
*Color:* Light airy green to deep blue. The color range is fantastic.
*Soil:* Prefers well-drained moist soil; will perform in clay soils.
*Maintenance:* Pruning is not necessary but they tolerate heavy pruning in hedging; transplants well because of shallow root system.
*Problems:* Canker, rust, wood decay, spruce gall aphid, cooley spruce gall aphid, spruce budworm, sawflies, spruce spider mite, bagworm.

P. ABIES **Norway Spruce**
Grows in any soil and puts up with dreadful conditions; deep green foliage, 50' (15 m) high; **'Pendula'**, **'Inversa'** are good weeping forms; zone 2 to 5.

P. ENGELMANNII **Engelmann Spruce**
Rocky Mountain species; adaptable, grows to 100' (30 m), conical in shape; zone 2.

P. GLAUCA **White Spruce**
Light green foliage burns in windy sites, formal conical shape; zone 1. **'Densata'** doesn't burn as badly; contorted appearance, 20' (6 m) darker blue-green needles.

P. G. **'Conica'** (or **'Aertiana Conica'**)
Dwarf Alberta spruce, burns in sunny, windy sites; bright green, slow growing, 2" - 4" (2 cm - 10 cm) to 10' (3 m); formal; zone 2.

P. MARIANA **'Nana' Black Spruce**
Mounds out from the center, lying flat at the edges; blue-green and dense; zone 2.

P. PUNGENS **Colorado Spruce**
Unkillable; a good background plant.
P. P. **'Hoopsii'**, very blue, dense pyramidal form and the best grower. **'Bakeri'** is smaller, 8' by 3' (2.5 m by 1 m) and pyramidal. **'Compacta'** is flat on top 2' by 2' (.5 m by .5 m). **'Globosa'** is round 2' by 2' (.5 m by .5 m); zone 2.

PIERIS JAPONICA (py-EE-ris) **Japanese Andromeda, Lily-of-the-valley Bush**
*ZONE:* 5, 4 with protection, to 8.
*Origin:* Japan.
*Value:* Does well in shrub border with other broadleaf evergreens.
*Hardiness:* Requires protection from the frost, late spring frosts destroy early budding.
*Size:* 9' - 12' (3 m - 3.5 m) high, 6' - 8' (2 m - 2.5 m) spread.
*Color:* Dark green foliage; fragrant flowers are white, borne in March-April.
*Soil:* Moist, acid, well-drained soil, supplemented with peat moss or compost.
*Maintenance:* Prune hard for shape after flowering.
*Problems:* Leaf spot, dieback, mites, chlorosis. Some cultivars: **'Bisbee Dwarf'**, compact bushy plant, leaves half the size of specimen plant, dark green foliage, zone 5. **'Flamingo'**, deep rose-red flowers, zone 5. **'Mountain Fire'**, new growth is fire red, flowers white, zone 5. **'Valley Valentine'**, dark red flowers, red buds all winter, zone 5.

P. FLORIBUNDA **Mountain Pieris**
Much hardier than P. JAPONICA, will resist leaf burn, grows in some lime without chlorosis, needs lots of water; flowers from March to May; up to 6' (2 m); zone 5.

PINUS (PY-nus) **Pine**
*ZONE:* 2 to 8, depending on variety.
There are 90 species throughout the Northern Hemisphere. Pines come in every form from dwarf shrubs to huge trees and they tolerate even more difficult soil and climate than PICEA or ABIES.
*Origin:* Northern temperate zone.
*Value:* As a huge plant for a focal point or background, this one is perfect. Be careful in small sites.
*Hardiness:* Out of its range, it will succumb to windburn.
*Size:* Various heights and shapes, difficult to stereotype a pine.
*Color:* From deep green to bluish green.
*Soil:* Any soil conditions.
*Maintenance:* Nothing special.
*Problems:* Root rot, dieback, tip blight, needle blight, needle rust, shrub pine needle rust, bark beetles, white pine weevil.

P. DENSIFLORA **Japanese Red Pine**
*ZONE:* 3 to 7.
Unusually shaped specimen that becomes exotic early in its life.
*Origin:* Japan, Korea, parts of China.
*Value:* Decorative orange-red bark is interesting, especially in the winter garden.
*Hardiness:* Slow growth.
*Size:* 40' (12 m) high, similar spread; can grow to 100' (30 m).
*Color:* Leaf is a lustrous dark green.
*Soil:* Sunny location, well-drained acid soil. Some cultivars: **'Pendula'**, weeping form with rich green needles, used in raised planters, over rock walls, zone 5. **'Umbraculifera'**, dwarf umbrella-like head, average 9' (3 m) high, branches dense and upright, snow may damage the branches of mature large trees, goes by the name of **'Tanyosho'**; origin Japan; zone 3b to 8.

P. MUGO **Swiss Mountain Pine, Mugo Pine** *ZONE:* 2 to 7.
*Origin:* Mountains of central Europe.
*Value:* Species seldom used, but there are many varieties and cultivars; dwarf plants can be used as background plants or as focal points; as foundation plants they can be striking.
*Size:* 15' - 20' (4.5 m - 6 m) high, 25' - 30' (8 m - 9 m) spread.
*Color:* Medium green, yellowish green in the winter.
*Soil:* Prefers sun, deep moist sandy loam.
*Maintenance:* Transplants well if balled and roots are pruned.
*Problems:* Rusts, wood rots, borers, sawflies and especially scale.

P. M. **'Gnom'**, 25-year-old plant is only 15' (4.5 m) high and 36' (10.5 m) wide, dark green mound, dense and compact; zone 2.

P. M. **Dwarf Mugo**
6' - 8' (2 m - 2.5 m) high and usually about 1½ times as wide, flat-topped. It is a rounded to flat-topped mound.

P. M. PUMILIO **Prostrate Mugo**
Twisted new growth make this a fascinating ground-covering plant; slightly more wind tolerant than other varieties; 12" - 24" (30 cm - 60 cm) high, 10' - 30' (3 m - 9 m) spread.

POTENTILLA FRUTICOSA (po-ten-TILL-a) **Bush Cinquefoil** *ZONE:* 2 to 7.
*Origin:* Northern Hemisphere.
*Value:* An asset to any garden because of its longevity. Can be used as a hedge, in the shrub border, massing or as edging plant.
*Size:* 1' - 4' (30 cm - 1.2 m) high, 2' - 4' (.5 m - 1.2 m) spread.
*Color:* Bright to dark green leaves in summer, turning to yellow-brown; bright yellow flowers bloom in June until frost.

*Soil:* Withstands dry and poor soils, prefers well-drained soils in full sun but will tolerate partial shade.

*Maintenance:* Transplants well, softwood cuttings root easily in moist peat moss.

Some cultivars: **'Abbotswood'**, dark bluish green foliage, large white flowers, spreading habit; zone 2. **'Coronation Triumph'**, soft green foliage, dense, full, compact, bright yellow flowers; zone 2. **'Dart's Gold-digger'**, large, golden flowers, delicate bright green leaves, low-spreading habit, zone 3. **'Daydawn'**, white flowers, tall mounded form with medium green foliage; zone 3. **'Forrestii'**, medium yellow, abundant large flowers, gray-green leaves, low, mounded form, bronze color in late summer, zone 3. **'Friedrichsenii'**, creamy white to pale yellow, sparse flowering, zone 3. **'Grandiflora'**, flowers bright yellow, large dark leaves, 6' (2 m) high, zone 3. **'Jackmanii'**, dark green foliage, bright yellow flowers, 3' - 4' (1 m - 1.2 m) high, zone 3. **'Klondike'**, dwarf compact shrub, 2' (.5 m) high, deep yellow flowers, zone 3. **'Red Ace'**, red-flowering form, weak grower, zone 3. **'Royal Flush'**, rosy pink, compact, 12" - 18" (30 cm - 45 cm) high, dark green; in hot weather it loses its color and fades to soft pink or cream, zone 3.

## PRUNUS (PROO-nus) ❧ Cherries, Plums, Peaches, Apricots, Almonds

P. BESSEYI **Sand Cherry** ZONE: 3 to 6.
*Origin:* North America.
*Hardiness:* Dry climates and conditions.
*Size:* Spreading habit, 4' - 6' (1.2 m - 2 m) high.
*Color:* Gray-green foliage glows with pure white flowers in April to May, then purplish black fruit ripens in July and August.
*Soil:* Well-drained soil.

P. GLANDULOSA **Dwarf Flowering Almond** Zone 4 to 8. Apart from the flashy show of blossoms in spring, this plant is pretty ordinary. Origin is central China and northern Japan. Grows 4' - 5' (1.2 m - 1.5 m) high, 3' - 4' (1 m - 1.2 m) spread. Foliage is dull green in summer; single or double flowers are abundant in late April to early May, pink or white; fruits are rarely produced but are red. Not fussy about soil, few problems.

P. PENSYLVANICA **Pin or Wild Red Cherry** ZONE: 2.
*Origin:* North America.
*Hardiness:* Intolerant of shade.
*Size:* 25' - 40' (8 m - 12 m) high, 18' - 25' (5.5 m - 8 m) spread.
*Color:* Deep green foliage, changes to yellow and red in the fall; flowers are white, borne in May and June; fruit is a light red, ripens in July through August.
*Soil:* Adaptable to many soil conditions.
*Maintenance:* Propagate by softwood cuttings.

P. SERRULATA **Japanese Flowering Cherry** ZONE: 5 to 6.
*Origin:* Japan, Korea, China.
*Value:* Good border plant for woodland areas; this is one of the first nurse plants, lives until other plants have had a chance to establish, excellent for the wildlife garden as birds delight in the fruit. Magnificent bark.
*Size:* 50' - 75' (15 m - 23 m) high; cultivars grow on average 20'- 35' (6 m - 11 m).
*Color:* Foliage is lustrous green turning a bronze-red in the fall; flowers are single or double and range in quantity according to variety, borne in April to early May, white or pink, come with the leaves along the stems; fruit is reddish, ripening in late August.
*Soil:* Any soil conditions.
*Maintenance:* Nothing special.
*Problems:* Short-lived.

Some cultivars: **'Kwanzan'** (syn. **'Kanzan'**, **'Hisakuna'**, **'Sekiyama'**), the most popular and hardiest, double flowers of deep pink, foliage is bronze-orange in the fall, 40' (12 m) high tree on its own roots, when grafted it grows about 4' - 6' (1.2 m - 2 m) in perfect form; zone 6. **'Shirofugen'**, pink buds open to white flowers in early spring, deep bronze leaves, fast grower; zone 6. **'Shirotae'**, white fragrant semi-double flowers, pale green foliage with a bronze tinge, spreads; zone 6.

PSEUDOTSUGA MENZIESII GLAUCA (soo-do-SUGA) ❧ **Rocky Mountain Douglas-fir** ZONE: 3 to 6.
*Origin:* North America.
*Value:* Noble forest tree, ornamental, needs space, excellent specimen for massing, windbreaks; a natural as a Christmas tree.
*Hardiness:* This tree will survive in eastern Alberta in -62°F (-51°C). Find out where the seeds came from to judge its hardiness.
*Size:* 40' - 80' (12 m - 24 m) in landscape conditions, 12' - 20' (3.5 m - 6 m) spread; it can grow to 200' (60 m) in its native habitat.
*Color:* Yellow-green foliage, rose-red flowers borne on 3-year-old trees.
*Soil:* Prefers slightly acid or neutral soil, well-drained, moist, in sunny locations; does poorly on dry soils.
*Maintenance:* Needs a good trimming.
*Problems:* Canker, leaf casts, Douglas-fir bark beetle, gypsy moth, pine butterfly, budworm. *Leaf Cast*—yellow spots appear in the fall, turn reddish brown in the spring, tree looks scorched; there is no control for the disease. *Douglas-fir bark beetle*—proper pruning helps control this small black beetle; eggs run across grain of the wood. Don't trim or cut off too many healthy branches.

Some cultivars: **'Compacta'**, compact conical form, short dark green needles; zone 7. **'Fastigiata'**, conical, crowded branches, good looking clone; zone 7. **'Pendula'**, blue cascading form.

PYRACANTHA COCCINEA (py-ra-KAN-tha) ❧ **Scarlet Firethorn** ZONE: 6 to 9, zone 5.
*Origin:* China.
*Value:* Good for informal hedging, or against shady cool walls; can be trained to grow up trellis or espaliered; the fruit is its best asset.
*Hardiness:* Wind chill damages young growth, takes temperatures to -20°F (-30°C).
*Size:* 6' (2 m) high with an equal spread.
*Color:* Dark green foliage that turns brown in winter unless plant is situated well; flowers in April, whitish, showy, with an unpleasant odor; quite spectacular berry-like fruit is orange-red ripening in September and hanging on until winter, keeps the wildlife fed.
*Soil:* Amazingly tolerant of dry or wet soil but does best in well-drained moist soil, full sun produces best fruit.
*Maintenance:* Needs considerable pruning to control; propagate from semiripe cuttings taken in the summer; transplants poorly.
*Problems:* Susceptible to fireblight, twig blight, root rot, leaf blight, aphids, scales.

Some cultivars: **'Chadwickii'**, hardy to zone 6, prolific fruiter, orange-red. **'Gnome'**, this is usually mislabelled as P. ANGUSTIFOLIA 'Gnome'; it is smaller all-round; zone 6. **'Kasan'**, orange-red fruit, Russian origin, scab susceptible; zone 6. **'Lalandei'**, most widely known, red fruits, 10' - 15' (3 m - 4.5 m) high, scab susceptible, hardiest; zone 6. **'Walker's Pride'**, dense and compact; only one for zone 5, says Sabuco.

P. CRENULATA ROGERSIANA **'Teton'**
Adaptable to zone 5 if in full sun. When planting, cut back almost to the ground. Takes 3 to 4 years to recover, so don't give up.

PYRUS CALLERYANA (PY-rus) ❧ **Bradford Callery Pear** ZONE: 4 to 8.
*Origin:* China.
*Value:* A very elegant tree that forms a great wall even in a small city garden.
*Size:* 30' - 50' (9 m - 15 m) high with a spread of 20' - 35' (6 m - 11 m).
*Color:* Glossy green foliage in summer, turning to glossy purple or scarlet in the fall; flowers are white, borne in early May; the tree looks like a large white cloud and is well known for its spring show; fruit is small, rounded and hidden by the foliage.
*Soil:* Adaptable to many different soils.
*Maintenance:* Transplant in late winter or in early spring, never when in bloom or leaf.

*Problems:* Older trees might split because of its habit of forming a tight crotch; pest free. Some cultivars: **'Bradford'**, the most commonly available, but Sabuco thinks it's overplanted. The following are preferable: **'Autumn Blaze'**, cold hardy, tougher because it can be grown on its own roots; consistent purple-red fading to maroon fall color, zone 4. **'Chanticleer'**, the hardiest of the grafted specimens; pyramidal shape, might be used in areas where there is not room for the spread of **'Bradford'**; zone 4. **'Redspire'**, pyramidal form, shiny dark green leaves turn more yellow than red in fall, thornless; zone 5.

PYRUS SALICIFOLIA **Willowleaf Pear**
This variety has graceful, silver-gray leaves; 15' - 25' (4.5 m - 8 m) high; susceptible to fireblight. More ornamental is the cultivar P. s. **'Pendula'** with its elegant drooping branches; flowers are pure white, fruits are typical pear shape, origin is southeastern Europe, Asia. This is a choice tree for a small garden; zone 4. A new cultivar is P. S. **'Silver Frost'**, with very silvery narrow leaves.

QUERCUS ALBA (KWER-kus) **White Oak** *ZONE:* 2b.
About 40 types are available in North American nurseries.
*Origin:* Northern Temperate zones.
*Value:* Slow growth, not widely used, unless native to the area, a majestic tree for a very large garden.
*Size:* 100' (30 m) high, 50' - 80' (15 m - 24 m) spread.
*Color:* Dark green leaves in summer, turning a rich red to a wine color that lasts a long time.
*Soil:* Found in many types of soil, prefers well-drained, moist, acid soils.
*Maintenance:* Prune in winter or early spring; transplants well as a small tree; grow from seed sown directly in soil.
*Problems:* White oak is a durable long-living tree; however, there is a long list of problems that have been reported on all oaks.

Q. BICOLOR **Swamp White Oak**
Needs lots of water, adaptable to clay, wet soil and some shade. Forms a round pyramid when young, with glossy leaves that are white felty underneath, exfoliate bark exposes orange-brown; leaves may hang on until spring; zone 4b.

Q. GARRYANA **Oregon White Oak, Western Oak**
Native to the West Coast, this beautiful tree grows to 90' (27 m) and does well on dry gravelly soils; zone 8.

Q. IMBRICARIA **Shingle Oak**
Easily grown and easy to prune, laurel-like leaves, red when they open, to burnt sienna in autumn; zone 4b.

Q. RUBRA **Red Oak** *ZONE:* 3.
*Origin:* Eastern North America.
*Value:* Fast growing oak, good street tree.
*Hardiness:* Tolerates pollution but not heat.
*Size:* Grows to 75' (23 m) with a spread of 40' to 50' (12 m - 15 m).
*Color:* Pinkish to red as leaves unfold, lustrous green in summer turning russet to bright red in fall.
*Soil:* Sandy loam soil, well-drained, on the acid side.
*Maintenance:* Transplants well.
*Problems:* A bit less susceptible to problems than other oaks.

RHAMNUS CATHARTICA (RAM-nus)
**Common Buckthorn** *ZONE:* 5.
*Origin:* Europe and Asia.
*Value:* Also suitable as a hedge or backdrop and excellent for difficult areas; requires pruning to keep under control. Because the berries are all over the place, the trees sprout up all over the place.
*Hardiness:* Will grow in areas where other trees will not, very tolerant of the urban landscape.
*Size:* 18' - 25' (5.5 m - 8 m) high, with equal spread.
*Color:* Dark glossy leaves, no fall color to speak of; flowers are unimportant; black berry-like fruit attracts birds.
*Soil:* Very adaptable, will grow in difficult soil conditions.
*Maintenance:* Easily transplanted, birds carry seeds and plants become weed-like.
*Problems:* Leaf spot, rust, powdery mildew.

R. FRANGULA **Alder Buckthorn** *ZONE:* 3b.
*Origin:* Europe, Asia, North Africa.
*Value:* Dirr finds the species weedlike but good for a wildlife garden.
*Size:* 10' - 12' (2 m - 3.5 m) high with 8' - 12' (2.5 m - 3.5 m) spread.
*Color:* Dark glossy green leaf, fall color a poor green-yellow; bees love the small creamy green flowers, borne in May, not showy; red to purple-black fruit is berry-like and ripens July through to September.
*Soil:* Well-drained soil, adaptable.
*Maintenance:* Transplants well, seeds prolifically.

RHODODENDRONS AND AZALEAS
*ZONE:* 4 to 6, depending on the species.
*Origin:* China, Japan, Europe and North America. There are over 900 species with thousands of cultivars. It's important to check on the origin to ensure plant will be hardy.
*Value:* Can be used effectively in a woodland setting, in combination with smaller-leaved plants, in shrub borders, as specimens (some get to be enormous) and even in containers. They mingle handsomely together, as well as with heathers and dwarf conifers.

*Hardiness:* They are sensitive to winter chill, susceptible to injury if not protected, and are best planted in slightly shaded areas, protected from wind and strong winter sun.
*Size:* Depends on cultivar and growing conditions; they average between 3' and 6' (1 m to 2 m) high with an equal or greater spread.
*Color:* Lavender, purple, magenta flowers are the most common; leaves are glossy dark green.
*Soil:* Sensitive to salinity, likes acid soil but some species can adapt to less acidity. The larger the leaf the more shade the plant needs. Add lots of organic matter to the soil.
*Maintenance:* When planting, the root ball should sit either on top of the soil or level with it. Add loam, and then mulch with leaf mold and compost to about 4" (10 cm) deep, but not touching the trunk of the plant. Deadhead carefully—the new buds are side by side with old blooms. Snap off the dead bloom at the base. Prune only to keep in shape by removing anything that looks ratty over 3 years.
*Problems:* They have fine shallow roots that won't stand up to competition so be careful where you place them.

R. ARBORESCENS, **Sweet Azalea**, deciduous; white blooms in June; 6' - 10' (2 m - 3 m); survives -20°F (-25°C), zone 4.

R. ARBOREUM, from the Himalayas, evergreen, pink or red flowers, 6' (2 m); zone 7.

R. CANADENSE, **Rhodora**, 3' - 4' (1 m - 1.2 m) high and wide; rose-colored flowers; zone 4.

R. CAROLINIANUM, **Carolina Rhododendron**, a parent of **'PJM'**, pink-rose, lavender; cut back after flowering for more blooms; early spring. **'Album'** is white; **'Luteum'** is pale yellow; all zone 5.

R. FASTIGIATUM, small upright evergreen 12" - 18" (30 cm - 45 cm) with purple blooms; blue-green leaves; zone 5.

R. IMPEDITUM, **Cloudland Rhododendron**, must have snow cover in zone 5; dwarf, 12" (30 cm), dark blue or purple flowers. The foliage is blue—just lovely; zone 5.

R. LUTEUM has yellow fragrant flowers; 3' - 4' (1 m - 1.2 m); zone 5.

R. MICRANTHUM, **Manchurian Rhododendron**, evergreen, drought tolerant; tiny leaves and delicate little white flowers; up to 4' (1.2 m); zone 3 (only under snow).

R. MUCRONULATUM, **Korean Azalea**, early rosy blooms, light green small leaves, spicy fragrance; 6' (2 m); zone 5.

R. SCHLIPPENBACHII, **Royal Azalea**, hates direct summer sun; unusually shaped leaves; delicate pink blooms in May; 4' - 5' (1.2 m - 1.5 m); zone 5.

RHODODENDRONS YAKUSIMANUM 'Ken Janek', large pink flowers, excellent foliage, compact plant, zone 5. 'Mist Maiden', apple blossom pink flowers that turn white with age, excellent foliage, compact, zone 5. 'Whitney's Dwarf Form' is tolerant of harsh conditions; 2' (.5 m); dark red bud opens to pink, felt-like indumentum on the bottom of leaf; zone 5.

R. YEDOENSE POUKHANENSE, Yodogawa Azalea, tolerates lime; sometimes semi-evergreen, lovely fall color; magenta flowers; 2' - 3' (.5 m - 1 m); zone 5.

There are so many hybrids and cultivars that it's possible to find any color you want. Look for ones that are bred in your region and follow the instructions above. Particularly wonderful rhodos are 'Aglo'; Catawbiense Hybrids, 'English Roseum'; Exbury Hybrid Azaleas; 'Olga Mezitt'; 'PJM'; 'Roseum elegans'.

RHODOTYPOS SCANDENS (ro-DO-tip-us) ❀ Jetbead ZONE: 6.
Origin: China, Korea, Japan.
Value: A modest, not flashy, shade plant for difficult areas.
Hardiness: Tough, durable plant.
Size: 3' - 6' (1 m - 2 m) high with a spread of 5' - 10' (1.5 m - 2 m).
Color: Dark green foliage during summer, green-yellow in fall; flowers are white, borne at end of twigs in May-June; shiny black fruit ripens in October.
Soil: Tolerant of different soils, full sun or partial shade.
Maintenance: Remove one-third of old wood after flowering to encourage rejuvenation; transplants easily.

RHUS AROMATICA (RUSS) ❀ Fragrant Sumac ZONE: 3 to 9.
Origin: Ontario to Minnesota, south to Florida and Texas.
Value: Fast-growing cover, stabilizes banks and hillsides, good background to shrub border and as a screen.
Hardiness: Low, irregularly shaped shrub, suckers from the root and produces a dense tangle of stems and leaves.
Size: 6' - 9' (2 m - 1.8 m) high, width is often twice the height.
Color: Leaf color is medium green, almost a blue-green, and glossy; leaves start turning in August-September; yellowish flowers borne in March-April.
Soil: Prefers acid soil but is very adaptable.
Maintenance: Prune off suckers; transplants easily. Spreads everywhere in the garden.
R. A. 'Grow Low' does just that, about 30" (75 cm) and about 8' (2.5 m) wide.

RHUS TYPHINA ❀ Staghorn Sumac ZONE: 3 to 8.
Origin: Eastern North America.

Value: Good for naturalizing or massing on banks and in waste areas; also as a screen, foundation planting, or container planting. I know that some think it's a weed, but in the right situation, and with its magnificent scarlet color in autumn, it is a treat.
Size: 15' - 25' (4.5 m - 8 m) high under cultivation, twice that in the wild.
Color: Leaves are bright green in summer, yellow, orange and scarlet in fall; fruit is crimson, late August through to April; greenish yellow flowers June to July.
Soil: Well-drained or dry, sterile soil.
Maintenance: Cut to ground to rejuvenate; easily transplanted.
Problems: Suckers easily from the root.

RIBES ALPINUM (RY-beez) ❀ Alpine Currant ZONE: 2 to 7.
Origin: Europe.
Value: Used as hedge, for mass planting, screening; good in semishade areas.
Size: 3' - 6' (1 m - 2 m) high and just as wide.
Color: Leaf is deep green in summer, yellow in fall; one of the first shrubs to leaf out in the spring; flowers in April, greenish yellow; scarlet juicy berries ripen in June-July.
Soil: Tolerant of any soil.
Maintenance: Prune older stems and cut back anything that gets out of control; transplants easily, softwood cuttings taken in June root well with rooting treatment.
Problems: Cane blight, leaf spot, rust, currant aphid, scale.
Some cultivars: 'Aureum', dwarf type, yellow-green leaves, best in full sun, zone 2. 'Green Mound', dwarf, dense, 2' - 3' (.5 m - 1 m) high, male shows resistance to leaf diseases; Dirr also lists 'Nana', 'Pumila', 'Compacta'.

R. SANGUINEUM, Red Flowering Currant
Cannot be grown in wheat areas because it is an alternate host for black stem wheat rust; other than that it is trouble-free; zone 5.

ROBINIA PSEUDOACACIA (ro-BIN-ia) ❀ Black Locust, False Acacia, Yellow Locust ZONE: 3 to 8.
Origin: Eastern United States.
Value: Will grow in poor and dry soils; survives under the worst conditions, good for highways, stripped mine areas. Attractive to bees. Will add bright yellow to the garden and is a good tree for the cottage or country. It's not so dense as to block a view.
Hardiness: Tolerates dry conditions.
Size: 30' - 50' (9 m - 15 m) high with a spread of 20' - 35' (6 m - 11 m).
Color: Leaf is dull, dark blue-green; fragrant white flowers after leaves have developed; fruit matures in October.
Soil: Varied soils, does not like wet soils, maximum development is on limestone, moist rich soil.

Maintenance: Transplants easily.
Problems: Two serious pests: the locust borer and locust leaf miner. Locust borer: bark is discolored and disfigured; insect is a small black beetle; control with cutting and destroying infested trees, kill young borer in trunk by inserting Borox into burrows and sealing the openings with chewing gum. Locust leaf miner: beetles live through the winter and attack the leaves in May, second generation is born in September from larvae under the leaves; control by removing any infested leaves and getting rid of them, but don't put them in the compost. Keep well cultivated and weedfree.
Some cultivars: 'Frisia', leaves are golden yellow and hold color all summer, this is the best yellow form; zone 4. 'Umbraculifera', dense umbrella-like canopy shape, 20' (6 m) high and wide, few if any flowers, prominent in European landscapes; zone 4.

ROSA (RO-sa) ❀ Rose
Roses have evolved over millions of years. Botanically they belong to a single genus, but thousands of varieties exist. They are designated by classes. Roses that grow in the wild belong to the class of species roses. The other classes are made up of cultivars that have been bred by crossing species roses with hybrids.

Cultivated rose classes are further divided into modern and old roses. The dividing year is 1867, the year that a French botanist crossed a hybrid with a tea rose and bred the first Western rose to bloom repeatedly from spring to fall. There are some 18 classes.

Hybrid Tea Roses; Shrub Roses or Old-Fashioned Roses or Rugosa Roses; Floribundas; Grandifloras; Climbers and Ground Covers are the best bets for Canadian gardens.

Climbers: An assortment of types that share a tendency to produce long, flexible flowering canes. Climbers may be Hybrid Teas or Floribundas.
Maintenance: Remove an old cane for every new one produced, cut it at the base. Remove dead or diseased canes. If there is not enough bloom, then a good pruning is required. Cut back several laterals leaving 4 to 8 buds, remove all suckers, and where there is overcrowding, thin the canes. Prune when dormant, between late fall and early spring. Tie new canes with a material that will disintegrate—wire will damage the canes.

Floribundas: Feature clusters of flowers in a wide variety of colors. Usually hardy, they will bloom throughout the season. Use as a mass planting, hedge or a single plant. Floribundas are grafted like Hybrid Teas, grow no more than 3' (1 m).

*Grandifloras:* The flowers are clusters with Hybrid Tea-like blooms in a wide variety of colors. They bloom constantly and are easy to grow. They reach heights of 3' - 4' (1 m - 1.2 m).

*Hybrid Teas:* The most popular of the roses. Long slender buds that become beautiful double blooms, they are highly fragrant. There are numerous varieties of color. They grow 3' - 4' (1 m - 1.2 m) high. The top is grafted onto the roots. They have hardy rootstalks.

*Shrub Roses* (R. RUGOSA): These pillar-type roses are modern roses. They stand independently and have a shrub- or tree-like growth. Some have double or semi-double blooms and they tend to repeat flowering. They require light pruning of spent blooms after early-summer flowering.

ROSA RUGOSA ❧ **Japanese Rose, Rugosa Rose**
*ZONE:* 2 to 7.
*Origin:* Northern China, Korea, Japan.
*Value:* Hedges, banks, sandy soils, difficult sites, tolerates salt sea spray.
*Hardiness:* Sturdy shrub, vigorous, grows fast.
*Size:* 4' - 6' (1.2 m - 2 m) high, equal spread.
*Color:* Deep green foliage in summer, yellow in fall; flowers June through to August, rose-purple to white; brick red rose hips.
*Soil:* Prefers organic, well-drained soil, slightly acid is best, but tolerates alkalinity; will grow under almost any conditions.
*Maintenance:* As above.
*Problems:* A complete listing of problems is impossible, they have too many according to Dirr.
Some cultivars: '**Alba**', single white flower. '**Albo-plena**', double white flower. '**Plena**', double fuchsia-purple flower. '**Rosea**', single rose flowers.

***Species Roses***
There are several hundred types of species roses. They flower in late spring: single flowers, five-petalled. Here are two:

R. GLAUCA (syn. RUBRIFOLIA) *ZONE:* 2 to 7.
*Origin:* Central and southern Europe.
*Value:* Shrub border.
*Hardiness:* Adaptable to many conditions.
*Size:* Grows 5' - 7' (1.5 m - 2.1 m) high.
*Color:* Foliage is coppery or purplish color with a gray or silver cast; cane is covered in purplish bloom; flowers are a clear pink.
*Soil:* Almost any.
*Maintenance:* Prune for shape after blooming or try the Japanese method of creating a pendulous shrub: tie a container of pebbles to the top of a branch—just light enough to bend the cane—in spring add pebbles to make the container progressively heavier.

R. HUGONIS **Father Hugo Rose** *ZONE:* 5.
A species rose often found in older gardens.
*Origin:* Central China.
*Value:* Medium-sized shrub, free-flowering, Dirr says it looks ragged when not in flower.
*Size:* Grows 6' - 8' (2 m - 2.5 m) high.
*Color:* Flowers are single canary yellow, blooming in May-June; canes are often reddish; fruit is scarlet, turns blackish red, ripens in August.

SALIX ALBA (SAY-lix) ❧ **White Willow**
*ZONE:* 2 to 8.
*Origin:* Europe, North Africa, Asia.
*Value:* Too dirty for the street or in most gardens; excellent for moist areas.
*Hardiness:* Damaged in ice and wind storms.
*Size:* Grows 75' (23 m) high.
*Color:* Leaf is bright green almost a silver-green in summer; male flowers are showy and create a pussy willow effect.
*Soil:* Prefers moist soils; found along streams, ponds, rivers and other moist areas.
*Problems:* Twig blight, crown gall, leaf blight, black canker, gray scab, leaf spot, powdery mildew, tar spot, rust, imported willow leaf beetle, pine cone gall, basket willow gall, willow lace bug, willow flea weevil, willow shoot sawfly, mottled willow borer.

S. BABYLONICA **Babylon Weeping Willow**
A golden tree that grows to 40' (12 m) with similar spread, broad crown of weeping branches; origin is China; zone 7.

S. CAPREA **Goat Willow**
An erect small tree, grows up to 25' (8 m), male catkins appear in March or early April and are known as pussy willows; this is not the true pussy willow of S. DISCOLOR; origin is Europe, Iran, northern Asia; zone 4 to 8.

S. GRACILISTYLA **'Melanostachys' Black Willow**
Black catkins with red anthers, bushy shrub, grows 10' - 12' (3 m - 3.5 m), zone 4 to 9.

S. LANATA, **Woolly Willow**
A great plant for winter interest; zone 1.

S. SACHALINENSIS **'Sekka'**
Favorite of arrangers. Wonderful flattened and curled stems. Large useful shrub for pondside, zone 4.

SAMBUCUS CANADENSIS (sam-BEW-kus) ❧ **American Elder** *ZONE:* 3 to 9.
*Origin:* Nova Scotia and Manitoba to Florida and Texas.
*Value:* Fruit can be used for jellies and wine; poor unkempt habit for the home garden, good for naturalizing or in wetlands.
*Hardiness:* Found in rich moist soil.
*Size:* 5' - 12' (1.5 m - 3.5 m) high, depending on habitat.
*Color:* Bright green in summer; white flowers are borne in June-July covering the entire plant; fruit is purple-black berry-like, ripens in August-September.
*Soil:* Does best in moist soils but tolerates dry conditions.
*Maintenance:* Nothing special.
*Problems:* Leaf spot, powdery mildew, canker, borers.
Some cultivars: '**Aurea**', cherry red fruit, yellow foliage, vigorous grower, zone 3. '**Maxima**', rose-purple flowers in large clusters, vigorous, zone 3.

S. NIGRA **European Elder**
Grows 30' (9 m) high, dark green foliage in summer, stinks; flowers are yellow-white, borne in June; fruit is dark black, ripens in September. There are yellow-leaved varieties as well as purple; origin is Europe, North Africa, western Asia; zone 4.

SCHIZOPHRAGMA HYDRANGEOIDES (sky-zo-FRAG-ma) ❧ **Japanese Hydrangea Vine** *ZONE:* 5.
*Origin:* Asia.
*Value:* This self-clinging vine blooms much earlier than H. ANOMALA PETIOLARIS. The leaves are more matte and serrated than the latter.
*Size:* Climbs 30' (9 m) or more.
*Color:* Long lasting white flowers look like tarnished lace when they turn brown.
*Soil:* Not fussy but does prefer moist soil; semishade.
*Maintenance:* It will hang back at first and then start to cling onto the nearest fence or tree.
Some cultivars: '**Moonlight**', dark green leaves with silver overlay. '**Roseum**', the pink version; if you can ever find it, grab it. '**Strawberry Leaf**', dark green strawberry shaped leaves, pleasant bark, white flowers.

SENECIO GREYI (sen-EE-sio) ❧ **Shrubby Ragwort** *ZONE:* 9 to 10.
*Origin:* New Zealand.
*Value:* Used as low-growing shrub in borders or, if planted far enough apart, as hedging; also used in containers along paths.
*Hardiness:* The true species S. GREYI is very tender.
*Size:* Maximum height at maturity is 3' (1 m).
*Color:* Foliage is a sensuous silver-gray, downy and soft; clusters of daisy-shaped yellow flowers borne in June; fruit is insignificant.
*Soil:* Well-drained open soil, dislikes being water-logged.
*Maintenance:* Annual trim to keep shrub looking healthy, best done in spring; cut old wood back to ground to rejuvenate. Semiripe cuttings in summer, container-grown plants transplant well.
*Problems:* Can become woody.
S.G. '**Sunshine**' is an attractive and popular hybrid, zone 7 to 8.

SHEPHERDIA CANADENSIS (shep-HER-dia)
🌿 **Russet Buffaloberry** *ZONE:* 1 to 6.
*Origin:* North America.
*Value:* Highways and difficult areas. A good plant for windbreaks. Fixes nitrogen in soil.
*Hardiness:* Seems to appreciate abuse.
*Size:* 3' - 8' (1 m - 2.5 m) high and as wide.
*Color:* Silver-green to gray-green foliage in summer; does not color well in the fall; single yellowish flowers not showy, in April to early May; fruit ripens in June to a yellowish red.
*Soil:* Tolerates the poorest of soils, in fact, the poorer the better; prefers open sunny location.
*Maintenance:* None whatsoever, but it will sucker and you can end up with quite a hedge. Never fertilize.
*Problems:* The usual: leaf spot, powdery mildew.

S. ARGENTEA, **Silver Buffaloberry**, thorny shrub, tree-like, grows to 10' (3 m) high; foliage is silvery, all else is similar to above; zone 2.

S. SHEPARDIA, **Roundleaf Buffaloberry**, a Rocky Mountain native, likes sun, little wind; thick silvery leaves; zone 5.

SKIMMIA JAPONICA (SKIM-ia) 🌿 **Japanese Skimmia** *ZONE:* 7 to 8, possibly 6 to 9.
*Origin:* Japan.
*Value:* Woodland gardens, shrub borders, tub plantings, foundations.
*Hardiness:* Tolerates temperatures to 5°F (-15°C), needs winter protection in colder areas, full sun prevents discoloring.
*Size:* Grows 4' (1.2 m) high with similar spread, but can grow to 6' (2 m) and larger in the right conditions.
*Color:* Compared to other evergreens, lighter green foliage; flowers are slightly fragrant, borne in March-April, glossy maroon red in bud, creamy white when open, males are fragrant; red fruit is found only on the female.
*Soil:* Acid to neutral soil, dislikes alkalinity, dislikes dry or water-logged conditions; light shade is acceptable with enough moisture.
*Maintenance:* Rooted suckers or semiripe cuttings taken in midsummer transplant easily.

SORBUS ALNIFOLIA (SOR-bus) 🌿 **Korean Mountain Ash** *ZONE:* 3 to 7.
*Origin:* Central China, Korea, Japan.
*Value:* Specimen tree for lawns, not good for streets or downtown areas.
*Hardiness:* Tolerates poor soil conditions but tends to get stressed in polluted urban sites.
*Size:* Grows 50' (15 m) high with a smaller spread.
*Color:* Bark is gray on old trunks; leaves a lustrous green in summer, turning yellow, orange and golden brown in fall; flowers are a perfect white, borne in May; round, orange-red to scarlet red fruit ripens in September.
*Soil:* Survives in any soil.

*Maintenance:* Nothing special.
*Problems:* Fireblight.

S. AUCUPARIA **European Mountain Ash** *ZONE:* 3 to 6, maybe 7.
*Origin:* Europe to western Asia and Siberia.
*Value:* Excellent fruit effect, but susceptible to many pests.
*Hardiness:* Problems in severe summer heat.
*Size:* Grows 40' (12 m) with a spread of two-thirds of height.
*Color:* Flat dull green in summer, fall color ranges from green, orange, yellow to red; flowers are flat-topped corymbs in mid to late May, not showy; berry-like fruit, orange-red in August, birds love the fruit.
*Soil:* Prefers acid soil.
*Maintenance:* Be vigilant for all the pests.
*Problems:* Fireblight can wipe it out, crown gall, canker, leaf rust, scab, aphids, pear leaf blister, Japanese leafhopper, roundheaded borer, mountain ash sawfly. Dirr says the best defense is a vigorous, healthy tree.

S. AMERICANA, **American Mountain Ash**, northern species, a small tree, grows 30' (9 m) high, hardy to zone 2, found in cold swamps; on dry soils is stunted, short-lived, slow growing; flowers are white, fruits are orange-red; origin is eastern North America.

S. ARIA, **Whitebeam Mountain Ash**, tree with rounded shape, 35' - 45' (11 m - 14 m) high, lustrous leather-like leaves, white flowers, orange-red fruit ripens in September-October, native to Europe, zone 5.

S. CASHMIRIANA, **Kashmir Mountain Ash**, has a lovely flower, pink in bud, opening to deeper pink with white and pink fruit; zone 5.

SPIRAEA (spy-REE-a)
Spireas fall into 2 groups: spring-blooming and summer-blooming. Can also be classified as tall or short; vary in height and form. Native to the Himalayas through China and Japan.

S. ALBIFLORA 🌿 **Japanese White Spirea** *ZONE:* 4.
Equated with the white flowering S. 'Anthony Waterer'. Dirr thinks this could be listed as a cultivar of S. JAPONICA.
*Value:* Good for borders, containers or mass plantings.
*Size:* Low growing, 18" (45 cm), rounded habit.
*Color:* Medium to dark green leaves; white flowers appear in late June or early July.
*Soil:* Prefers acid soil.
*Maintenance:* Flowers on new growth so can be cut back each spring; roots readily from cuttings.
*Problems:* None; considered superior to the spireas that become unkempt in appearance.

S. X BILLIARDII 🌿 **Billiard Spirea**
Cross between S. DOUGLASII and S. SALICIFOLIA.
Upright habit to 6' (2 m). Dense dark green foliage; rose-colored flowers bloom June to August, 4" - 8" (10 cm - 20 cm) long panicles, pyramidal shape. Remove flowers when they fade to ugly brown. Susceptible to iron chlorosis; plant in acid soil only, zone 3.

S. BULLATA 🌿 **Crispleaf Spirea**
Excellent low ground cover. 12" - 15" (30 cm - 45 cm) high. Dark green foliage; deep rosy-pink dense corymbs borne in June and July, zone 4.

S. X BUMALDA 🌿 **Bumald Spirea**
An overused ground cover, low massing. Grows 3' (1 m) high, 3' - 5' (1 m - 1.5 m) wide. Pinkish to reddish new foliage, dark bluish green in summer, turns almost bronze in fall; flowers white to deep pink, borne June into August. Tolerant of many soils, except wet ones, prefers full sun. Easy to transplant, suckers easily; zone 2b to 8.

S. X CINEREA 'Grefsheim'
An early-flowering spirea with small white flowers that clothe the leafless branches in April; looks like a cloud, dense arching foliage, 4' - 5' (1.2 m - 1.5 m) high and wide; Norwegian origin; zone 4.

S. JAPONICA 🌿 **Japanese Spirea**
This is the most readily available spirea. Has upright stiff branches. Native to Japan where it grows wild. Many cultivars have been developed over the centuries. Grows 5' (1.5 m) high. Pale to deep pink to white flowers, June through July. Blooms on current wood, so cut it back almost to the ground in early spring, zone 3 to 8.
var. ALPINA or 'Nana', dainty fine-textured low-growing type with pink flowers, June-July, grows to 6' (2 m) in width, good edging plant, grouping or ground cover, some evidence of chlorosis. 'Anthony Waterer' (syn S. X BUMALDA), to 4' (1.2 m) high, flowers deep carmine-pink, numerous clones, found in many older gardens, overused, foliage is reddish purple in the spring; zone 3. 'Coccinea' same size and shape as 'Little Princess' but has darker rose flowers; zone 3. 'Crispa' (syn S. X BUMALDA), twisted leaves, grows to 3' (1 m) high, rose-pink flowers in June-July, zone 3. 'Froebellii' (syn S. X BUMALDA), to 3' (1 m) high, deep pink flowers; compact plant; zone 3. 'Gold Flame' (syn S. X BUMALDA), to 3' (1 m) high, new foliage is mottled with red, copper, and orange and repeated in the fall, compact pinkish flowers, foliage is yellow to yellow-green in summer; zone 3. 'Little Princess', pink flowers all summer; zone 3.

SPIRAEA NIPPONICA 'Snowmound' (spy-REE-a) ❦ Snowmound Nippon Spirea
Origin is Japan. Grows 5' (1.5 m) high and wide. Dark blue-green leaves, white flowers bloom in late May to June; dense form, zone 3 to 8.

S. THUNBERGII Thunberg Spirea
Grows to 5' (1.5 m) high with the same width; bushy, slender branches, twiggy; yellowish green foliage in summer, tinged with orange and bronze in fall; flowers are white, borne in March-April before the leaves; native to China; zone 3 to 8.

S. TRILOBATA Threelobe Spirea
The most shade-tolerant small shrub, grows 5' (1.5 m) high, dense and compact, leaves are bluish green, flowers are pure white and in great profusion in May; native to northern China to Siberia; zone 2.

STEPHANANDRA INCISA (steff-an-AND-ra) ❦ Cutleaf Stephanandra ZONE: 3 to 7.
Origin: Japan, Korea.
Value: Good for hedges, massing, screens, shrub border, bank cover, ground cover.
Hardiness: Grows in full sun or light shade. Fast grower.
Size: Grows to 7' (2.1 m) high, equal or greater spread.
Color: Bright green, red-purple in fall; yellowish white flowers like those of spirea borne in May-June; flowers are insignificant.
Soil: Prefers moist acid soil, well-drained, supplemented with peat moss or leaf mold.
Maintenance: Just plant and let grow; transplants readily.
Problems: None serious; will develop chlorosis in very limy soils.

STEWARTIA PSEUDOCAMELLIA (stew-ART-ia) ❦ Japanese Stewartia ZONE: 5 to 8.
Origin: Japan.
Value: Excellent tree with late-blooming flowers in July or August; has beautiful gray, orange, yellow and red bark in winter. Good in woodlands.
Hardiness: Has been known to take temperatures -25°F (-32°C).
Size: Grows 50' (15 m).
Color: Dark green leaves, turning yellow, red to dark reddish purple in fall; white flowers with orange anthers bloom in July.
Soil: Moist, loamy acid soil.
Maintenance: Not a troublesome plant.
Problems: Keep roots protected from hot sun.
S. P. 'Cascade' is a weeping form; var. KOREANA is slightly hardier; grows to 35' (11 m); zone 5.
S. OVATA GRANDIFLORA is a splendid understorey plant with white flowers 4" (10 cm), purple stamens and golden anthers. Brilliant red leaves in fall; zone 6.

STYRAX JAPONICUS (STY-rax) ❦ Japanese Snowbell ZONE: 5.
Origin: China, Japan.
Value: Small tree, excellent near the patio or pool where the lovely scent can be appreciated in the evening; good in the shrub border, on hillsides, slopes or as a specimen.
Hardiness: Tolerates -20°F (-30°C) but will be injured at lower temperatures.
Size: Grows 30' (9 m) with equal spread.
Color: Medium to dark green foliage in summer, turning yellowish to red in fall; white, yellow-stamened flowers, slightly fragrant, bell-shaped, May-June; fruit is grayish; bark has gray and orange streaks.
Soil: Runs rampant and produces too much soft growth in rich soil; full sun out of wind.
Maintenance: None and it is pest free.
Some varieties and cultivars: 'Fargesii', more tree-like, larger leaves. 'Pink Chimes', pink blooms that are slightly smaller than the species. S. OBASSIA, a lovely plant that is less well known; needs lots of moisture; pure white heavily scented flowers produced in racemes (clusters) 6" (15 cm) long; grows 30' (9 m) high, zone 6. S. AMERICANA likes a slightly acid soil with cool root run, white bell-shaped fragrant flowers, some dieback in severe winters; zone 5.

SYMPHORICARPOS ALBUS (sim-for-ik-KAR-pos) ❦ Common Snowberry ZONE: 2.
Origin: North America and Mexico.
Value: Small genus grown mainly for its white or rose-colored berries—indispensable in the winter garden. Not bad as a hedge. Shade tolerant; a good understorey plant.
Size: Grows 6' (2 m) high.
Color: Pink flowers in June; white berries.
Soil: Any soil.
Maintenance: Prune hard in early spring to remove suckers and cut the rest in half; flowers on new growth; easily divided, suckers root.
Problems: Cannot stand wet feet in winter.

S. X CHENAULTII takes both sun and shade, any soil; can withstand drought; disease resistant. Good for really difficult sites; zone 3.

S X C. 'Hancock', a ground cover shrub. Sabuco thinks this is a better plant than COTONEASTER APICULATUS or C. HORIZONTALIS; he says it is hardier, showier and more disease resistant. I'll take them all. Zone 3.

S. X DORRENBOSII 'Mother of Pearl', an excellent clone with pale pink tint to the fruit. Very drought tolerant; grows 3' (1 m) high; adaptable to zone 3.

S. ORBICULATUS 'Foliis Variegatis', grows 3' - 5' (1 m - 1.5 m) high, bright green leaves with yellow edge, dense shrub; zone 2 or 3.

SYMPLOCOS PANICULATA (SIM-plo-kos) ❦ Sapphire Berry ZONE: 4 to 8.
Origin: Himalayas to China and Japan.
Value: Best used in the back of shrub border, as a screen, small specimen tree or to attract birds. Plant several to cross-pollinate.
Size: 10' - 20' (3 m - 6 m) high.
Color: Dark green oval leaves with white flowers in May to June; but it's the turquoise blue to pure blue berries in autumn that are the main attraction.
Soil: Well-drained soil, full sun.
Maintenance: Prune during winter; transplants well, cuttings root easily in July.

SYRINGA VULGARIS
There are more than 24 species and over 500 varieties in North America. Depending on variety blooms from early May to late June. Look for the more interesting ones that have been micro-propagated on their own roots.
Maintenance: Needs space for air circulation (to avoid powdery mildew), excellent drainage and lots of mulching during the first 3 years. After that they are pretty much drought tolerant. Most like alkaline soil—add some horticultural lime every 2 years to keep soil neutral. Full sun. Keep mulched—they will suck all the nutrients from everything around them.
Prune the plants according to type:
Slow-growing forms: no pruning needed except to keep tidy. Cut back stems.
Large-flowered forms: deadheading will discourage fungus; prune out dead or diseased branches after flowering is over. To bring back an unruly old clump: cut back stems to 6" (15 cm) from ground in spring.

SYRINGA MEYERI (si-RING-ga) ❦ Meyer Lilac
This is a disease-resistant lilac that usually isn't prone to mildew. Origin is Northern China. Wonderfully fragrant small-leaved variety with a fairly long blooming period. Grows 6' - 8' (1 m - 2.5 m) high and up to 10' (3 m) wide. Flowers are purple to violet, zone 3.

S. VULGARIS: the cultivars of this species are the most commonly available. 'Charles Joly', double wine red. 'Lavender Lady'. 'Ludwig Spaeth', wine red. 'Katherine Havemeyer', double purple-lavender. 'Michel Buchner', double lavender. 'Sensation', purple-red.
The Preston Hybrids were developed by Isabella Preston in Ottawa and are late blooming in reds and pink. They are, of course, very hardy. 'Isabella' is one of the best.

S. AMURENSIS JAPONICA Japanese Tree Lilac, white flowers in mid to late June.

S. DILATATA, a variety with better autumn color than most; zone 2.

SYRINGA PATULA (syn S. VELUTINA) **Korean Lilac**

The most famous cultivar is '**Miss Kim**'. Very easy to grow and to transplant. At 12' (3.5 m) high is not exactly dwarf. Buds open pink and fade to pale lavender-blue, very floriferous. Likes alkaline soil. Slow growing, zone 3.

TAMARIX RAMOSISSIMA (TAM-ar-ix) ❦ **Five-stamen Tamarix** *ZONE:* 2.
*Origin:* Europe, Africa, Asia.
*Value:* Foliage makes it a good background plant. Good for the seashore.
*Hardiness:* Likes full sun, salt tolerant.
*Size:* Grows 15' (4.5 m) with similar spread.
*Color:* Light green scale-like leaf, rosy pink flowers, borne in dense racemes June-July, lasts 6 to 8 weeks.
*Soil:* Thrives in poor, infertile, but well-drained soil.
*Maintenance:* For early-flowering species, prune back in early spring since it flowers on new growth. Prune autumn-flowering ones every few years in spring to 1" (2.5 cm) of old wood; sparse root system, transplant carefully, softwood cuttings will take easily.
*Problems:* Canker, powdery mildew, root rot, wood rot and scale.
T. R. '**Pink Cascade**', shell pink flowers. Var. RUBRA, deeper pink flowers.

TAXODIUM DISTICHUM (tax-O-dium) ❦ **Bald Cypress** *ZONE:* 4.
*Origin:* North America, East Asia, Tasmania.
*Value:* A conifer for infertile swampy places. Has unusual, long knobby knee-like roots to hold it out of water on wet ground.
*Hardiness:* Has been known to withstand -42°F (-40°C).
*Size:* Columnar growth to 125' (38 m), 30' - 40' (9 m - 12 m) in 15 to 20 years.
*Color:* Pale green leaves over red bark, which may exfoliate, exposing even deeper red bark beneath.
*Problems:* Chlorosis. Correct with ferric ammonium citrate or chelated iron.

TAXUS CUSPIDATA (TAX-us) ❦ **Japanese Yew** *ZONE:* 4.
*Origin:* Japan, Korea, Manchuria.
*Value:* The worst use of this plant is to shear it off in grotesque shapes for foundation planting. It has a beautiful natural form and makes a superb background for lighter plants. From zone 7, use TAXUS BACCATA as an evergreen hedge, slightly clipped over each year; use it as an informal barrier between garden rooms, for a Mediterranean garden or for tapestry hedges.
*Hardiness:* Some cultivars are resistant to burn at -38°F (-39°C).
*Size:* Pyramidal form to 50' (15 m).
*Color:* Dark green foliage, reddish brown bark and seeds.

*Soil:* Prefers acid soils, moist, well-drained, sandy loam.
*Maintenance:* None; cuttings root easily; can be pruned.
*Problems:* Taxus mealybug, black vine weevil, scale, yew-gall midge.

T. BACCATA, **English Yew,** is the traditional form for hedges.

T. B. '**Fastigiata Aurea**', **Golden Irish Yew**
An elegant form that grows to 6' (2 m); makes a thick impenetrable hedge, pleasant yellow edge to the leaves, good screen for swimming pools; grows slowly.

THUJA (thew-YA) ❦ **Arborvitae**
Medium-sized evergreen with 5 species in North America. Usually dense, pyramidal trees, narrow to broad. Cultivars range from dwarf, rounded shaped to globe to marrow types with foliage colors of yellow, bluish and various greens. Combine in a shrub border as a foil for contrasting textures. Good as hedges, screens and windbreaks—to the point of stereotyping them in these roles. Rub needles slightly to release a tantalizing scent.

T. OCCIDENTALIS **American Arborvitae, White Cedar** *ZONE:* 2 to 8.
*Origin:* Eastern North America.
*Hardiness:* Needs humidity and medium soil, moisture; damaged by strong winds, snow and ice.
*Size:* Grows 60' (18 m), usually less, spreads 15' (4.5 m).
*Color:* Tends to go yellow or brown-green in winter but it comes back.
*Soil:* Deep well-drained soils, full sun, tolerant of limestone soil, thrives in marshy loam.
*Maintenance:* Survives considerable pruning to shape. Transplants easily, cuttings taken from new wood root well when the heel is taken. Here's a tip from a hortbuddy: if transplanting from a farmer's field or from the side of the road, don't dig the plant, just pull it up. The roots will come away from the soil easily and suffer less damage. Plant immediately and use lots of water—the water is more important than the soil type.
*Problems:* Nothing serious except browning and needles dropping off.
Some cultivars: '**Aurea**', broad conical shrub with golden yellow leaves. '**Boothii**', dwarf globular dense foliage, bright green. '**Douglasii Aurea**', pyramidal, slender, tall, sprays yellow. '**Ellwangerana**', juvenile form, conical, slow growing. '**Ericoides**', juvenile form, dwarf, compact, rounded, 3' (1 m). '**Globosa**', dwarf globular leaves, slightly gray in winter. '**Hetz Midget**', dense globe shape, fine rich green, to 4' (1.2 m). '**Holmstrup**', compact, slow growing, pyramidal form, to 10' (3 m). '**Rheingold**', a remarkable shrub with unique rich amber gold color, grows to 10' (3 m).

T. ORIENTALIS **Oriental Arborvitae** *ZONE:* 5 to 9.
*Origin:* Korea, Manchuria, Northern China.
*Value:* Attractive small, shapely, conical tree.
*Hardiness:* Does not tolerate wet winters.
*Size:* 18' - 25' (5.5 m - 8 m) high.
*Color:* Dark green in maturity.
*Soil:* Most soils.
*Maintenance:* Difficult to root, transplants well.
T. O. '**Aurea Nana**', very popular, 6' (2 m) high.

THUJA PLICATA **Giant Arborvitae, Western Cedar** *ZONE:* 5 to 7.
*Origin:* Alaska to California.
*Value:* Hedges in formal settings, nice touch to the winter garden. Fast-growing pyramidal shape. Responds well to clipping.
*Hardiness:* Prefers moist atmosphere, full sun.
*Size:* Grows 70' (21 m).
*Color:* Dark green in summer and winter.
*Soil:* Prefers moist well-drained, fertile soil; growth is stunted in dry soils.
*Maintenance:* On older specimens it is necessary to remove dead wood. Easily transplanted, cuttings root well if taken in January.
*Problems:* Bagworm, heart rot.

TILIA CORDATA (TIL-ia) ❦ **Littleleaf Linden** *ZONE:* 3 to 7.
*Origin:* Europe.
*Value:* Excellent shade tree for large gardens, streets, parks since it is pollution resistant. It's possible to use this tree in pleaching since it can be clipped and trained.
*Hardiness:* Tolerant of pollution.
*Size:* 60' - 80' (18 m - 24 m) high.
*Color:* Dark green leaves, shiny, often turning yellow in fall; flowers are yellow and fragrant, late June or early July. Orange-red of young wood is warm-looking in winter.
*Soil:* Moist well-drained soil, found on limestone in the wild, obviously adaptable.
*Maintenance:* Can be pruned into hedges; transplants easily.
*Problems:* Leaf blight, canker, powdery mildew, leaf miner, linden bark borer; leaves develop a brownish cast in fall, unsightly but not life threatening.

T. TOMENTOSA ❦ **Silver Linden** *ZONE:* 4 to 7.
*Origin:* China, Mongolia.
*Value:* Good street tree, more ornamental than other lindens.
*Hardiness:* Survives drought and hot weather.
*Size:* 50' - 70' (15 m - 21 m) high.
*Color:* Light gray, very smooth bark makes this tree memorable; gleaming dark green leaves, silvery beneath; flowers are yellowish and fragrant, late June to early July.
*Soil:* Same as other lindens.
T. T. '**Fastigiata**', upright clone; with age, it is similar to species.

TILIA MONGOLICA, **Mongolian Linden**, a small graceful tree.

TSUGA CANADENSIS (TSOO-ga) ❦ **Canada Hemlock** ZONE: 3 to 8.
*Origin:* Nova Scotia to Alabama.
*Value:* Combines well with other plants for contrast. This is Marion Jarvie's combination: ABIES PROCERA 'Glauca Prostrata', an end-of-the-century variety, with a prostrate form, along with TSUGA CANADENSIS 'Jeddeloh', which is also prostrate and can be mounded over a rock. It is a graceful evergreen in any garden; good for hedging, screening, accent plant or foundation.
*Hardiness:* Can take fierce conditions, tolerates shade.
*Size:* 40' - 70' (12 m - 21 m) high.
*Color:* Glossy green.
*Soil:* Fine in most soils, prefers well-drained, moist, acid soil, rocky bluffs or sandy soils. Sabuco says it is also drought tolerant.
*Maintenance:* Can be pruned for shaping; transplants well.
*Problems:* Once adapted to the site there should be few problems.
Some cultivars: 'Albospica', tipped with white, good focal point. 'Pendula', **Sargent's Weeping Hemlock**, 15' (4.5 m) by 40' (12 m) wide; discolors slightly in winter. 'Gracilis', dwarf, new growth turns from yellow to dark green. 'Jeddeloh', very hardy dwarf, blue-green, 4' (1.2m) high by 6' (2 m) wide.

T. HETEROPHYLLA, shiny dark green with bright red fruit, native to the Rockies and West Coast; zone 4, northern section; zone 6, more humid coastal climes.

T. MERTENSIANA, droopy central leaders give this a fascinating shape; zone 3 for interior Northern Rockies; westerly, zone 6.

VACCINIUM CORYMBOSUM (VAC-sin-ium) ❦ **Highbush Blueberry** ZONE: 3 to 7.
*Origin:* North America, East Asia.
*Value:* Shrub border, small garden plot, provides berries for baking, jams and the birds.
*Hardiness:* Full sun or partial shade.
*Size:* 6' - 12' (2 m - 3.5 m) high, spreads 8' - 12' (2.5 m - 3.5 m).
*Color:* Leaf a dark blue-green in summer, changing to yellow bronze, orange to red; flowers are white, possibly pink, borne in May; berries are blue-black, late July early August, edible with plenty of sugar.
*Soil:* Moist, acid soil; native to swamps; also does well in acid, sandy conditions; likes mulch.
*Maintenance:* Prune after the fruit; mulch around the roots to reduce root injury and keep the plant moist; softwood cuttings collected in June root easily.

*Problems:* If you want the fruit, you will have to battle the insects; if you just want the ornamental value of this plant, don't worry about it; grow it for the birds.
V. CRASSIFOLIUM, zone 5; V. SEMPERVIRENS, very durable, zone 5.

VANCOUVERIA HEXANDRA (van-koo-VEE-ria) ❦ **American Barrenwort** ZONE: 4.
*Origin:* West Coast of North America.
*Value:* This is a lovely woodland ground cover that must be grown in dense shade without competition.
*Hardiness:* Snow cover is essential; heat above 90°F (33°C) can be fatal.
*Size:* 18" (45 cm) high.
*Color:* White flowers from May to June.
*Maintenance:* Add lots of humus.

V. PLANIPETALA, same culture as above; evergreen turning to bronze in fall with white flowers; zone 5.

VIBURNUM (vy-BER-num) ❦ **Viburnum**
ZONE: Deciduous viburnums to zone 2; semi-evergreen and evergreen forms to zone 5.
There are some 225 species. Some are deciduous, others are semi-evergreen and evergreen. The size ranges from 2' or 3' to 30' (.5 to 9 m). The white and pink flowers have a fragrance that ranges from delicious to offensive; fruit ranges from yellow, orange, red-pink, blue to black.
*Origin:* North America, Europe, Asia.
*Value:* In combination with other shrubs and perennials they are nonpareil.
*Soil:* Most like full sun or light shade; they all need well-drained loamy soil and should be watered once a week during the growing season. They like a good organic mulch.
*Size:* From a few feet to tree size.
*Maintenance:* Most keep shapely without pruning. Remove crossed branches or twigs. To renew old plants take out large older branches at base. Do any pruning after flowering—they flower on new wood.

V. X BURKWOODII **Burkwood Viburnum**
ZONE: 4 to 8.
*Origin:* Central China.
*Value:* Good in the shrub border. Fragrance is desirable in any garden. First-rate companion for broad-leaved evergreens; tolerates pollution.
*Hardiness:* Tolerates cold and hot climates, thrives in polluted areas, semi-evergreen in zone 5, injured at -25°F (-32°C); in zone 6 and warmer, keeps most of its foliage.
*Size:* 8' - 10' (2.5 m - 3 m) high with ⅔ spread. Needs lots of room.

*Color:* Dark green lustrous leaves, light gray-brown beneath, red-wine color in fall; flowers pink in bud, white in flower, spicy fragrance, April; fruit is red, changing to black in July-August, insignificant ornamental factor.
*Soil:* Slightly moist soil, well-drained, slightly acid situations preferred.
*Maintenance:* Cuttings of softwood root easily if taken in June-July; transplants well, the smaller the plant the easier to transplant.

VIBURNUM CARLESII **Korean Spice Viburnum** ZONE: 4 to 7.
*Origin:* Japan.
*Value:* Most valuable for its fragrance.
*Hardiness:* Full sun to partial shade.
*Size:* Grows 5' (1.5 m) high, with same width.
*Color:* Dull dark green foliage in summer and red-wine in fall, but not outstanding; flowers are pink to red in bud and opening white, April-May, outstanding fragrance; fruit in August-September, red to black berries, nothing to write home about.
*Soil:* Well-drained slightly acid soil.
*Maintenance:* Prune after flowering; dislikes root disturbance, hard to transplant successfully.
*Problems:* Bacterial leaf spot.
V. C. 'Compactum' cultivar, after reaching 4' quickly becomes more dense.

V. X CARLCEPHALUM **Fragrant Viburnum**
Dark green foliage, white flowers, fragrant, April-May; fruit is red to black; easily rooted from softwood cuttings; 6' - 10' (2 m -3 m) high, not as fine a shrub as V. X JUDDII.

V. DAVIDII **David Viburnum**
A good specimen—rugose leaves; blue fruit in October. Origin is western China. Use with other broad-leaved shrubs. Requires a moderate even climate. Dense white flowers in April-May which are breathtakingly beautiful. Grows to 3' - 5' (1 m - 1.5 m) mound, zone 7 to 8.

V. DENTATUM **Arrowwood Viburnum** ZONE: 2.
*Origin:* New Brunswick, Florida to Texas.
*Value:* Screenings, hedges, massing, group plantings and for naturalizing.
*Hardiness:* Adaptable to most situations, full sun to partial shade.
*Size:* Grows to 15' (4.4 m) with similar spread.
*Color:* Lustrous dark green foliage, fall color of leaves ranges from yellow, red to red-purple; white flowers on yellow stems create impression of cream color, the smell is unpleasant, May to June; fruit blue to blue-black, late September through October, birds like the fruit and seeds.
*Soil:* Well-drained soils, extremely adaptable.

*Maintenance:* Suckers easily; restrict the suckering to control the bounds of the shrub; to revive, cut back to the ground; softwood cuttings root easily.

*Problems:* Keep suckers under control, birds transport seeds throughout garden; no serious problems.

### VIBURNUM FARRERI  Fragrant Viburnum

Loose, unkempt and unruly, one of the earliest to flower; dark green foliage, changing to reddish purple in fall; flowers are pink to red in bud and white in flower, mid-April, fragrant; fruit is red to black, July to August; late frost can damage the shrub. Origin is China.

### V. X JUDDII

More adaptable than one of its parents, v. CARLESII, dense with large flowers, very fragrant white flowers. Slow grower, grows 7' (2.1 m) high, 9' (3 m) wide; zone 3.

### V. LANTANA  Wayfaring Tree  ZONE: 3 to 8 but not vigorous in 8.

*Origin:* Europe, western Asia.
*Value:* Hedges, screens, massing, shrub border.
*Hardiness:* Withstands dry soils, full sun or partial shade.
*Size:* 10' - 20' (3 m - 6 m) high, ⅔ in spread.
*Color:* Leaves are dull green, leathery texture, fall a purplish red; flowers are white and fragrant borne in May; fruit is yellow changing to red and finally black in August to late September.
*Soil:* Well-drained loamy situations.
*Maintenance:* Very little required; grows from seed, softwood cuttings root easily.

### V. OPULUS  European Cranberry Bush, Guelder Rose

There are better viburnums—this one gets hit constantly with plant lice and aphids that make it look terribly ratty. It has to be cut back but will recover; zone 3.

### V. PLICATUM TOMENTOSUM  Doublefile Viburnum, Japan Snowball

This is one of the most beautiful forms of all with horizontal branches laden with flowers in spring. Grows to 9' (3 m). Pure white flowers, with red and black fruit—flowers are fertile so keep it out of the wind and insects will be able to do their job. Very little maintenance is needed. Origin is Japan and China, zone 5. Some cultivars: 'Lanarth', very wide spreading. 'Mariesii', glorious fall color from August to October. 'Shasta', gorgeous large white flowers; 'Summer Snowflake' is a Royal Botanical Garden introduction and a beauty; it blooms almost all summer.

### V. X RHYTIDOPHYLLOIDES

Has long semi-evergreen leaves with red fruit turning black; zone 3; it's deciduous farther north than zone ·5. One cultivar v. x R. 'Alleghany' has bright red fruit and I've had the leaves hang on until February in zone 6. Keep out of the wind and winter sun.

### V. SARGENTII  Sargent Cranberry Bush

Yellow to red leaves in autumn, 12' - 15' (3.5 m - 4.5 m) high with comparable spread; sun or shade; zone 3 to 7.

### VINCA MINOR (VIN-ka) ❧ Common Periwinkle  ZONE: 3 to 8, and farther north if protected by snow.

*Origin:* Europe and western Asia.
*Value:* Excellent ground cover, grows in shade, flowers over a long period.
*Hardiness:* Fills in fast in well-drained soil.
*Size:* 3" - 6" (7.5 cm - 15 cm) ground hugging plant.
*Color:* Dark blue-green foliage, loses some of its shine in winter.
*Soil:* Tolerates any soil but does best in well-drained soils full of organic matter.
*Maintenance:* Except for removing ratty looking bits it doesn't require much maintenance; divides easily and cuttings root quickly—pin down a branch; once it has taken, cut away from the mother plant.
*Problems:* Dieback is a serious problem, along with blight, canker, leaf spot and root rot.

### VITIS RIPARIA (VY-tis) ❧ Riverbank Grape  ZONE: 2.

*Origin:* Eastern United States.
*Value:* A really good looking vine that attaches itself by tendrils, thus provides a dappled shade; maple-like leaves.
*Color:* Bright green leaves.
*Soil:* Will take almost anything except extremely dry sites.
*Maintenance:* Little is required. It can be propagated by cuttings.
*Problems:* None.

### V. COIGNETIAE, the ornamental grape vine from Japan has purple fruit, leaves are a spectacular crimson or scarlet in fall, will cover enormous spaces—1000 square feet (90 square meters); zone 5.

### V. VINIFERA 'Purpurea', claret red leaves turning purple, good grown with silver and gray leaved plants or with PYRUS SALICIFOLIA 'Pendula'.

### WEIGELA FLORIDA VENUSTA (wy-GEE-la) ❧ Old Fashioned Weigela  ZONE: 3 to 8.

*Origin:* China.
*Value:* Shrub border, massing, groupings, foundation plantings; blooms on and on for months. Blooms on new and old wood.
*Hardiness:* Full sun, pollution tolerant.
*Size:* 6' - 9' (2 m - 3 m) high, 9'- 12' (3 m - 3.5 m) wide.
*Color:* Leaf a nondescript green; rosy pink flowers borne in May-June on last year's growth.
*Soil:* In full sun adaptable to heavy clay but prefers well-drained soil.

*Maintenance:* Cut back after blooming and take out old stems to base, thin during the summer; roots easily from softwood cuttings collected in June-July-August.
*Problems:* Dieback may occur, prune after flowering to control.
Some cultivars: 'Bristol Ruby', brilliant ruby red blooms; zone 3. 'Dropmore Pink', an introduction from Canada and it is a beauty; grows 8' (2.5 m); 'x Red Prince', dwarf with reddish foliage, deep red flowers, very hardy, blooms all summer; transplants easily; zone 5.

### WISTERIA FLORIBUNDA (wis-TEE-ria) ❧ Japanese Wisteria, Wisteria  ZONE: 4 to 9.

*Origin:* Japan.
*Value:* An excellent vine for patios; adds architectural interest to buildings; can give an almost Mediterranean feeling to a deck. Will even create a very beautiful standard with proper pruning and training.
*Hardiness:* Slow to establish, use named cultivars for best success, full sun, tolerates -25°F (-32°C).
*Size:* Grows 30' (9 m) or more, limited usually by support or structure.
*Color:* Bright green leaf; flowers are a perfect violet-blue, slightly fragrant, numerous blooms, April-May.
*Soil:* Needs a sunny spot that's sheltered in deep, moist, well-drained loam.
*Maintenance:* To get this plant to flower, let the leader sprout and grow to the desired length, then pinch the ends of all 6 or 7 branches. These will send out side shoots; cut these back to 4 leaf nodes from the main covering branches. It can be pruned twice a year—after blooming and in midsummer, prune out all long shoots back to about 6" (15 cm) on new growth. It is slow to establish but will transplant well with some cutting back.

### W. SINENSIS

This has more leaflets and is therefore lighter and better suited to the smaller garden. Prune in late winter to size desired; for flower production reduce the side shoots to 2 buds in the middle of summer; this won't affect foliage at all. When it flowers, it is magnificent, but you have to be brutal to get it to do this. I have one that hasn't bloomed in 25 years. Can become quite heavy. Twines clockwise. Make sure you buy a grafted plant if you want it to bloom within 10 years.

w. s. 'Alba' twines counter-clockwise. Should be a grafted plant or it will take about 10 years to flower. Can create a fragrant roof or arch; flows over pergolas and walkways; trees may be linked with this climber.

w. s. 'Black Dragon' has very deep blue flowers.

YUCCA FILAMENTOSA (YUK-ka) ⅋ **Adam's Needle Yucca** ZONE: 5.
*Value:* Good plant for winter interest; sharp architectural contrast to more sensual plants.
*Hardiness:* Very hardy in intolerable situations.
*Size:* Low evergreen, in July-August conical panicles shoot up to 6' (2 m) high.
*Color:* Yellow-green foliage, yellow flowers in July-August, best show when massed.
*Soil:* Any type if moist.
*Maintenance:* Very little required.
Some cultivars: **'Bright Edge'**, **'Golden Sword'**, **'Variegata'**.

Y. GLAUCA, even more tolerant of wet than the previous listings; slightly waxy film on leaves; same size as others, less showy flowers; zone 2.

## Listings of Ornamental Grasses

These are choice plants for the xeriscaped garden: they require little water, are low maintenance and disease and pest free. They adapt to extreme weather conditions and many kinds of soil.

Species from the family GRAMINEAE are most drought-tolerant, followed by bamboos, sedges and true rushes, JUNCUS. Many grasses grow very large. Be sure to check with your grower what size they will become and plant them in a suitable location. They always look good with evergreens.

ARUNDINARIA JAPONICA (PSEUDOTSUGA METAKE) **Japanese Bamboo, Arrow Bamboo**
Good as decorative screen, also for hedges and tubs. Propagate from rhizomes; slow to spread. Stalk 10' - 13' (3 m - 4 m) high, ¾" (2 cm) diameter. Shade-tolerant. Origin is Europe, zone 7.

A. PUMILA **Dwarf Bamboo**
Grows 2' (60 cm) high, leaf blades to 6" (15 cm) long; bright green, hairy on both sizes. Origin is Japan, zone 8.

A. VIRIDISTRIATA **Running Bamboo**
Good patio plant. Grows 6' (2 m) high, canes 8" (20 cm) wide; new shoots creamy gold; bright green, narrow, tapered leaves, with golden stripes in sun, muted in shade. Cut to ground late autumn for improved showing the following year, zone 7.

CALAMAGROSTIS ACUTIFLORA STRICTA **Feather Reed Grass**
This grass has a striking vertical line; yellow flower spikes last into winter. Grows 5' (1.5 m), if in full sun, zone 6.

C. BRACHYTRICHA **Feather Reed Grass**
Ideal for the winter garden. Purple-pink flower heads in the fall; needs full sun, zone 6.

CAREX BUCHANANII **Buchanan's Sedge, Leatherleaf Sedge**
This densely tufted evergreen is good for the water garden or mixed border. Grows 2' (60 cm); coppery brown with curled leaf tips, mass of fine straw-colored stems. Full sun; zone 6.

C. MORROWII **'Aureo-variegata'**
Variegated Japanese sedge. Mound forming to 1' (30 cm). Leaves flat, semi-evergreen, color combines cream and green.

C. M. **'Variegata'**
Needs part shade, cool moist soil. Dark green leaves with white margins. Grows 1' (30 cm) high. Good for edging or damp rock gardens, zone 5.

FESTUCA OVINA **'Glauca'** (syn. F. CAESIA) **Blue Fescue**
Silvery blue foliage on slender stems. Grows 8" - 12" (20 cm - 30 cm) high. If the center of the plant dies out, divide, reset and cut back, zone 4.

HELICTOTRICHON SEMPERVIRENS **Blue Oat Grass**
A favorite of mine in the winter garden when the blue spikes turn to brown; sun or shade; grows 2' (60 cm), zone 4.

IMPERATA CYLINDRICA **'Red Baron' Japanese Blood Grass**
Upright tufting habit with a brilliant red color. Mass in sun or part shade, zone 5.

LIRIOPE MUSCARI **Big Blue Lilyturf**
Violet colored flowers, cut back in spring, sun or part shade, zone 6.

MISCANTHUS SINENSIS **'Autumn Light'**
Hardy maiden grass, flowers in September in full sun, fine slender leaves. Grows 9' (3 m).

M. S. STRICTUS **Porcupine Grass**
Very showy with green leaves banded in yellow. Excellent beside a swimming pool. Grows 3' - 6' (1 m - 2 m).

MOLINIA CAERULEA **Moor Grass**
Grows in dark tufts, good for wild areas or by ponds; blooms in July in moist acid soil, sun or partial shade. Grows 18" (45 cm).

OPHIOPOGON PLANISCAPUS **'Ebony Knight' Black Mondo Grass**
Distinctive black leaves with white flowers and black berries. Grows in sun or shade or containers. Grows 6" (15 cm). Tender so use it as an annual.

PENNISETUM ALOPECUROIDES **Fountain Grass**
Purple feathery plumes bloom in August. Grows 1' - 3' (30 cm - 100 cm) high in full sun, zone 6.

PHYLLOSTACHYS AUREA **Golden Bamboo**
A good screen or hedge. Prune to shape in summer, sun or shade, zone 5 or 6.

### Other Bamboos

Also look for bamboos under ARUNDINARIA, PLEOBLASTUS, PSEUDOSASA, SASA, SEMIARUNDINARIA and SHIBATAEA in nurseries.

# GLOSSARY

*Acaulescent*: Stemless or without a visible stem.

*Acicular*: Needle-shaped.

*Acuminate*: Tapering to a slender tip.

*Allee*: A broad path cut through woodland.

*Alternate*: Leaves or branches arranged at different heights on either side of a stem.

*Anther*: The pollen-bearing part of the stamen, borne on top of the filament in the male reproductive part of a flower.

*Apex*: The tip or terminal end.

*Axis*: The central part of a longitudinal support on a stem or branch.

*Basal*: Forming the base of the plant.

*Bipinnate*: Having primary leaflets that are further divided into secondary leaflets.

*Calcareous*: Containing lime, chalky.

*Calyx*: Collectively describes the sepals or outer circle of floral parts; usually green.

*Caudate*: Having a tail-like appendage.

*Caulescent*: Having an obvious above-ground stem (opposite of acaulescent).

*Cilia*: Hairs along the edges or margins.

*Cleft*: Divided or incised, usually in the middle.

*Clone*: Any plant propagated vegetatively and, therefore, true to its parent. Hybrids propagated by seed usually don't come true to the parent.

*Columnar*: Shaped like a column or pillar.

*Compound*: Composed of two or more similar parts. A compound leaf is divided into leaflets.

*Corolla*: All the petals in a flower considered collectively.

*Cultivar*: A cultivated variety of plant.

*Decumbent*: Trailing or reclining plants, but with the tip ascending or erect.

*Dentate*: Sharply toothed leaf, with teeth perpendicular to the leaf margin.

*Dioecious*: Having male and female flowers on separate plants.

*Fastigiate*: Having erect and parallel branches.

*Foliaceous*: Leaflike in texture and appearance.

*Frond*: An often large, divided leaf, usually applied to ferns and palms.

*Genus*: A taxonomic category referring to related species.

*Glabrous*: Smooth and hairless.

*Glaucous*: Covered with a waxy bloom.

*Incised*: Sharply notched or deeply divided—usually irregularly—leaf.

*Indumentum*: Dense covering of hair.

*Inflorescence*: Flowering portion of a plant.

*Laciniate*: Narrow, irregular incisions or lobes.

*Lanate*: Woolly, with matted hairs.

*Lanceolate*: Shaped like a lance.

*Lepidote*: Covered with small scales.

*Ligneous*: Woody.

*Monoecious*: Having stamens (male) and pistils (female) on separate flowers on the same plant.

*Native*: An indigenous plant.

*Obcordate*: Heart-shaped.

*Orbicular*: Circular.

*Osier*: A tough, flexible twig or branch, often used for wickerwork.

*Palmate*: Lobe or leaflets radiating from a common basal point.

*Panicle*: A branched raceme.

*Pannose*: Feltlike in texture.

*Pedicel*: The stalk of an individual flower in a cluster; a small stalk.

*Peduncle*: A stalk that supports either a flower cluster or a solitary flower.

*Peltate*: Having a leaf that is attached to the stalk near the center of the leaf or inside its margin.

*Perianth*: The calyx or corolla—or both—of a flower.

*Petiolate*: Having a petiole: a slender stalk that attaches a leaf to a stem.

*Pilose*: Covered with soft hairs.

*Pinnate*: Having leaflets arranged on opposite sides of a common petiole.

*Pistil*: The female reproductive part of a flower, consisting of ovary, style and stigma.

*Plicate*: Folded into plaits, like a fan.

*Plumose*: Having hairs set on each side of an axis, like a feather.

*Procumbent*: Trailing or lying on the ground, but not putting forth roots.

*Pubescent*: Covered with fine short hairs.

*Punctate*: Marked with minute spots or depressions.

*Raceme*: A simple indeterminate inflorescence in which the stalked flowers are arranged singly along a common elongated axis.

*Rachis*: The axis of a compound leaf or inflorescence.

*Reticulate*: Forming a network.

*Revolute*: Rolled or turned backward at the leaf tip or margin toward the undersurface.

*Rootstock*: A root and its growth buds.

*Roseate*: Rose-colored.

*Rosette*: A circular cluster of basal leaves.

*Rostrate*: Having a beak; curved at the tip.

*Rosulate*: Like the petals of a rose, turning outward and downward.

*Rugose*: Wrinkled and rough.

*Runcinate*: Coarsely toothed, with the teeth curved backward.

*Scale*: (Also called bud scale.) A specialized leaf, enclosing an immature leaf bud.

*Scape*: A leafless flower-bearing stem coming up from the ground.

*Semi-evergreen*: Any plant that's green for only a part of the winter.

*Sepal*: Makes up the outer ring of floral parts—usually green.

*Serrate*: Sharp-toothed and notched, pointing toward the apex of a leaf.

*Sheath*: A tubular structure, such as a leaf base, enclosing the stem.

*Shrub*: A woody plant, usually smaller than a tree, branching from the base with one or more main stems.

*Simple*: Usually applied to leaves, means not divided into leaflets; a stem that has no branches.

*Spathe*: A bract or leaf surrounding or partly enclosing an inflorescence.

*Species*: A group of like individuals within a genus. Each species is distinct and reproduces from seed with only slight variation. Second word in a plant's name is the species.

*Spike*: An unbranched inflorescence in which the flowers are without stalks and along a long axis (for example, liatris).

*Spine*: A woody, sharp-pointed outgrowth.

*Spur*: A tubular or sac-like projection at the base of the corolla or calyx; a short compact twig with little or no internodal development.

*Stalk*: The stem of any organ on a plant.

*Stamen*: The pollen-bearing, male reproductive part of a flower. It comprises the filament and the anther.

*Sterile*: Any plant incapable of reproducing sexually; bearing no stamens or pistils.

*Stigma*: The part of pistil that receives pollen.

*Stoma*: Pores or small slits in the epidermis of leaves and stems through which gasses are exchanged.

*Style*: Stalklike tube that rises from the ovary and terminates with the stigma in the female reproductive part of a flower.

*Tendril*: A slender leafless organ for climbing, formed by a modified leaf, a branch or inflorescence.

*Umbel*: An inflorescence with numerous pedicels springing from the end of the primary flower stalk.

*Variety*: A category within a species, based on some hereditary difference.

*Vegetative*: Reproduction that doesn't involve seed production.

*Verticil*: A whorl of more than two similar leaves, hairs, etc., arranged around a node.

*Wing*: Any leaflike expansion.

*Xerophyte*: Any plant that can withstand long periods of drought.

# BIBLIOGRAPHY

Ashley, Anne & Peter. *The Canadian Plant Sourcebook*. Ottawa: 93 Fentiman Ave., K1S OT7, 1990.

Billington, Jill. *Architectural Foliage*. London; New York: Ward Lock, 1991.

Bloom, Alan & Adrian. *Blooms of Bressingham Garden Plants*. London: Harper Collins, 1992.

Boisset, Caroline. *Town Gardens*. Boston: Little, Brown and Co., 1989.

—. *Vertical Gardening*. New York: Weidenfeld & Nicolson, 1988.

Brookes, John. *The Book of Garden Design*. New York: Macmillan, 1991.

Church, Thomas. *Your Private World; A Study of Intimate Gardens*. San Francisco: Chronicle Books, [1969].

Cole, Trevor. *The Ontario Gardener*. Vancouver: Whitecap Books, 1991.

Cox, Jeff. *Flowers for all Seasons*. Emmaus, Pa.: Rodale Press, 1987.

—. *Landscaping with Nature*. Emmaus, Pa.: Rodale Press, 1991.

Crowe, Sylvia. *Garden Design*. New York: Hearthside Press, 1959, 1958.

Davis, Brian. *The Gardener's Illustrated Encyclopedia of Trees & Shrubs*. Emmaus, Penn.: Rodale, 1987.

Dirr, Michael A. *Manual of Woody Landscape Plants*. Champaign, Ill.: Stipes Publishing, 1983.

Ellefson, Connie Lockhart. *Xeriscape Gardening*. New York: Macmillan, 1992.

Fearnley-Whittingstall. *Ivies*. New York: Random House, 1992.

Fox, Robin Lan. *Better Gardening*. Harmondsworth, Middlesex: Penguin, 1982.

Frederick, William H., Jr. *The Exuberant Garden and the Controlling Hand*. Boston: Little, Brown, 1992.

Garland, Sarah. *The Herb Garden*. New York: Viking, 1984.

Glattstein, Judy. *Garden Design with Foliage*. Pownal, Vt.: Storey Communications, 1991.

Hannebaum, Leroy G. *Landscape Design*. 2nd ed. New Jersey: Prentice Hall, 1990.

Harris, Marjorie. *The Canadian Gardener*. Toronto: Random House, 1990.

—. *Ecological Gardening*. Toronto: Random House, 1991.

—. *The Canadian Gardener's Year*. Toronto: Random House, 1992.

Huxley, Anthony. *An Illustrated History of Gardening*. New York: Paddington Press, 1978.

Gayton, Don. *The Wheatgrass Mechanism: Science and Imagination in the Western Canadian Landscape*. Saskatoon: Fifth House Publishers, 1990.

Kelly, John. *Foliage in Your Garden*. New York: Penguin Books, 1989.

Knowles, R. H. *Woody Ornamentals for the Prairie Provinces*. Edmonton: Faculty of Agriculture and Forestry, U. of Alberta, 1975.

Lacey, Stephen. *The Startling Jungle*. Harmondsworth, Middlesex; N.Y.: Viking, 1986.

Lacy, Allen. *The Garden in Autumn*. New York: Atlantic Monthly Press, 1990.

Lloyd, Christopher. *Clematis*. Deer Park, WI: Capability's Books, 1989.

—. *Foliage Plants*. Middlesex, England: Viking, 1985.

Motloch, John L. *Introduction to Landscape Design*. New York: Van Nostrand Reinhold, 1991.

*Native Trees and Woodland Shrubs of Prince Edward Island*. Charlottetown, P.E.I.: Department of Agriculture, n.d.

Oehme, Wolfgang. *Bold Romantic Gardens*. Reston, VA: Acropolis Books, c1990.

Osborne, Robert. *Roses for Canadian Gardens*. Toronto: Key Porter, 1992.

Page, Russell. *The Education of a Gardener*. London: Collins, 1962.

Paul, Anthony, & Yvonne Rees. *Designing with Trees*. Topsfield, Mass.: Salem House, 1989.

Phillips, Roger. *Trees of North America and Europe*. New York: Random House, 1978.

Phillips, Roger, & Martyn Rix. *The Random House Book of Shrubs*. New York: Random House, 1989.

Pirone, P.P., ed. *Tree Maintenance*. New York: Oxford University Press, 1988.

Pollan, Michael. *Second Nature*. New York: Atlantic Monthly Press, 1991.

Rae-Smith, William. *The Complete Book of Water Gardening*. London: Bracken Books, 1989.

Sabuco, John J. *The Best of the Hardiest*. Flossmoor, Ill. Plantsmen's Publications, 1990.

Shigo, Alex L. *A New Tree Biology*. Durham, NH: Shigo and Trees, 1991.

—. *Tree Pruning; A Worldwide Photo Guide*. Durham, NH: Shigo and Trees, 1991.

Simonds, John Ormsbee. *Landscape Architecture; A Manual of Site Planning and Design*, 2nd ed. New York: McGraw Hill, 1983.

Stearn, William T. *Botanical Latin*. Newton Abbot; North Pomfret, Vt.: David & Charles, 1991.

Straley, Gerald B. *Trees of Vancouver*. Vancouver: UBC Press, 1992.

Street, John. *Rhododendrons*. Chester, Conn.: Globe Pequot Press, 1987.

Suzuki, David T. *Sciencescape*. Toronto: Oxford University Press, 1986.

Taylor, Patrick. *Planting in Patterns*. New York: Harper & Row, 1989.

Thomas, Graham Stuart. *Plants for Ground-Cover*. Portland, Or.: Sagapress/Timber Press, 1990, c1970.

Toogood, Alan. *Conifers and Heather*. London: Tiger Books International, 1989.

Van Zuylen, Gabrielle. *The Gardens of Russell Page*. New York: Stewart, Tabori & Chang, 1991.

Verey, Rosemary. *Classic Garden Design*. New York: Random House, 1989.

Wyman, Donald. *Trees for American Gardens*. New York: Macmillan, 1990.

Yiesla, Sharon A., & Floyd A. Giles. *Shade Trees for the Central and Northern United States and Canada*. Champaign, Ill.: Stipes, 1992.

Zucker, Isabel. *Flowering Shrubs & Small Trees*. New York: Grove Weidenfeld, 1990.

# REFERENCE WORKS

*Encyclopaedia of the American Horticultural Society*.

*Hortus Third*. New York: Macmillan, 1976.

*Sunset Western Garden Book*. Sunset Books. Menlo Park, Ca.: Lane Publishing, 1988.

Wyman, Donald. *Wyman's Gardening Encyclopedia*. New York: Macmillan, 1986.

# PERIODICALS

*Bulletin of the American Rock Garden Society*
*Fine Gardening*
*Garden Design*
*Gardens West*
*Horticulture*
*Hortus*
*Journal of the Ontario Rock Garden Society*
*The Island Grower*
*Trellis* (Civic Garden Centre, Toronto)
*Wildflower* (Journal of the Canadian Wildflower Society)

# INDEX